*Christina Rossetti*

"Buy from us with a golden curl"

# The Works of
# *Christina Rossetti*

❦

*with an Introduction by Martin Corner,
and Bibliography*

*Wordsworth Poetry Library*

This edition published 1995 by Wordsworth Editions Ltd,
Cumberland House, Crib Street, Ware, Hertfordshire SG12 9ET.

ISBN 1-85326-429-6

Printed and bound in Denmark by Nørhaven.

The paper in this book is produced from pure wood
pulp, without the use of chlorine or any other substance
harmful to the environment. The energy used in its
production consists almost entirely of hydroelectricity
and heat generated from waste materials, thereby
conserving fossil fuels and contributing little to the
greenhouse effect.

# INTRODUCTION

CHRISTINA ROSSETTI was one of the most prolific and popular poets of the English nineteenth century; no reading of the poetry of the period would be complete without her. Even in her own country she attracted high praise from sometimes surprising quarters: Philip Larkin admired her 'steely stoicism', and Lionel Trilling and Harold Bloom described her as the most considerable woman poet in England before the twentieth century.

But there are problems for modern readers. A glance into her works will suggest a sensibility marked by features that we, a hundred years on, find hard to accept: an apparent rejection of life, a fascination, sometimes self-indulgent, with death. Nor do the poems known to contemporary readers, such as 'Goblin Market' and 'In the bleak mid-winter' ('A Christmas Carol'), properly represent the balance of her achievement; neither is easily paralleled elsewhere in her writing. Her full quality, which is considerable and often surprising, only begins to emerge when one moves to less familiar and less immediately appealing work.

If readers have found her problematical, this is no more than she found her own life. She was born in London in 1830, the fourth and youngest child of Gabriele Rossetti, an Italian emigré, and his half-Italian wife, Frances Polidori. The lives of the children led in strikingly different directions: Maria, the eldest, became a nun in one of the newly-established Anglo-Catholic orders; Dante Gabriel was, like Christina, a poet and also a painter, and one of the founders of the Pre-Raphaelite Brotherhood; and William, who survived to edit Christina's collected poems, a civil servant. The family grew up among artistic friends and political exiles, and in some economic insecurity. The children spoke Italian with their father and English with their mother; in later life, Christina was to write Italian poetry as well as English. She began to write at an early age, and in 1847 her maternal grandfather rewarded her precocity with a private edition of her poems.

These were the years in which Dante Gabriel was gathering the Pre-Raphaelite painters around him, and it was to a minor member of that group, James Collinson, that Christina was briefly engaged. Collinson wavers between the Church of England and Rome; and when, in 1850, he settled for Rome, Christina renounced him. This loss was to mark her for the rest of her life. Her choice reveals the strength of her commitment to the post-Tractarian wing of the Church of England; she was to make a similar renunciation in 1866, when she broke with the writer Charles Cayley on the grounds of his agnosticism. She came to see her life as a test of her power to renounce: to live on very little as the world sees it, in the hope and expectation of a fuller reward. But this was essentially an inward disposition; though never at the centre of society, she was not out of touch with Victorian life. At the age of 24 during the Crimean war, she volunteered to nurse under Florence Nightingale in the Scutari hospital; rejected, she worked among the London poor. Dante Gabriel's circle introduced her to a wider world, and she knew such as Edmund Gosse, Hall Caine, and (towards the end of her life) Katharine Tynan. She read Whitman and Dickinson. After 1873 her health declined and she devoted herself more and more to religious writing. She died of cancer in 1894.

Her first success was *Goblin Market and Other Poems*

(1862), which was widely read and reviewed, so that she came to be seen, rather misleadingly, as the poet of the Pre-Raphaelite movement. In fact nothing could have been further from her than their largely aesthetic religiosity. Other collections followed in 1866 (*The Prince's Progress and Other Poems*) and 1881 (*A Pageant and Other Poems*). The degree of her popularity can be gauged from the last volume published in her lifetime: *Verses* (1893), a collection of devotional poems selected from several earlier volumes, was by 1904 into its twentieth thousand. Her brother William edited her *Poetical Works* in 1904.

Rossetti might at first appear to be a poet of exclusively private experience; but this is less than the whole truth. Much of her poetry is a sensitive and intimate following-through of the life of feeling and of faith, rendered with directness and a freedom from the usual Victorian encrustation of poetic diction that makes it forceful and telling. But there is also an alertness to the world around her; in her own way she registers the cosmic despair of her age, so visible in the work of Tennyson and Arnold, and there is a strong social awareness in her consciousness of the inequities of women's lives in her time.

But it is the inner life that dominates. Much of her poetry is driven by the tension between irrecoverable loss and unattainable hope. Her exploration of loss is complex and based on the disappointments of her own life. Generally the loss flows from her own decision (as in 'A Portrait'); but there are also poems (such as 'Winter: My Secret') in which she is less the chooser than the victim of trauma, only half able to reveal even to herself the wound that she has suffered. The consequences of this fracture of love were deep loneliness and a sense of exclusion. 'Chilly Night' is a Gothic nightmare of desolation, in which all human love has failed and her mother appears only as a blank, eyeless terror. 'Shut Out' conveys, even more bleakly, the sense of being excluded from the life she should have lived: in detail suggestive of Kafka, a spirit first shows her the garden of her life and then builds a wall between her and it.

Rossetti's constant effort was to turn raw loss into renunciation, an act of her own will that might, despite its pain, restore her being in another direction. 'Three Stages' is one of many poems in which this struggle is described. Its outcome is hope on a different level, but this is perhaps not its most important benefit for her. A poem like 'Memory' suggests that the real fruit of renunciation was a strength of self-sufficiency and independence: that only in this way could a woman in Rossetti's position free herself from the dependency of conventional gender relationships.

Nevertheless hope is central to these poems: hope for a fullness of love that life has denied her. This has a human and a divine form. On the human level, she is capable of anger at the paucity and thinness of the love that has been offered her. In 'The Heart Knoweth Its Own Bitterness' (written in 1852, not long after the break with Collinson) she appeals in erotic terms for a love that will 'probe my quick core and sound my depth'. 'Enrica', which contrasts an Italian woman with the English, reveals a fear that she may herself, at least in her English identity, share this emotional thinness. When she allows herself to imagine a fulfilled love, it is noticeable that the images are as often of love for women as for men. 'Two Thoughts on Death', 'Is and Was', and 'In The Lane' are all poems of love for women.

Most of these threads draw together in 'Goblin Market', which deserves its place as Rossetti's central achievement because it is here that her imagination finds both its own form and its fullest freedom. All the central themes are here: renunciation set against indulgence, sexuality against a spiritual asceticism, the love and solidarity of women broken by the intrusion of men. The fulfilment of (heterosexual) desire destroys itself and leaves an arid, insatiable craving, whereas the love between the sisters is restorative and life-giving. This is a poem of real depth, and we should not condescend to its author and first readers by suggesting that they did not fully understand it.

In her search for the love of God, Rossetti wrote many poems that do little more than versify the pieties of Victorian High Anglicanism. But some are better than that. 'In the bleak mid-winter' is justly famous as an expression of an ideal simplicity of love for God, and there are several poems, such as 'Dost Thou Not Care?', 'Lord, What Have I To Offer?' and 'The Fields Are White' in which she comes close to the freshness of Herbert's dialogic spiritual realism. 'What Good Shall My Life Do Me?', with its toughness of thought, feeling and form, convincingly conveys a love larger than the failures of human love.

The public significances of Rossetti's poems are necessarily secondary to the private, but real nevertheless. Her poems of loneliness and desolation speak for the age as well as for herself; such pieces as 'From the Antique' ('The wind shall lull us yet...') and 'One Certainty' catch the Victorian bleakness of Godless time which is also there in Arnold and Tennyson. 'From the antique' ('It's a weary life, it is, she said...') and 'Long Barren' are explicit on the disadvantages of many women's lives, and such as 'Seeking Rest' celebrate the resource of women's solidarity. 'Mary Magdalene' reverses the gospel to see the meeting between Mary and Christ from the woman's perspective; the same reversal of perspective occurs in the 'Monna Innominata' sonnets, a courtly-love sequence in which it is the woman who initiates, speaks, and looks towards the man. These sonnets are polished and emotionally persuasive, and stand well beside the sonnet-sequences of Elizabeth Barrett Browning and George Meredith. Apart form her sonnets, Rossetti's contact with the wider tradition of Victorian poetry, not always easy to trace, is perhaps most visible in her ballad poems, such as 'Noble

Sisters', 'Maude Clare', and 'The Convent Threshold', where she displays an unexpected crispness in medievalising narrative that links her with Morris.

*Martin Corner*
*Kingston University*

FURTHER READING

Battiscombe, G., *Christina Rossetti: A Divided Life* (1981)
Charles, E.K., *Christina Rossetti: Critical Perspectives* (1988)
Crump, R.W. (ed.), *The Complete Poems of Christina Rossetti*, 3 vols. (1979-90)
Jones, K., *Learning Not To Be First: The Life of Christina Rossetti* (1991)
Packer, L.M., *Christina Rossetti* (1963)
Roe, S. (ed.), *Women Reading Women's Writing* (1987)

TO

## MY MOTHER,

IN ALL REVERENCE AND LOVE,

I INSCRIBE THIS BOOK.

# CONTENTS.

## THE FIRST SERIES.

# THE SECOND SERIES.

PAGE

# THE FIRST SERIES

# GOBLIN MARKET.

MORNING and evening
    Maids heard the goblins cry:
" Come buy our orchard fruits,
Come buy, come buy :
Apples and quinces,
Lemons and oranges,
Plump unpecked cherries,
Melons and raspberries,
Bloom-down-cheeked peaches,
Swart-headed mulberries,
Wild free-born cranberries,
Crab-apples, dewberries,
Pine-apples, blackberries,
Apricots, strawberries ;—
All ripe together
In summer weather,—
Morns that pass by,
Fair eves that fly ;
Come buy, come buy :
Our grapes fresh from the vine,
Pomegranates full and fine,

Dates and sharp bullaces,
Rare pears and greengages,
Damsons and bilberries,
Taste them and try :
Currants and gooseberries,
Bright-fire-like barberries,
Figs to fill your mouth,
Citrons from the South,
Sweet to tongue and sound to eye ;
Come buy, come buy."

Evening by evening
Among the brookside rushes,
Laura bowed her head to hear,
Lizzie veiled her blushes :
Crouching close together
In the cooling weather,
With clasping arms and cautioning lips,
With tingling cheeks and finger tips.
"Lie close," Laura said,
Pricking up her golden head :
"We must not look at goblin men,
We must not buy their fruits :
Who knows upon what soil they fed
Their hungry thirsty roots ?"
"Come buy," call the goblins
Hobbling down the glen.
"Oh," cried Lizzie, "Laura, Laura,
You should not peep at goblin men."
Lizzie covered up her eyes,

Covered close lest they should look ;
Laura reared her glossy head,
And whispered like the restless brook :
" Look, Lizzie, look, Lizzie,
Down the glen tramp little men.
One hauls a basket,
One bears a plate,
One lugs a golden dish
Of many pounds weight.
How fair the vine must grow
Whose grapes are so luscious ;
How warm the wind must blow
Through those fruit bushes."
" No," said Lizzie : " No, no, no ;
Their offers should not charm us,
Their evil gifts would harm us."
She thrust a dimpled finger
In each ear, shut eyes and ran :
Curious Laura chose to linger
Wondering at each merchant man.
One had a cat's face,
One whisked a tail,
One tramped at a rat's pace,
One crawled like a snail,
One like a wombat prowled obtuse and furry
One like a ratel tumbled hurry skurry.
She heard a voice like voice of doves
Cooing all together :
They sounded kind and full of loves
In the pleasant weather.

Laura stretched her gleaming neck
Like a rush-imbedded swan,
Like a lily from the beck,
Like a moonlit poplar branch,
Like a vessel at the launch
When its last restraint is gone.

Backwards up the mossy glen
Turned and trooped the goblin men,
With their shrill repeated cry,
" Come buy, come buy."
When they reached where Laura was
They stood stock still upon the moss,
Leering at each other,
Brother with queer brother ;
Signalling each other,
Brother with sly brother.
One set his basket down,
One reared his plate ;
One began to weave a crown
Of tendrils, leaves, and rough nuts brown
(Men sell not such in any town) ;
One heaved the golden weight
Of dish and fruit to offer her :
" Come buy, come buy," was still their cry
Laura stared but did not stir,
Longed but had no money :
The whisk-tailed merchant bade her taste
In tones as smooth as honey,
The cat-faced purr'd,

The rat-paced spoke a word
Of welcome, and the snail-paced even was heard;
One parrot-voiced and jolly
Cried "Pretty Goblin" still for "Pretty Polly;"—
One whistled like a bird.

But sweet-tooth Laura spoke in haste:
"Good Folk, I have no coin;
To take were to purloin:
I have no copper in my purse,
I have no silver either,
And all my gold is on the furze
That shakes in windy weather
Above the rusty heather."
"You have much gold upon your head,"
They answered all together:
"Buy from us with a golden curl."
She clipped a precious golden lock,
She dropped a tear more rare than pearl,
Then sucked their fruit globes fair or red:
Sweeter than honey from the rock,
Stronger than man-rejoicing wine,
Clearer than water flowed that juice;
She never tasted such before,
How should it cloy with length of use?
She sucked and sucked and sucked the more
Fruits which that unknown orchard bore;
She sucked until her lips were sore;
Then flung the emptied rinds away
But gathered up one kernel stone,

And knew not was it night or day
As she turned home alone.

    Lizzie met her at the gate
Full of wise upbraidings :
"Dear, you should not stay so late,
Twilight is not good for maidens ;
Should not loiter in the glen
In the haunts of goblin men.
Do you not remember Jeanie,
How she met them in the moonlight,
Took their gifts both choice and many,
Ate their fruits and wore their flowers
Plucked from bowers
Where summer ripens at all hours ?
But ever in the noonlight
She pined and pined away ;
Sought them by night and day,
Found them no more, but dwindled and grew grey
Then fell with the first snow,
While to this day no grass will grow
Where she lies low :
I planted daisies there a year ago
That never blow.
You should not loiter so."
"Nay, hush," said Laura :
"Nay, hush, my sister :
I ate and ate my fill,
Yet my mouth waters still
To-morrow night I will

Buy more;" and kissed her:
" Have done with sorrow ;
I'll bring you plums to-morrow
Fresh on their mother twigs,
Cherries worth getting ;
You cannot think what figs
My teeth have met in,
What melons icy-cold
Piled on a dish of gold
Too huge for me to hold,
What peaches with a velvet nap,
Pellucid grapes without one seed :
Odorous indeed must be the mead
Whereon they grow, and pure the wave they drink
With lilies at the brink,
And sugar-sweet their sap."

Golden head by golden head,
Like two pigeons in one nest
Folded in each other's wings,
They lay down in their curtained bed ·
Like two blossoms on one stem,
Like two flakes of new-fall'n snow,
Like two wands of ivory
Tipped with gold for awful kings.
Moon and stars gazed in at them,
Wind sang to them lullaby,
Lumbering owls forebore to fly
Not a bat flapped to and fro
Round their rest :

Cheek to cheek and breast to breast
Locked together in one nest.

Early in the morning
When the first cock crowed his warning,
Neat like bees, as sweet and busy,
Laura rose with Lizzie :
Fetched in honey, milked the cows,
Aired and set to rights the house,
Kneaded cakes of whitest wheat,
Cakes for dainty mouths to eat,
Next churned butter, whipped up cream,
Fed their poultry, sat and sewed ;
Talked as modest maidens should :
Lizzie with an open heart,
Laura in an absent dream,
One content, one sick in part ;
One warbling for the mere bright day's delight,
One longing for the night.

At length slow evening came :
They went with pitchers to the reedy brook ;
Lizzie most placid in her look,
Laura most like a leaping flame.
They drew the gurgling water from its deep ;
Lizzie plucked purple and rich golden flags,
Then turning homeward said: "The sunset flushes
Those furthest loftiest crags ;
Come, Laura, not another maiden lags.
No wilful squirrel wags,

The beasts and birds are fast asleep."
But Laura loitered still among the rushes
And said the bank was steep.

And said the hour was early still,
The dew not fall'n, the wind not chill,
Listening ever, but not catching
The customary cry,
"Come buy, come buy,"
With its iterated jingle
Of sugar-baited words :
Not for all her watching
Once discerning even one goblin
Racing, whisking, tumbling, hobbling.
Let alone the herds
That used to tramp along the glen,
In groups or single,
Of brisk fruit-merchant men.

Till Lizzie urged, "O Laura, come ;
I hear the fruit-call, but I dare not look :
You should not loiter longer at this brook
Come with me home.
The stars rise, the moon bends her arc,
Each glowworm winks her spark,
Let us get home before the night grows dark :
For clouds may gather
Though this is summer weather,
Put out the lights and drench us through ;
Then if we lost our way what should we do ?'

Laura turned cold as stone
To find her sister heard that cry alone,
That goblin cry,
" Come buy our fruits, come buy."
Must she then buy no more such dainty fruit !
Must she no more such succous pasture find,
Gone deaf and blind ?
Her tree of life drooped from the root :
She said not one word in her heart's sore ache ;
But peering thro' the dimness, nought discerning,
Trudged home, her pitcher dripping all the way ;
So crept to bed, and lay
Silent till Lizzie slept ;
Then sat up in a passionate yearning,
And gnashed her teeth for baulked desire, and wep
As if her heart would break.

Day after day, night after night,
Laura kept watch in vain
In sullen silence of exceeding pain.
She never caught again the goblin cry :
"Come buy, come buy ; "—
She never spied the goblin men
Hawking their fruits along the glen :
But when the noon waxed bright
Her hair grew thin and grey ;
She dwindled, as the fair full moon doth turn
To swift decay and burn
Her fire away.

One day remembering her kernel-stone
She set it by a wall that faced the south ;
Dewed it with tears, hoped for a root.
Watched for a waxing shoot,
But there came none ;
It never saw the sun,
It never felt the trickling moisture run :
While with sunk eyes and faded mouth
She dreamed of melons, as a traveller sees
False waves in desert drouth
With shade of leaf-crowned trees,
And burns the thirstier in the sandful breeze

She no more swept the house,
Tended the fowls or cows,
Fetched honey, kneaded cakes of wheat,
Brought water from the brook :
But sat down listless in the chimney-nook
And would not eat.

Tender Lizzie could not bear
To watch her sister's cankerous care
Yet not to share.
She night and morning
Caught the goblins' cry :
" Come buy our orchard fruits,
Come buy, come buy : "—
Beside the brook, along the glen,
She heard the tramp of goblin men
The voice and stir

Poor Laura could not hear;
Longed to buy fruit to comfort her,
But feared to pay too dear.
She thought of Jeanie in her grave,
Who should have been a bride;
But who for joys brides hope to have
Fell sick and died
In her gay prime,
In earliest Winter time,
With the first glazing rime,
With the first snow-fall of crisp Winter time

Till Laura dwindling
Seemed knocking at Death's door:
Then Lizzie weighed no more
Better and worse;
But put a silver penny in her purse,
Kissed Laura, crossed the heath with clumps of furze
At twilight, halted by the brook:
And for the first time in her life
Began to listen and look.

Laughed every goblin
When they spied her peeping:
Came towards her hobbling,
Flying, running, leaping,
Puffing and blowing,
Chuckling, clapping, crowing,
Clucking and gobbling,
Mopping and mowing,

Full of airs and graces,
Pulling wry faces,
Demure grimaces,
Cat-like and rat-like,
Ratel- and wombat-like,
Snail-paced in a hurry,
Parrot-voiced and whistler,
Helter skelter, hurry skurry,
Chattering like magpies,
Fluttering like pigeons,
Gliding like fishes,—
Hugged her and kissed her:
Squeezed and caressed her:
Stretched up their dishes,
Panniers, and plates:
" Look at our apples
Russet and dun,
Bob at our cherries,
Bite at our peaches,
Citrons and dates,
Grapes for the asking,
Pears red with basking
Out in the sun,
Plums on their twigs;
Pluck them and suck them,
Pomegranates, figs."—

"Good folk," said Lizzie,
Mindful of Jeanie:
"Give me much and many:"—

Held out her apron,
Tossed them her penny.
" Nay, take a seat with us,
Honour and eat with us,"
They answered grinning :
" Our feast is but beginning.
Night yet is early,
Warm and dew pearly,
Wakeful and starry :
Such fruits as these
No man can carry ;
Half their bloom would fly,
Half their dew would dry,
Half their flavour would pass bv.
Sit down and feast with us,
Be welcome guest with us,
Cheer you and rest with us."—
" Thank you," said Lizzie : "But one waits
At home alone for me :
So without further parleying,
If you will not sell me any
Of your fruits though much and many,
Give me back my silver penny
I tossed you for a fee."—
They began to scratch their pates,
No longer wagging, purring,
But visibly demurring,
Grunting and snarling.
One called her proud,
Cross-grained, uncivil ;

Their tones waxed loud,
Their looks were evil.
Lashing their tails
They trod and hustled her,
Elbowed and jostled her,
Clawed with their nails,
Barking, mewing, hissing, mocking,
Tore her gown and soiled her stocking,
Twitched her hair out by the roots,
Stamped upon her tender feet,
Held her hands and squeezed their fruits
Against her mouth to make her eat.

White and golden Lizzie stood,
Like a lily in a flood,—
Like a rock of blue-veined stone
Lashed by tides obstreperously,—
Like a beacon left alone
In a hoary roaring sea,
Sending up a golden fire,—
Like a fruit-crowned orange-tree
White with blossoms honey-sweet
Sore beset by wasp and bee,—
Like a royal virgin town
Topped with gilded dome and spire
Close beleaguered by a fleet
Mad to tug her standard down.

One may lead a horse to water,
Twenty cannot make him drink.

Though the goblins cuffed and caught her,
Coaxed and fought her,
Bullied and besought her,
Scratched her, pinched her black as ink,
Kicked and knocked her,
Mauled and mocked her,
Lizzie uttered not a word;
Would not open lip from lip
Lest they should cram a mouthful in:
But laughed in heart to feel the drip
Of juice that syrupped all her face,
And lodged in dimples of her chin,
And streaked her neck which quaked like curd
At last the evil people,
Worn out by her resistance,
Flung back her penny, kicked their fruit
Along whichever road they took,
Not leaving root or stone or shoot;
Some writhed into the ground,
Some dived into the brook
With ring and ripple,
Some scudded on the gale without a sound,
Some vanished in the distance.

In a smart, ache, tingle,
Lizzie went her way;
Knew not was it night or day;
Sprang up the bank, tore thro' the furze,
Threaded copse and dingle,
And heard her penny jingle

Bouncing in her purse,—
Its bounce was music to her ear.
She ran and ran
As if she feared some goblin man
Dogged her with gibe or curse
Or something worse :
But not one goblin skurried after,
Nor was she pricked by fear ;
The kind heart made her windy-paced
That urged her home quite out of breath with haste
And inward laughter.

She cried, " Laura," up the garden.
" Did you miss me ?
Come and kiss me.
Never mind my bruises,
Hug me, kiss me, suck my juices
Squeezed from goblin fruits for you,
Goblin pulp and goblin dew.
Eat me, drink me, love me ;
Laura, make much of me ;
For your sake I have braved the glen
And had to do with goblin merchant men."

Laura started from her chair,
Flung her arms up in the air,
Clutched her hair :
" Lizzie, Lizzie, have you tasted
For my sake the fruit forbidden ?
Must your light like mine be hidden,

Your young life like mine be **wasted,**
Undone in mine undoing,
And ruined in my ruin,
Thirsty, cankered, goblin ridden ? "—
She clung about her sister,
Kissed and kissed and kissed her :
Tears once again
Refreshed her shrunken eyes,
Dropping like rain
After long sultry drouth ;
Shaking with aguish fear, and pain,
She kissed and kissed her with a hungry mouth.

Her lips began to scorch,
That juice was wormwood to her tongue,
She loathed the feast :
Writhing as one possessed she leaped and sung,
Rent all her robe, and wrung
Her hands in lamentable haste,
And beat her breast.
Her locks streamed like the torch
Borne by a racer at full speed,
Or like the mane of horses in their flight,
Or like an eagle when she stems the light
Straight toward the sun,
Or like a caged thing freed,
Or like a flying flag when armies run.

Swift fire spread through her veins. knocked at
her heart,

Met the fire smouldering there
And overbore its lesser flame ;
She gorged on bitterness without a name :
Ah ! fool, to choose such part
Of soul-consuming care !
Sense failed in the mortal strife :
Like the watch-tower of a town
Which an earthquake shatters down,
Like a lightning-stricken mast,
Like a wind-uprooted tree
Spun about,
Like a foam-topped waterspout
Cast down headlong in the sea,
She fell at last ;
Pleasure past and anguish past,
Is it death or is it life ?

   Life out of death.
That night long Lizzie watched by her,
Counted her pulse's flagging stir,
Felt for her breath,
Held water to her lips, and cooled her face
With tears and fanning leaves :
But when the first birds chirped about their eaves
And early reapers plodded to the place
Of golden sheaves,
And dew-wet grass
Bowed in the morning winds so brisk to pass,
And new buds with new day
Opened of cup-like lilies on the stream,
Laura awoke as from a dream,

Laughed in the innocent old way,
Hugged Lizzie but not twice or thrice
Her gleaming locks showed not one thread of grey
Her breath was sweet as May
And light danced in her eyes.

Days, weeks, months, years
Afterwards, when both were wives
With children of their own ;
Their mother-hearts beset with fears,
Their lives bound up in tender lives :
Laura would call the little ones
And tell them of her early prime,
Those pleasant days long gone
Of not-returning time :
Would talk about the haunted glen,
The wicked, quaint fruit-merchant men,
Their fruits like honey to the throat
But poison in the blood ;
(Men sell not such in any town) :
Would tell them how her sister stood
In deadly peril to do her good,
And with the fiery antidote :
Then joining hands to little hands
Would bid them cling together,
" For there is no friend like a sister
In calm or stormy weather ;
To cheer one on the tedious way,
To fetch one if one goes astray,
To lift one if one totters down,
To strengthen whilst one stands."

## THE PRINCE'S PROGRESS.

TILL all sweet gums and juices flow.
   Till the blossom of blossoms blow,
The long hours go and come and go,
   The bride she sleepeth, waketh, sleepeth,
Waiting for one whose coming is slow :—
   Hark ! the bride weepeth.

" How long shall I wait, come heat come rime ?"—
" Till the strong Prince comes, who must come in
      time "
(Her women say), " there's a mountain to climb,
   A river to ford, sleep, dream and sleep ;
Sleep " (they say) : " we've muffled the chime,
   Better dream than weep."

In his world-end palace the strong Prince sat,
Taking his ease on cushion and mat,
Close at hand lay his staff and his hat.
   " When wilt thou start ? the bride waits, O youth."
" Now the moon's at full ; I tarried for that,
   Now I start in truth.

" But tell me first, true voice of my doom,
Of my veiled bride in her maiden bloom ;
Keeps she watch through glare and through gloom,

Watch for me asleep and awake ?"—
"Spell-bound she watches in one white room,
    And is patient for thy sake.


" By her head lilies and rosebuds grow ;
The lilies droop, will the rosebuds blow ?
The silver slim lilies hang the head low ;
    Their stream is scanty, their sunshine rare :
Let the sun blaze out, and let the stream flow,
    They will blossom and wax fair.


" Red and white poppies grow at her feet,
The blood-red wait for sweet summer heat,
Wrapped in bud-coats, hairy and neat ;
    But the white buds swell, one day they will burst
Will open their death cups drowsy and sweet—
    Which will open the first ? "


Then a hundred sad voices lifted a wail,
And a hundred glad voices piped on the gale :
"Time is short, life is short," they took up the tale :
    " Life is sweet, love is sweet, use to-day while you
        may ;
Love is sweet, and to-morrow may fail ;
    Love is sweet, use to-day."


While the song swept by, beseeching and meek,
Up rose the Prince with a flush on his cheek,
Up he rose to stir and to seek,

Going forth in the joy of his strength ;
Strong of limb if of purpose weak,
    Starting at length.

Forth he set in the breezy morn,
Across green fields of nodding corn,
As goodly a Prince as ever was born,
    Carolling with the carolling lark ;—
Sure his bride will be won and worn,
    Ere fall of the dark.

So light his step, so merry his smile,
A milkmaid loitered beside a stile,
Set down her pail and rested awhile,
    A wave-haired milkmaid, rosy and white ;
The Prince, who had journeyed at least a mile,
    Grew athirst at the sight.

" Will you give me a morning draught ? "—
" You're kindly welcome," she said, and laughed
He lifted the pail, new milk he quaffed ;
    Then wiping his curly black beard like silk :
" Whitest cow that ever was calved
    Surely gave you this milk."

Was it milk now, or was it cream ?
Was she a maid, or an evil dream ?
Her eyes began to glitter and gleam ;
    He would have gone, but he stayed instead ;
Green they gleamed as he looked in them :
    " Give me my fee," she said.—

" I will give you a jewel of gold."-
" Not so ; gold is heavy and cold."—
" I will give you a velvet fold
    Of foreign work your beauty to deck."—
" Better I like my kerchief rolled
      Light and white round my neck." -

" Nay," cried he, " but fix your own fee."—
She laughed, " You may give the full moon to me,
Or else sit under this apple-tree
    Here for one idle day by my side ;
After that I'll let you go free,
      And the world is wide."

Loth to stay, yet to leave her slack,
He half turned away, then he quite turned back :
For courtesy's sake he could not lack
    To redeem his own royal pledge ;
Ahead too the windy heaven lowered black
      With a fire-cloven edge.

So he stretched his length in the apple-tree shade
Lay and laughed and talked to the maid,
Who twisted her hair in a cunning braid
    And writhed it in shining serpent-coils,
And held him a day and night fast laid
      In her subtle toils.

At the death of night and the birth of day,
When the owl left off his sober play,
And the bat hung himself out of the way,

Woke the song of mavis and merle,
And heaven put off its hodden grey
    For mother-o'-pearl.

Peeped up daisies here and there,
Here, there, and everywhere;
Rose a hopeful lark in the air,
    Spreading out towards the sun his breast;
While the moon set solemn and fair
      Away in the West.

"Up, up, up," called the watchman lark,
In his clear réveillée : "Hearken, oh hark !
Press to the high goal, fly to the mark.
    Up, O sluggard, new morn is born;
If still asleep when the night falls dark,
      Thou must wait a second morn."

"Up, up, up," sad glad voices swelled :
"So the tree falls and lies as it's felled.
Be thy bands loosed, O sleeper, long held
    In sweet sleep whose end is not sweet.
Be the slackness girt and the softness quelled
      And the slowness fleet."

Off he set.   The grass grew rare,
A blight lurked in the darkening air,
The very moss grew hueless and spare,
    The last daisy stood all astunt;
Behind his back the soil lay bare,
      But barer in front.

A land of chasm and rent, a land
Of rugged blackness on either hand :
If water trickled its track was tanned
   With an edge of rust to the chink ;
If one stamped on stone or on sand
     It returned a clink.

A lifeless land, a loveless land,
Without lair or nest on either hand :
Only scorpions jerked in the sand,
   Black as black iron, or dusty pale ;
From point to point sheer rock was manned
     By scorpions in mail.

A land of neither life nor death,
Where no man buildeth or fashioneth,
Where none draws living or dying breath ;
   No man cometh or goeth there,
No man doeth, seeketh, saith,
     In the stagnant air.

Some old volcanic upset must
Have rent the crust and blackened the crust ,
Wrenched and ribbed it beneath its dust,
   Above earth's molten centre at seethe,
Heaved and heaped it by huge upthrust
     Of fire beneath.

Untrodden before, untrodden since :
Tedious land for a social Prince ;
Halting, he scanned the outs and ins.

Endless, labyrinthine, grim,
Of the solitude that made him wince,
Laying wait for him.

By bulging rock and gaping cleft,
Even of half mere daylight reft,
Rueful he peered to right and left,
Muttering in his altered mood :
" The fate is hard that weaves my weft,
Though my lot be good."

Dim the changes of day to night,
Of night scarce dark to day not bright.
Still his road wound towards the right,
Still he went, and still he went,
Till one night he spied a light,
In his discontent.

Out it flashed from a yawn-mouthed cave,
Like a red-hot eye from a grave.
No man stood there of whom to crave
Rest for wayfarer plodding by :
Though the tenant were churl or knave
The Prince might try.

In he passed and tarried not,
Groping his way from spot to spot,
Towards where the cavern flare glowed hot :
An old, old mortal, cramped and double,
Was peering into a seething-pot,
In a world of trouble.

The veriest atomy he looked,
With grimy fingers clutching and crooked,
Tight skin, a nose all bony and hooked,
    And a shaking, sharp, suspicious way ;
Blinking, his eyes had scarcely brooked
        The light of day.

Stared the Prince, for the sight was new ;
Stared, but asked without more ado :
" May a weary traveller lodge with you,
    Old father, here in your lair ?
In your country the inns seem few,
        And scanty the fare."

The head turned not to hear him speak ;
The old voice whistled as through a leak
(Out it came in a quavering squeak) :
    "Work for wage is a bargain fit :
If there's aught of mine that you seek
        You must work for it.

" Buried alive from light and air
This year is the hundredth year,
I feed my fire with a sleepless care,
    Watching my potion wane or wax :
Elixir of Life is simmering there,
        And but one thing lacks.

" If you're fain to lodge here with me,
Take that pair of bellows you see—
Too heavy for my old hands they be—

Take the bellows and puff and puff:
When the steam curls rosy and free
    The broth's boiled enough.

"Then take your choice of all I have;
I will give you life if you crave.
Already I'm mildewed for the grave,
    So first myself I must drink my fill:
But all the rest may be yours, to save
    Whomever you will."

"Done," quoth the Prince, and the bargain stood
First he piled on resinous wood,
Next plied the bellows in hopeful mood;
    Thinking, "My love and I will live.
If I tarry, why life is good,
    And she may forgive."

The pot began to bubble and boil;
The old man cast in essence and oil,
He stirred all up with a triple coil
    Of gold and silver and iron wire
Dredged in a pinch of virgin soil,
    And fed the fire.

But still the steam curled watery white;
Night turned to day and day to night;
One thing lacked, by his feeble sight
    Unseen, unguessed by his feeble mind:
Life might miss him, but Death the blight
    Was sure to find.

So when the hundredth year was full
The thread was cut and finished the school.
Death snapped the old worn-out tool,
    Snapped him short while he stood and stirred
(Though stiff he stood as a stiff-necked mule)
        With never a word.

Thus at length the old crab was nipped.
The dead hand slipped, the dead finger dipped
In the broth as the dead man slipped,—
    That same instant, a rosy red
Flushed the steam, and quivered and clipped
        Round the dead old head.

The last ingredient was supplied
(Unless the dead man mistook or lied).
Up started the Prince, he cast aside
    The bellows plied through the tedious trial,
Made sure that his host had died,
        And filled a phial.

"One night's rest," thought the Prince: "This done,
Forth I speed with the rising sun :
With the morrow I rise and run,
    Come what will of wind or of weather.
This draught of life when my bride is won
        We'll drink together."

Thus the dead man stayed in his grave,
Self-chosen, the dead man in his cave ;
There he stayed, were he fool or knave.

Or honest seeker who had not found :
While the Prince outside was prompt to crave
    Sleep on the ground.

" If she watches, go bid her sleep ;
Bid her sleep, for the road is steep :
He can sleep who holdeth her cheap,
    Sleep and wake and sleep again.
Let him sow, one day he shall reap,
    Let him sow the grain.

" When there blows a sweet garden rose,
Let it bloom and wither if no man knows :
But if one knows when the sweet thing blows
    Knows, and lets it open and drop,
If but a nettle his garden grows
    He hath earned the crop."

Through his sleep the summons rang,
Into his ears it sobbed and it sang.
Slow he woke with a drowsy pang,
    Shook himself without much debate,
Turned where he saw green branches hang,
    Started though late.

For the black land was travelled o'er,
He should see the grim land no more.
A flowering country stretched before
    His face when the lovely day came back
He hugged the phial of Life he bore,
    And resumed his track.

By willow courses he took his path,
Spied what a nest the kingfisher hath,
Marked the fields green to aftermath,
    Marked where the red-brown field-mouse ran
Loitered a while for a deep stream bath,
        Yawned for a fellow-man.

Up on the hills not a soul in view,
In the vale not many nor few ;
Leaves, still leaves and nothing new.
    It's oh for a second maiden, at least,
To bear the flagon, and taste it too,
        And flavour the feast.

Lagging he moved, and apt to swerve ;
Lazy of limb, but quick of nerve.
At length the water-bed took a curve,
    The deep river swept its bankside bare ;
Waters streamed from the hill-reserve—
        Waters here, waters there.

High above, and deep below,
Bursting, bubblir.g, swelling the flow,
Like hill torrents after the snow,—
    Bubbling, gurgling, in whirling strife,
Swaying, sweeping to and fro,—
        He must swim for his life.

Which way ?—which way ?—his eyes grew dim
With the dizzying whirl—which way to swim ?
The thunderous downshoot deafened him ;

Half he choked in the lashing spray :
Life is sweet, and the grave is grim—
     Which way?—which way?

A flash of light, a shout from the strand :
" This way—this way ; here lies the land ! "
His phial clutched in one drowning hand ;
     He catches—misses—catches a rope ;
His feet slip on the slipping sand :
     Is there life?—is there hope?

Just saved, without pulse or breath—
Scarcely saved from the gulp of death ;
Laid where a willow shadoweth—
     Laid where a swelling turf is smooth.
(O Bride ! but the Bridegroom lingereth
     For all thy sweet youth.)

Kind hands do and undo,
Kind voices whisper and coo :
" I will chafe his hands "—" And I "—" And you
     Raise his head, put his hair aside."
(If many laugh, one well may rue :
     Sleep on, thou Bride.)

So the Prince was tended with care :
One wrung foul ooze from his clustered hair ;
Two chafed his hands, and did not spare ;
     But one propped his head that drooped awry :
Till his eyes oped, and at unaware
     They met eye to eye.

Oh, a moon face in a shadowy place,
And a light touch and a winsome grace,
And a thrilling tender voice which says :
    "Safe from waters that seek the sea—
Cold waters by rugged ways—
        Safe with me."

While overhead bird whistles to bird,
And round about plays a gamesome herd :
"Safe with us "—some take up the word—
    "Safe with us, dear lord and friend :
All the sweeter if long deferred
        Is rest in the end."

Had he stayed to weigh and to scan,
He had been more or less than a man :
He did what a young man can,
    Spoke of toil and an arduous way --
Toil to-morrow, while golden ran
        The sands of to-day.

Slip past, slip fast,
Uncounted hours from first to last,
Many hours till the last is past,
    Many hours dwindling to one—
One hour whose die is cast,
        One last hour gone.

Come, gone—gone for ever--
Gone as an unreturning river—
Gone as to death the merriest liver—

Gone as the year at the dying fall—
To-morrow, to-day, yesterday, never—
　　Gone once for all.

Came at length the starting-day,
With last words, and last, last words to say,
With bodiless cries from far away—
　　Chiding wailing voices that rang
Like a trumpet-call to the tug and fray ;
　　And thus they sang :

" Is there life ?—the lamp burns low ;
Is there hope ?—the conring is slow :
The promise promised so long ago,
　　The long promise, has not been kept.
Does she live ?—does she die ?—she slumbers so
　　Who so oft has wept.

" Does she live ?—does she die ?—she languisheth
As a lily drooping to death,
As a drought-worn bird with failing breath,
　　As a lovely vine without a stay,
As a tree whereof the owner saith,
　　' Hew it down to-dav.' "

Stung by that word the Prince was fain
To start on his tedious road again.
He crossed the stream where a ford was plain,
　　He clomb the opposite bank though steep,
And swore to himself to strain and attain
　　Ere he tasted sleep.

Huge before him a mountain frowned
With foot of rock on the valley ground,
And head with snows incessant crowned,
    And a cloud mantle about its strength,
And a path which the wild goat hath not found
        In its breadth and length.

But he was strong to do and dare :
If a host had withstood him there,
He had braved a host with little care
    In his lusty youth and his pride,
Tough to grapple though weak to snare.
        He comes, O Bride.

Up he went where the goat scarce clings,
Up where the eagle folds her wings,
Past the green line of living things,
    Where the sun cannot warm the cold,—
Up he went as a flame enrings
        Where there seems no hold.

Up a fissure barren and black,
Till the eagles tired upon his track,
And the clouds were left behind his back,
    Up till the utmost peak was past,
Then he gasped for breath and his strength fell slack
        He paused at last.

Before his face a valley spread
Where fatness laughed, wine, oil, and bread,
Where all fruit-trees their sweetness shed.

Where all birds made love to their kind,
Where jewels twinkled, and gold lay red
    And not hard to find.

Midway down the mountain side
(On its green slope the path was wide)
Stood a house for a royal bride,
    Built all of changing opal stone,
The royal palace, till now descried
    In his dreams alone.

Less bold than in days of yore,
Doubting now though never before,
Doubting he goes and lags the more:
    Is the time late? does the day grow dim?
Rose, will she open the crimson core
    Of her heart to him?

Above his head a tangle glows
Of wine-red roses, blushes, snows,
Closed buds and buds that unclose,
    Leaves, and moss, and prickles too;
His hand shook as he plucked a rose,
    And the rose dropped dew.

Take heart of grace! the potion of Life
May go far to woo him a wife:
If she frown, yet a lover's strife
    Lightly raised can be laid again:
A hasty word is never the knife
    To cut love in twain.

Far away stretched the royal land,
Fed by dew, by a spice-wind fanned
Light labour more, and his foot would stand
 On the threshold, all labour done ;
Easy pleasure laid at his hand,
  And the dear Bride won.

His slackening steps pause at the gate—
Does she wake or sleep ?—the time is late—
Does she sleep now, or watch and wait ?
 She has watched, she has waited long,
Watching athwart the golden grate
  With a patient song.

Fling the golden portals wide,
The Bridegroom comes to his promised Bride ;
Draw the gold-stiff curtains aside,
 Let them look on each other's face,
She in her meekness, he in his pride—
  Day wears apace.

Day is over, the day that wore.
What is this that comes through the door,
The face covered, the feet before ?
 This that coming takes his breath ;
This Bride not seen, to be seen no more
  Save of Bridegroom Death ?

Veiled figures carrying her
Sweep by yet make no stir ;
There is a smell of spice and myrrh,

A bride-chant burdened with one name;
The bride-song rises steadier
　　Than the torches' flame:

" Too late for love, too late for joy,
　　Too late, too late !
You loitered on the road too long,
　　You trifled at the gate :
The enchanted dove upon her branch
　　Died without a mate ;
The enchanted princess in her tower
　　Slept, died, behind the grate ;
Her heart was starving all this while
　　You made it wait.

" Ten years ago, five years ago,
　　One year ago,
Even then you had arrived in time,
　　Though somewhat slow ;
Then you had known her living face
　　Which now you cannot know :
The frozen fountain would have leaped,
　　The buds gone on to blow,
The warm south wind would have awaked
　　To melt the snow.

Is she fair now as she lies ?
　　Once she was fair ;
Meet queen for any kingly king,
　　With gold-dust on her hair.

Now these are poppies in her locks,
   White poppies she must wear;
Must wear a veil to shroud her face
   And the want graven there:
Or is the hunger fed at length,
   Cast off the care?


"We never saw her with a smile
   Or with a frown;
Her bed seemed never soft to her,
   Though tossed of down;
She little heeded what she wore,
   Kirtle, or wreath, or gown;
We think her white brows often ached
   Beneath her crown,
Till silvery hairs showed in her locks
   That used to be so brown.


"We never heard her speak in haste:
   Her tones were sweet,
And modulated just so much
   As it was meet:
Her heart sat silent through the noise
   And concourse of the street.
There was no hurry in her hands,
   No hurry in her feet;
There was no bliss drew nigh to her,
   That she might run to greet.

" You should have wept her yesterday,
  Wasting upon her bed :
But wherefore should you weep to-day
  That she is dead ?
Lo, we who love weep not to-day,
  But crown her royal head.
Let be these poppies that we strew,
  Your roses are too red :
Let be these poppies, not for you
  Cut down and spread."


## MAIDEN-SONG.

LONG ago and long ago,
  And long ago still,
There dwelt three merry maidens
  Upon a distant hill.
One was tall Meggan,
  And one was dainty May,
But one was fair Margaret,
  More fair than I can say,
Long ago and long ago.


When Meggan plucked the thorny rose,
  And when May pulled the brier,
Half the birds would swoop to see,
  Half the beasts draw nigher ;

Half the fishes of the streams
    Would dart up to admire :
But when Margaret plucked a flag-flower
    Or poppy hot aflame,
All the beasts and all the birds
    And all the fishes came
To her hand more soft than snow.

Strawberry leaves and May-dew
    In brisk morning air,
Strawberry leaves and May-dew
    Make maidens fair.
" I go for strawberry leaves,"
    Meggan said one day :
" Fair Margaret can bide at home,
    But you come with me, May ;
Up the hill and down the hill,
    Along the winding way
You and I are used to go."

So these two fair sisters
    Went with innocent will
Up the hill and down again,
    And round the homestead hill :
While the fairest sat at home,
    Margaret like a queen,
Like a blush-rose, like the moon
    In her heavenly sheen,
Fragrant-breathed as milky cow
    Or field of blossoming bean,

Graceful as an ivy bough
    Born to cling and lean ;
Thus she sat to sing and sew.

When she raised her lustrous eyes
    A beast peeped at the door ;
When she downward cast her eyes
    A fish gasped on the floor ;
When she turned away her eyes
    A bird perched on the sill,
Warbling out its heart of love,
    Warbling warbling still,
With pathetic pleadings low.

Light-foot May with Meggan
    Sought the choicest spot,
Clothed with thyme-alternate grass :
    Then, while day waxed hot,
Sat at ease to play and rest,
    A gracious rest and play ;
The loveliest maidens near or far,
    When Margaret was away,
Who sat at home to sing and sew.

Sun-glow flushed their comely cheeks,
    Wind-play tossed their hair,
Creeping things among the grass
    Stroked them here and there ;
Meggan piped a merry note,
    A fitful wayward lay

While shrill as bird on topmost twig
   Piped merry May ;
Honey-smooth the double flow.


Sped a herdsman from the vale,
   Mounting like a flame,
All on fire to hear and see,
   With floating locks he came.
Looked neither north nor south,
   Neither east nor west,
But sat him down at Meggan's feet
   As love-bird on his nest,
And wooed her with a silent awe,
   With trouble not expressed ;
She sang the tears into his eyes,
   The heart out of his breast :
So he loved her, listening so.


She sang the heart out of his breast,
   The words out of his tongue ;
Hand and foot and pulse he paused
   Till her song was sung.
Then he spoke up from his place
   Simple words and true :
"Scanty goods have I to give,
   Scanty skill to woo ;
But I have a will to work,
   And a heart for you :
Bid me stay or bid me go."

Then Meggan mused within herself:
   " Better be first with him,
Than dwell where fairer Margaret sits,
   Who shines my brightness dim,
For ever second where she sits,
   However fair I be :
I will be lady of his love,
   And he shall worship me ;
i will be lady of his herds
   And stoop to his degree,
At home where kids and fatlings grow."

Sped a shepherd from the height
   Headlong down to look,
(White lambs followed, lured by love
   Of their shepherd's crook) :
He turned neither east nor west,
   Neither north nor south,
But knelt right down to May, for love
   Of her sweet-singing mouth ;
Forgot his flocks, his panting flocks
   In parching hill-side drouth ;
Forgot himself for weal or woe.

Trilled her song and swelled her song
   With maiden coy caprice
In a labyrinth of throbs,
   Pauses, cadences ;
Clear-noted as a dropping brook,
   Soft-noted like the bees.

Wild-noted as the shivering wind
   Forlorn through forest trees :
Love-noted like the wood-pigeon
   Who hides herself for love,
Yet cannot keep her secret safe,
   But coos and coos thereof :
Thus the notes rang loud or low.

He hung breathless on her breath ;
   Speechless, who listened well ;
Could not speak or think or wish
   Till silence broke the spell.
Then he spoke, and spread his hands,
   Pointing here and there :
See my sheep and see the lambs,
   Twin lambs which they bare.
All myself I offer you,
   All my flocks and care,
Your sweet song hath moved me so."

In her fluttered heart young May
   Mused a dubious while :
" If he loves me as he says "—
   Her lips curved with a smile :
" Where Margaret shines like the sun
   I shine but like a moon ;
If sister Meggan makes her choice
   I can make mine as soon ;
At cockcrow we were sister-maids,
   We may be brides at noon."
Said Meggan, " Yes ;" May said not " No."

Fair Margaret stayed alone at home.
  Awhile she sang her song,
Awhile sat silent, then she thought
  " My sisters loiter long."
That sultry noon had waned away,
  Shadows had waxen great:
' Surely," she thought within herself,
  " My sisters loiter late."
She rose, and peered out at the door,
  With patient heart to wait,
And heard a distant nightingale
  Complaining of its mate;
Then down the garden slope she walked
  Down to the garden gate,
Leaned on the rail and waited so.

The slope was lightened by her eyes
  Like summer lightning fair,
Like rising of the haloed moon
  Lightened her glimmering hair,
While her face lightened like the sun
  Whose dawn is rosy white.
Thus crowned with maiden majesty
  She peered into the night,
Looked up the hill and down the hill,
  To left hand and to right,
Flashing like fire-flies to and fro.

Waiting thus in weariness
  She marked the nightingale

Telling, if any one would heed,
　　Its old complaining tale.
Then lifted she her voice and sang,
　　Answering the bird :
Then lifted she her voice and sang,
　　Such notes were never heard
From any bird when Spring's in blow

The king of all that country
　　Coursing far, coursing near,
Curbed his amber-bitted steed,
　　Coursed amain to hear ;
All his princes in his train,
　　Squire, and knight, and peer,
With his crown upon his head,
　　His sceptre in his hand,
Down he fell at Margaret's knees
　　Lord king of all that land,
To her highness bending low

Every beast and bird and fish,
　　Came mustering to the sound,
Every man and every maid
　　From miles of country round :
Meggan on her herdsman's arm,
　　With her shepherd May,
Flocks and herds trooped at their heels
　　Along the hill-side way ;
No foot too feeble for the ascent,
　　Not any head too grey ;
Some were swift and none were slow.

So Margaret sang her sisters home
   In their marriage mirth ;
Sang free birds out of the sky,
   Beasts along the earth,
Sang up fishes of the deep—
   All breathing things that move
Sang from far and sang from near
   To her lovely love ;
Sang together friend and foe ;

Sang a golden-bearded king
   Straightway to her feet,
Sang him silent where he knelt
   In eager anguish sweet.
But when the clear voice died away,
   When longest echoes died,
He stood up like a royal man
   And claimed her for his bride.
So three maids were wooed and won
   In a brief May-tide,
Long ago and long ago.

## DREAM LAND.

WHERE sunless rivers weep
　　Their waves into the deep,
She sleeps a charmèd sleep :
　　Awake her not.
Led by a single star,
She came from very far
To seek where shadows are
　　Her pleasant lot.

She left the rosy morn,
She left the fields of corn,
For twilight cold and lorn
　　And water springs.
Through sleep, as through a veil,
She sees the sky look pale,
And hears the nightingale
　　That sadly sings.

Rest, rest, a perfect rest
Shed over brow and breast ;
Her face is toward the west
　　The purple land.
She cannot see the grain
Ripening on hill and plain ;
She cannot feel the rain
　　Upon her hand.

Rest, rest, for evermore
Upon a mossy shore ;
Rest, rest at the heart's core
    Till time shall cease :
Sleep that no pain shall wake ;
Night that no morn shall break
Till joy shall overtake
    Her perfect peace.


## AT HOME.

WHEN I was dead, my spirit turned
        To seek the much-frequented house :
I passed the door, and saw my friends
    Feasting beneath green orange boughs ;
From hand to hand they pushed the wine,
    They sucked the pulp of plum and peach ;
They sang, they jested, and they laughed,
    For each was loved of each.

I listened to their honest chat :
    Said one : " To-morrow we shall be
Plod plod along the featureless sands,
    And coasting miles and miles of sea."
Said one : " Before the turn of tide
    We will achieve the eyrie-seat."
Said one : " To-morrow shall be like
    To-day, but much more sweet."

" To-morrow," said they, strong with hope,
　　And dwelt upon the pleasant way :
" To-morrow," cried they one and all,
　　While no one spoke of yesterday.
Their life stood full at blessed noon ;
　　I, only I, had passed away :
" To-morrow and to-day," they cried ;
　　I was of yesterday.

I shivered comfortless, but cast
　　No chill across the tablecloth ;
I all-forgotten shivered, sad
　　To stay and yet to part how loth :
I passed from the familiar room,
　　I who from love had passed away,
Like the remembrance of a guest
　　That tarrieth but a day.


# THE POOR GHOST.

" OH whence do you come, my dear friend, to me
　　With your golden hair all fallen below your knee,
And your face as white as snowdrops on the lea,
And your voice as hollow as the hollow sea ? "

" From the other world I come back to you,
My locks are uncurled with dripping drenching dew.
You know the old, whilst I know the new :
But to-morrow you shall know this too."

" Oh not to-morrow into the dark, I pray ;
Oh not to-morrow, too soon to go away :
Here I feel warm and well-content and gay :
Give me another year, another day."

" Am I so changed in a day and a night
That mine own only love shrinks from me with fright
Is fain to turn away to left or right
And cover up his eyes from the sight ? "

" Indeed I loved you, my chosen friend,
I loved you for life, but life has an end ;
Through sickness I was ready to tend :
But death mars all, which we cannot mend.

" Indeed I loved you ; I love you yet,
If you will stay where your bed is set,
Where I have planted a violet
Which the wind waves, which the dew makes wet."

" Life is gone, then love too is gone,
It was a reed that I leant upon :
Never doubt I will leave you alone
And not wake you rattling bone with bone.

" I go home alone to my bed,
Dug deep at the foot and deep at the head,
Roofed in with a load of lead,
Warm enough for the forgotten dead.

" But why did your tears soak through the clay,
And why did your sobs wake me where I lay?
I was away, far enough away:
Let me sleep now till the Judgment Day."


## GROWN AND FLOWN.

I LOVED my love from green of Spring
　　Until sere Autumn's fall;
But now that leaves are withering
　　How should one love at all?
　　One heart's too small
For hunger, cold, love, everything.

I loved my love on sunny days
　　Until late Summer's wane;
But now that frost begins to glaze
　　How should one love again?
　　Nay, love and pain
Walk wide apart in diverse ways.

I loved my love—alas to see
　　That this should be, alas!
I thought that this could scarcely be,
　　Yet has it come to pass:
　　Sweet sweet love was,
Now bitter bitter grown to me.

## A FARM WALK.

THE year stood at its equinox
    And bluff the North was blowing,
A bleat of lambs came from the flocks,
    Green hardy things were growing;
I met a maid with shining locks
    Where milky kine were lowing.

She wore a kerchief on her neck,
    Her bare arm showed its dimple,
Her apron spread without a speck,
    Her air was frank and simple.

She milked into a wooden pail
    And sang a country ditty,
An innocent fond lovers' tale,
    That was not wise nor witty,
Pathetically rustical,
    Too pointless for the city.

She kept in time without a beat
    As true as church-bell ringers,
Unless she tapped time with her feet,
    Or squeezed it with her fingers;
Her clear unstudied notes were sweet
    As many a practised singer's.

I stood a minute out of sight,
  Stood silent for a minute
To eye the pail, and creamy white
  The frothing milk within it;

To eye the comely milking maid
  Herself so fresh and creamy:
"Good day to you," at last I said;
  She turned her head to see me:
"Good day," she said with lifted head;
  Her eyes looked soft and dreamy,

And all the while she milked and milked
  The grave cow heavy-laden:
I've seen grand ladies plumed and silked,
  But not a sweeter maiden;

But not a sweeter fresher maid
  Than this in homely cotton,
Whose pleasant face and silky braid
  I have not yet forgotten.

Seven springs have passed since then, as I
  Count with a sober sorrow;
Seven springs have come and passed me by,
  And spring sets in to-morrow.

I've half a mind to shake myself
  Free just for once from London,
To set my work upon the shelf
  And leave it done or undone:

To run down by the early train,
   Whirl down with shriek and whistle,
And feel the bluff North blow again,
   And mark the sprouting thistle
Set up on waste patch of the lane
   Its green and tender bristle,

And spy the scarce-blown violet banks,
   Crisp primrose leaves and others,
And watch the lambs leap at their pranks
   And butt their patient mothers.

Alas, one point in all my plan
   My serious thoughts demur to :
Seven years have passed for maid and man,
   Seven years have passed for her too ;

Perhaps my rose is overblown,
   Not rosy or too rosy ;
Perhaps in farmhouse of her own
   Some husband keeps her cosy,
Where I should show a face unknown.
   Good-bye, my wayside posy.

## A PORTRAIT.

### I.

SHE gave up beauty in her tender youth,
    Gave all her hope and joy and pleasant ways;
  She covered up her eyes lest they should gaze
On vanity, and chose the bitter truth.
Harsh towards herself, towards others full of ruth,
    Servant of servants, little known to praise,
    Long prayers and fasts trenched on her nights and
        days:
She schooled herself to sights and sounds uncouth
That with the poor and stricken she might make
    A home, until the least of all sufficed
Her wants; her own self learned she to forsake,
Counting all earthly gain but hurt and loss.
So with calm will she chose and bore the cross
    And hated all for love of Jesus Christ.

### II.

They knelt in silent anguish by her bed,
    And could not weep; but calmly there she lay,
    All pain had left her; and the sun's last ray
Shone through upon her, warming into red
The shady curtains.   In her heart she said:
    "Heaven opens; I leave these and go away;
    The Bridegroom calls,—shall the Bride seek to
        stay?"
Then low upon her breast she bowed her head.

O lily flower, O gem of priceless worth,
　O dove with patient voice and patient eyes,
O fruitful vine amid a land of dearth,
　O maid replete with loving purities,
Thou bowedst down thy head with friends on earth
　To raise it with the saints in Paradise.


## BY THE SEA.

WHY does the sea moan evermore?
　　Shut out from heaven it makes its moan,
It frets against the boundary shore;
　All earth's full rivers cannot fill
　The sea, that drinking thirsteth still.


Sheer miracles of loveliness
　Lie hid in its unlooked-on bed:
Anemones, salt, passionless,
　Blow flower-like; just enough alive
　To blow and multiply and thrive.


Shells quaint with curve, or spot, or spike,
　Encrusted live things argus-eyed,
All fair alike, yet all unlike,
　Are born without a pang, and die
　Without a pang, and so pass by.

## GONE FOR EVER.

O HAPPY rosebud blooming
   Upon thy parent tree,
Nay, thou art too presuming;
For soon the earth entombing
   Thy faded charms shall be,
And the chill damp consuming.

O happy skylark springing
   Up to the broad blue sky,
Too fearless in thy winging,
Too gladsome in thy singing,
   Thou also soon shalt lie
Where no sweet notes are ringing.

And through life's shine and shower
   We shall have joy and pain;
But in the summer bower,
And at the morning hour,
   We still shall look in vain
For the same bird and flower.

## LOVE FROM THE NORTH.

I HAD a love in soft south land,
   Beloved through April far in May;
He waited on my lightest breath,
   And never dared to say me nay.

He saddened if my cheer was sad,
　But gay he grew if I was gay;
We never differed on a hair,
　My yes his yes, my nay his nay.

The wedding hour was come, the aisles
　Were flushed with sun and flowers that day;
I pacing balanced in my thoughts:
　" It's quite too late to think of nay."—

My bridegroom answered in his turn,
　Myself had almost answered " yea:"
When through the flashing nave I heard
　A struggle and resounding " nay."

Bridemaids and bridegroom shrank in fear,
　But I stood high who stood at bay:
" And if I answer yea, fair Sir,
　What man art thou to bar with nay?"

He was a strong man from the north,
　Light-locked, with eyes of dangerous grey:
" Put yea by for another time
　In which I will not say thee nay."

He took me in his strong white arms,
　He bore me on his horse away
O'er crag, morass, and hairbreadth pass,
　But never asked me yea or nay.

He made me fast with book and bell,
  With links of love he makes me stay ;
Till now I've neither heart nor power
  Nor will nor wish to say him nay.


## MAGGIE A LADY.

YOU must not call me Maggie, you must not call
    me Dear,
  For I'm Lady of the Manor now stately to see ;
And if there comes a babe, as there may some happy
    year,
  'Twill be little lord or lady at my knee.

Oh, but what ails you, my sailor cousin Phil,
  That you shake and turn white like a cockcrow ghost?
You're as white as I turned once down by the mill,
  When one told me you and ship and crew were lost :

Philip my playfellow, when we were boy and girl
  (It was the Miller's Nancy told it to me),
Philip with the merry life in lip and curl,
  Philip my playfellow drowned in the sea !

I thought I should have fainted, but I did not faint ;
  I stood stunned at the moment, scarcely sad,
Till I raised my wail of desolate complaint
  For you, my cousin, brother, all I had.

They said I looked so pale—some say so fair—·
　My lord stopped in passing to soothe me back to life
I know I missed a ringlet from my hair
　Next morning; and now I am his wife.

Look at my gown, Philip, and look at my ring
　I'm all crimson and gold from top to toe:
All day long I sit in the sun and sing,
　Where in the sun red roses blush and blow.

And I'm the rose of roses, says my lord;
　And to him I'm more than the sun in the sky,
While I hold him fast with the golden cord
　Of a curl, with the eyelash of an eye.

His mother said "fie," and his sisters cried "shame,'
　His highborn ladies cried "shame" from their place :
They said "fie" when they only heard my name,
　But fell silent when they saw my face.

Am I so fair, Philip? Philip, did you think
　I was so fair when we played boy and girl
Where blue forget-me-nots bloomed on the brink
　Of our stream which the mill-wheel sent awhirl?

If I was fair then sure I'm fairer now,
　Sitting where a score of servants stand,
With a coronet on high days for my brow
　And almost a sceptre for my hand.

You're but a sailor, Philip, weatherbeaten brown,
　A stranger on land and at home on the sea,
Coasting as best you may from town to town :
　Coasting along do you often think of me ?

I'm a great lady in a sheltered bower,
　With hands grown white through having nought to
　　do :
Yet sometimes I think of you hour after hour
　Till I nigh wish myself a child with you.


## FROM SUNSET TO STAR RISE.

GO from me, summer friends, and tarry not :
　　I am no summer friend, but wintry cold.
　A silly sheep benighted from the fold,
A sluggard with a thorn-choked garden plot.
Take counsel, sever from my lot your lot,
　Dwell in your pleasant places, hoard your gold ;
　Lest you with me should shiver on the wold,
Athirst and hungering on a barren spot.
For I have hedged me with a thorny hedge,
　I live alone, I look to die alone :
Yet sometimes when a wind sighs through the sedge
　Ghosts of my buried years and friends come back
My heart goes sighing after swallows flown
　On sometime summer's unreturning track.

## SPRING QUIET.

GONE were but the Winter,
  Come were but the Spring,
I would go to a covert
  Where the birds sing.

Where in the whitethorn
  Singeth a thrush,
And a robin sings
  In the holly-bush.

Full of fresh scents
  Are the budding boughs
Arching high over
  A cool green house:

Full of sweet scents,
  And whispering air
Which sayeth softly:
  "We spread no snare;

"Here dwell in safety,
  Here dwell alone,
With a clear stream
  And a mossy stone.

"Here the sun shineth
  Most shadily;
Here is heard an echo
  Of the far sea,
  Though far off it be."

## WINTER RAIN.

E VERY valley drinks,
    Every dell and hollow;
Where the kind rain sinks and sinks,
    Green of Spring will follow.

Yet a lapse of weeks
    Buds will burst their edges,
Strip their wool-coats, glue-coats, streaks,
    In the woods and hedges;

Weave a bower of love
    For birds to meet each other,
Weave a canopy above
    Nest and egg and mother.

But for fattening rain
    We should have no flowers,
Never a bud or leaf again
    But for soaking showers;

Never a mated bird
    In the rocking tree-tops,
Never indeed a flock or herd
    To graze upon the lea-crops.

Lambs so woolly white,
    Sheep the sun-bright leas on,

They could have no grass to bite
But for rain in season.

We should find no moss
In the shadiest places,
Find no waving meadow grass
Pied with broad-eyed daisies:

But miles of barren sand,
With never a son or daughter,
Not a lily on the land,
Or lily on the water.

## VANITY OF VANITIES.

### SONNET.

AH, woe is me for pleasure that is vain,
Ah, woe is me for glory that is past,
Pleasure that bringeth sorrow at the last,
Glory that at the last bringeth no gain!
So saith the sinking heart; and so again
It shall say till the mighty angel-blast
Is blown, making the sun and moon aghast,
And showering down the stars like sudden rain.
And evermore men shall go fearfully
Bending beneath their weight of heaviness;
And ancient men shall lie down wearily,
And strong men shall rise up in weariness;
Yea, even the young shall answer sighingly,
Saying one to another: How vain it is!

## DAYS OF VANITY.

A DREAM that waketh,
   Bubble that breaketh,
Song whose burden sigheth,
   A passing breath,
   Smoke that vanisheth,—
Such is life that dieth.

A flower that fadeth,
   Fruit the tree sheddeth,
Trackless bird that flieth,
   Summer time brief,
   Falling of the leaf,—
Such is life that dieth.

A scent exhaling,
   Snow waters failing,
Morning dew that drieth,
   A windy blast,
   Lengthening shadows cast,
Such is life that dieth.

A scanty measure,
   Rust-eaten treasure,
Spending that nought buyeth,
   Moth on the wing,
   Toil unprofiting,—
Such is life that dieth.

Morrow by morrow
Sorrow breeds sorrow,
For this my song sigheth;
From day to night
We lapse out of sight.—
Such is life that dieth.

## THE GHOST'S PETITION.

"THERE'S a footstep coming; look out and see."—
    " The leaves are falling, the wind is calling;
No one cometh across the lea."—

" There's a footstep coming; O sister, look."—
    " The ripple flashes, the white foam dashes;
No one cometh across the brook."—

" But he promised that he would come:
    To-night, to-morrow, in joy or sorrow,
He must keep his word, and must come home.

" For he promised that he would come:
    His word was given; from earth or heaven,
He must keep his word, and must come home

" Go to sleep, my sweet sister Jane;
    You can slumber, who need not number
Hour after hour, in doubt and pain.

" I shall sit here awhile, and watch;
    Listening, hoping, for one hand groping
In deep shadow to find the latch."

After the dark, and before the light,
  One lay sleeping; and one sat weeping,
Who had watched and wept the weary night.

After the night, and before the day,
  One lay sleeping; and one sat weeping—
Watching, weeping for one away.

There came a footstep climbing the stair;
  Some one standing out on the landing
Shook the door like a puff of air—

Shook the door and in he passed.
  Did he enter?   In the room centre
Stood her husband: the door shut fast.

" O Robin, but you are cold—
  Chilléd with the night-dew: so lily-white you
Look like a stray lamb from our fold.

" O Robin, but you are late:
  Come and sit near me—sit here and cheer me."—
(Blue the flame burnt in the grate.)

" Lay not down your head on my breast:
  I cannot hold you, kind wife, nor fold you
In the shelter that you love best.

" Feel not after my clasping hand:
  I am but a shadow, come from the meadow
Where many lie, but no tree can stand.

" We are trees which have shed their leaves :
  Our heads lie low there, but no tears flow there
Only I grieve for my wife who grieves.

" I could rest if you would not moan
  Hour after hour ; I have no power
To shut my ears where I lie alone.

" I could rest if you would not cry ;
  But there's no sleeping while you sit weeping—
Watching, weeping so bitterly."—

" Woe's me ! woe's me ! for this I have heard.
  Oh, night of sorrow !—oh, black to-morrow !
Is it thus that you keep your word ?

" O you who used so to shelter me
  Warm from the least wind—why, now the east wind
Is warmer than you, whom I quake to see.

" O my husband of flesh and blood,
  For whom my mother I left, and brother,
And all I had, accounting it good,

" What do you do there, underground,
  In the dark hollow ?   I'm fain to follow.
What do you do there ?—what have you found ? "—

" What I do there I must not tell :
  But I have plenty : kind wife, content ye :
It is well with us—it is well.

" Tender hand hath made our nest ;
    Our fear is ended, our hope is blended
With present pleasure, and we have rest."—

" Oh, but Robin, I'm fain to come
    If your present days are so pleasant,
For my days are so wearisome.

" Yet I'll dry my tears for your sake :
    Why should I tease you, who cannot please you
Any more with the pains I take ? "


## ONCE FOR ALL.

### (MARGARET.)

I SAID : This is a beautiful fresh rose.
    I said : I will delight me with its scent ,
    Will watch its lovely curve of languishment,
Will watch its leaves unclose, its heart unclose.
I said : Old earth has put away her snows,
    All living things make merry to their bent,
    A flower is come for every flower that went
In autumn, the sun glows, the south wind blows.
So walking in a garden of delight
    I came upon one sheltered shadowed nook
Where broad leaf shadows veiled the day with night
    And there lay snow unmelted by the sun :—
I answered : Take who will the path I took,
    Winter nips once for all ; love is but one.

## ENRICA, 1865.

SHE came among us from the South
   And made the North her home awhile ;
   Our dimness brightened in her smile,
Our tongue grew sweeter in her mouth.

We chilled beside her liberal glow,
   She dwarfed us by her ampler scale,
   Her full-blown blossom made us pale,
She summer-like and we like snow.

We Englishwomen, trim, correct,
   All minted in the self-same mould,
   Warm-hearted but of semblance cold,
All-courteous out of self-respect.

She woman in her natural grace,
   Less trammelled she by lore of school,
   Courteous by nature not by rule,
Warm-hearted and of cordial face.

So for awhile she made her home
   Among us in the rigid North,
   She who from Italy came forth
And scaled the Alps and crossed the foam

But if she found us like our sea,
   Of aspect colourless and chill,
   Rock-girt ; like it she found us still
Deep at our deepest. strong and free.

## A CHILL.

WHAT can lambkins do
        All the keen night through?
Nestle by their woolly mother
    The careful ewe.

What can nestlings do
    In the nightly dew?
Sleep beneath their mother's wing
    Till day breaks anew.

If in field or tree
    There might only be
Such a warm soft sleeping-place
    Found for me!


## SOMEWHERE OR OTHER.

SOMEWHERE or other there must surely be
    The face not seen, the voice not heard,
The heart that not yet—never yet—ah me!
    Made answer to my word.

Somewhere or other, may be near or far;
    Past land and sea, clean out of sight;
Beyond the wandering moon, beyond the star
    That tracks her night by night.

Somewhere or other, may be far or near;
　With just a wall, a hedge, between;
With just the last leaves of the dying year
　Fallen on a turf grown green.

## NOBLE SISTERS.

" NOW did you mark a falcon,
　　Sister dear, sister dear,
Flying toward my window
　In the morning cool and clear?
With jingling bells about her neck,
　But what beneath her wing?
It may have been a ribbon,
　Or it may have been a ring."—
　　" I marked a falcon swooping
　　　At the break of day:
　　And for your love, my sister dove,
　　　I 'frayed the thief away."—

" Or did you spy a ruddy hound,
　　Sister fair and tall,
Went snuffing round my garden bound,
　Or crouched by my bower wall?
With a silken leash about his neck;
　But in his mouth may be
A chain of gold and silver links,
　Or a letter writ to me."—

"I heard a hound, highborn sister,
  Stood baying at the moon :
I rose and drove him from your wall
  Lest you should wake too soon."—

"Or did you meet a pretty page
  Sat swinging on the gate ;
Sat whistling whistling like a bird,
  Or may be slept too late :
With eaglets broidered on his cap,
  And eaglets on his glove ?
If you had turned his pockets out,
  You had found some pledge of love."—
    "I met him at this daybreak,
      Scarce the east was red :
    Lest the creaking gate should anger you
      I packed him home to bed."—

"Oh patience, sister.  Did you see
  A young man tall and strong,
Swift-footed to uphold the right
  And to uproot the wrong,
Come home across the desolate sea
  To woo me for his wife ?
And in his heart my heart is locked,
  And in his life my life."—
    "I met a nameless man, sister,
      Who loitered round our door :
    I said : Her husband loves her much
      And yet she loves him more."—

"Fie, sister, fie, a wicked lie,
    A lie, a wicked lie,
I have none other love but him,
    Nor will have till I die.
And you have turned him from our door,
    And stabbed him with a lie:
I will go seek him thro' the world
    In sorrow till I die."—
        "Go seek in sorrow, sister,
            And find in sorrow too:
        If thus you shame our father's name
            My curse go forth with you."

## JESSIE CAMERON.

"JESSIE, Jessie Cameron,
    Hear me but this once," quoth he.
"Good luck go with you, neighbour's son,
    But I'm no mate for you," quoth she.
Day was verging toward the night
    There beside the moaning sea,
Dimness overtook the light
    There where the breakers be.
"O Jessie, Jessie Cameron,
    I have loved you long and true."—
"Good luck go with you, neighbour's son,
    But I'm no mate for you.

She was a careless, fearless girl,
    And made her answer plain,
Outspoken she to earl or churl,
    Kindhearted in the main,
But somewhat heedless with her tongue
    And apt at causing pain ;
A mirthful maiden she and young,
    Most fair for bliss or bane.
" Oh, long ago I told you so,
    I tell you so to-day :
Go you your way, and let me go
    Just my own free way."

The sea swept in with moan and foam
    Quickening the stretch of sand ;
They stood almost in sight of home ;
    He strove to take her hand.
" Oh, can't you take your answer then,
    And won't you understand ?
For me you're not the man of men,
    I've other plans are planned.
You're good for Madge, or good for Cis,
    Or good for Kate, may be :
But what's to me the good of this
    While you're not good for me ? "

They stood together on the beach,
    They two alone,
And louder waxed his urgent speech,
    His patience almost gone :

"Oh, say but one kind word to me,
    Jessie, Jessie Cameron."—
"I'd be too proud to beg," quoth she,
    And pride was in her tone.
And pride was in her lifted head,
    And in her angry eye,
And in her foot, which might have fled
    But would not fly.

Some say that he had gipsy blood,
    That in his heart was guile:
Yet he had gone through fire and flood
    Only to win her smile.
Some say his grandam was a witch,
    A black witch from beyond the Nile,
Who kept an image in a niche
    And talked with it the while.
And by her hut far down the lane
    Some say they would not pass at night,
Lest they should hear an unked strain
    Or see an unked sight.

Alas, for Jessie Cameron!—
    The sea crept moaning, moaning nigher.
She should have hastened to begone,—
    The sea swept higher, breaking by her:
She should have hastened to her home
    While yet the west was flushed with fire,
But now her feet are in the foam,
    The sea-foam sweeping higher.

O mother, linger at your door,
    And light your lamp to make it plain,
But Jessie she comes home no more,
    No more again.

They stood together on the strand,
    They only each by each ;
Home, her home, was close at hand,
    Utterly out of reach.
Her mother in the chimney nook
    Heard a startled sea-gull screech,
But never turned her head to look
    Towards the darkening beach :
Neighbours here and neighbours there
    Heard one scream, as if a bird
Shrilly screaming cleft the air :—
    That was all they heard.

Jessie she comes home no more,
    Comes home never ;
Her lover's step sounds at his door
    No more for ever.
And boats may search upon the sea
    And search along the river,
But none know where the bodies be
    Sea-winds that shiver,
Sea-birds that breast the blast,
    Sea-waves swelling,
Keep the secret first and last
    Of their dwelling.

Whether the tide so hemmed them round
  With its pitiless flow,
That when they would have gone they found
  No way to go ;
Whether she scorned him to the last
  With words flung to and fro,
Or clung to him when hope was past,
  None will ever know :
Whether he helped or hindered her,
  Threw up his life or lost it well,
The troubled sea for all its stir
  Finds no voice to tell.

Only watchers by the dying
  Have thought they heard one pray
Wordless, urgent ; and replying
  One seem to say him nay :
And watchers by the dead have heard
  A windy swell from miles away,
With sobs and screams, but not a word
  Distinct for them to say :
And watchers out at sea have caught
  Glimpse of a pale gleam here or there,
Come and gone as quick as thought,
  Which might be hand or hair.

## SPRING.

FROST-LOCKED all the winter,
    Seeds, and roots, and stones of fruit
What shall make their sap ascend
That they may put forth shoots?
Tips of tender green,
Leaf, or blade, or sheath;
Telling of the hidden life
That breaks forth underneath,
Life nursed in its grave by Death.

Blows the thaw-wind pleasantly,
Drips the soaking rain,
By fits looks down the waking sun:
Young grass springs on the plain;
Young leaves clothe early hedgerow trees;
Seeds, and roots, and stones of fruits,
Swollen with sap put forth their shoots;
Curled-headed ferns sprout in the lane;
Birds sing and pair again.

There is no time like Spring,
When life's alive in everything,
Before new nestlings sing,
Before cleft swallows speed their journey back
Along the trackless track—
God guides their wing,
He spreads their table that they nothing lack,—

Before the daisy grows a common flower,
Before the sun has power
To scorch the world up in his noontide hour.

There is no time like Spring,
Like Spring that passes by;
There is no life like Spring-life born to die,—
Piercing the sod,
Clothing the uncouth clod,
Hatched in the nest,
Fledged on the windy bough,
Strong on the wing:
There is no time like Spring that passes by,
Now newly born, and now
Hastening to die.

## SUMMER.

WINTER is cold-hearted,
　　　Spring is yea and nay,
Autumn is a weather-cock
　　Blown every way:
Summer days for me
When every leaf is on its tree;

When Robin's not a beggar,
　　And Jenny Wren's a bride,
And larks hang singing, singing, singing,

Over the wheat-fields wide,
  And anchored lilies ride,
And the pendulum spider
  Swings from side to side,

And blue-black beetles transact business,
  And gnats fly in a host,
And furry caterpillars hasten
  That no time be lost,
And moths grow fat and thrive,
And ladybirds arrive.

Before green apples blush,
  Before green nuts embrown,
Why, one day in the country
  Is worth a month in town ;
  Is worth a day and a year
Of the dusty, musty, lag-last fashion
  That days drone elsewhere.


## AUTUMN.

I DWELL alone—I dwell alone, alone,
  Whilst full my river flows down to the sea,
Gilded with flashing boats
  That bring no friend to me :
Love-songs, gurgling from a hundred throats,
  O love-pangs, let me be.

Fair fall the freighted boats which gold and stone
    And spices bear to sea :
Slim, gleaming maidens swell their mellow notes,
    Love-promising, entreating—
      Ah ! sweet, but fleeting—
    Beneath the shivering, snow-white sails.
    Hush ! the wind flags and fails—
Hush ! they will lie becalmed in sight of strand—
    Sight of my strand, where I do dwell alone ;
Their songs wake singing echoes in my land—
    They cannot hear me moan.

One latest, solitary swallow flies
    Across the sea, rough autumn-tempest tost,
    Poor bird, shall it be lost?
Dropped down into this uncongenial sea.
      With no kind eyes
      To watch it while it dies,
    Unguessed, uncared for, free :
      Set free at last,
      The short pang past,
In sleep, in death, in dreamless sleep locked fast.

Mine avenue is all a growth of oaks,
    Some rent by thunder strokes,
Some rustling leaves and acorns in the breeze ;
    Fair fall my fertile trees,
That rear their goodly heads, and live at ease.

A spider's web blocks all mine avenue ;
    He catches down and foolish painted flies
    That spider wary and wise.

Each morn it hangs a rainbow strung with dew
   Betwixt boughs green with sap,
   So fair, few creatures guess it is a trap:
     I will not mar the web,
Though sad I am to see the small lives ebb.

It shakes—my trees shake—for a wind is roused
     In cavern where it housed:
     Each white and quivering sail,
     Of boats among the water leaves
Hollows and strains in the full-throated gale:
     Each maiden sings again—
Each languid maiden, whom the calm
Had lulled to sleep with rest and spice and balm.
     Miles down my river to the sea
      They float and wane,
     Long miles away from me.

Perhaps they say: "She grieves,
     Uplifted, like a beacon, on her tower."
     Perhaps they say: "One hour
More, and we dance among the golden sheaves."
     Perhaps they say: "One hour
     More, and we stand,
     Face to face, hand in hand;
Make haste, O slack gale, to the looked-for land!"

     My trees are not in flower,
     I have no bower,
     And gusty creaks my tower,
And lonesome, very lonesome, is my strand.

## WINTER: MY SECRET

I TELL my secret? No indeed, not I:
  Perhaps some day, who knows?
But not to-day; it froze, and blows, and snows,
And you're too curious: fie!
You want to hear it? well:
Only, my secret's mine, and I won't tell.

  Or, after all, perhaps there's none:
Suppose there is no secret after all,
But only just my fun.
To-day's a nipping day, a biting day;
In which one wants a shawl,
A veil, a cloak, and other wraps:
I cannot ope to every one who taps,
And let the draughts come whistling through my hall;
Come bounding and surrounding me,
Come buffeting, astounding me,
Nipping and clipping through my wraps and all.
I wear my mask for warmth: who ever shows
His nose to Russian snows
To be pecked at by every wind that blows?
You would not peck? I thank you for good will,
Believe, but leave that truth untested still.

  Spring's an expansive time: yet I don't trust
March with its peck of dust,

Nor April with its rainbow-crowned brief showers,
Nor even May, whose flowers
One frost may wither through the sunless hours.

Perhaps some languid summer day,
When drowsy birds sing less and less,
And golden fruit is ripening to excess,
If there's not too much sun nor too much cloud,
And the warm wind is neither still nor loud,
Perhaps my secret I may say,
Or you may guess.


## AUTUMN VIOLETS.

KEEP love for youth, and violets for the spring :
　　Or if these bloom when worn-out autumn grieves,
　Let them lie hid in double shade of leaves,
Their own, and others dropped down withering ;
For violets suit when home birds build and sing,
　　Not when the outbound bird a passage cleaves ;
　　Not with dry stubble of mown harvest sheaves,
But when the green world buds to blossoming.
Keep violets for the spring, and love for youth,
　　Love that should dwell with beauty, mirth, and hope
　　Or if a later sadder love be born,
　Let this not look for grace beyond its scope,
But give itself, nor plead for answering truth—
　　A grateful Ruth tho' gleaning scanty corn.

## A DIRGE.

WHY were you born when the snow was falling?
  You should have come to the cuckoo's calling,
Or when grapes are green in the cluster,
Or, at least, when lithe swallows muster
    For their far off flying
    From summer dying.

Why did you die when the lambs were cropping?
You should have died at the apples' dropping,
When the grasshopper comes to trouble,
And the wheat-fields are sodden stubble,
    And all winds go sighing
    For sweet things dying.

## A BIRD'S-EYE VIEW.

" CROAK, croak, croak,"
    Thus the Raven spoke,
Perched on his crooked tree
As hoarse as hoarse could be.
Shun him and fear him,
Lest the Bridegroom hear him ;
Scout him and rout him
With his ominous eye about him.

Yet, " Croak, croak, croak,"
Still tolled from the oak ;
From that fatal black bird,
Whether heard or unheard :
" O ship upon the high seas,
Freighted with lives and spices,
Sink, O ship," croaked the Raven :
" Let the Bride mount to heaven."

In a far foreign land
Upon the wave-edged sand,
Some friends gaze wistfully
Across the glittering sea.
" If we could clasp our sister,"
Three say, " now we have missed her !"
" If we could kiss our daughter !"
Two sigh across the water.

Oh, the ship sails fast
With silken flags at the mast,
And the home-wind blows soft ;
But a Raven sits aloft,
Chuckling and choking,
Croaking, croaking, croaking :
Let the beacon-fire blaze higher ;
Bridegroom, watch ; the Bride draws nigher.

On a sloped sandy beach,
Which the spring-tide billows reach,
Stand a watchful throng
Who have hoped and waited long :

" Fie on this ship, that tarries
With the priceless freight it carries.
The time seems long and longer :
O languid wind, wax stronger ; "—

Whilst the Raven perched at ease
Still croaks and does not cease,
One monotonous note
Tolled from his iron throat :
" No father, no mother,
But I have a sable brother :
He sees where ocean flows to,
And he knows what he knows too."

A day and a night
They kept watch worn and white ;
A night and a day
For the swift ship on its way :
For the Bride and her maidens
—Clear chimes the bridal cadence—
For the tall ship that never
Hove in sight for ever.

On either shore, some
Stand in grief loud or dumb
As the dreadful dread
Grows certain though unsaid.
For laughter there is weeping,
And waking instead of sleeping,
And a desperate sorrow
Morrow after morrow.

Oh, who knows the truth,
How she perished in her youth,
And like a queen went down
Pale in her royal crown :
How she went up to glory
From the sea-foam chill and hoary,
From the sea-depth black and riven
To the calm that is in Heaven?

They went down, all the crew,
The silks and spices too,
The great ones and the small,
One and all, one and all.
Was it through stress of weather,
Quicksands, rocks, or all together?
Only the Raven knows this,
And he will not disclose this.—

After a day and a year
The bridal bell chimes clear ;
After a year and a day
The Bridegroom is brave and gay :
Love is sound, faith is rotten ;
The old Bride is forgotten :—
Two ominous Ravens only
Remember, black and lonely.

## FATA MORGANA.

A BLUE-EYED phantom far before
 Is laughing, leaping toward the sun :
Like lead I chase it evermore,
 I pant and run.

It breaks the sunlight bound on bound :
 Goes singing as it leaps along
To sheep-bells with a dreamy sound
 A dreamy song.

I laugh, it is so brisk and gay ;
 It is so far before, I weep :
I hope I shall lie down some day,
 Lie down and sleep.

## MEMORY.

### I.

I NURSED it in my bosom while it lived,
 I hid it in my heart when it was dead ;
In joy I sat alone, even so I grieved
 Alone and nothing said.

I shut the door to face the naked truth,
 I stood alone—I faced the truth alone,
Stripped bare of self-regard or forms or ruth
 Till first and last were shown.

I took the perfect balances and weighed ;
   No shaking of my hand disturbed the poise ,
Weighed, found it wanting : not a word I said,
     But silent made my choice.

None know the choice I made ; I make it still.
   None know the choice I made and broke my heart,
Breaking mine idol : I have braced my will
     Once, chosen for once my part.

I broke it at a blow, I laid it cold,
   Crushed in my deep heart where it used to live.
My heart dies inch by inch ; the time grows old,
     Grows old in which I grieve.


## II.

I have a room whereinto no one enters
   Save I myself alone :
   There sits a blessed memory on a throne,
There my life centres.

While winter comes and goes—oh tedious comer !—
   And while its nip-wind blows ;
   While bloom the bloodless lily and warm rose
Of lavish summer.

If any should force entrance he might see there
   One buried yet not dead,
   Before whose face I no more bow my head
Or bend my knee there ;

But often in my worn life's autumn weather
    I watch there with clear eyes,
    And think how it will be in Paradise
When we're together.


## "THEY DESIRE A BETTER COUNTRY."

### I.

I WOULD not if I could undo my past,
    Tho' for its sake my future is a blank;
My past for which I have myself to thank,
For all its faults and follies first and last.
I would not cast anew the lot once cast,
    Or launch a second ship for one that sank,
    Or drug with sweets the bitterness I drank,
Or break by feasting my perpetual fast.
I would not if I could: for much more dear
    Is one remembrance than a hundred joys,
      More than a thousand hopes in jubilee;
    Dearer the music of one tearful voice
      That unforgotten calls and calls to me,
"Follow me here, rise up, and follow here."


### II.

What seekest thou, far in the unknown land?
    In hope I follow joy gone on before;
    In hope and fear persistent more and more,
As the dry desert lengthens out its sand.

Whilst day and night I carry in my hand
 The golden key to ope the golden door
 Of golden home ; yet mine eye weepeth sore,
For long the journey is that makes no stand.
And who is this that veiled doth walk with thee
 Lo, this is Love that walketh at my right ;
  One exile holds us both, and we are bound
To selfsame home-joys in the land of light.
Weeping thou walkest with him ; weepeth he ?—
  Some sobbing weep, some weep and make no
  sound.

### III.

A dimness of a glory glimmers here
 Thro' veils and distance from the space remote
 A faintest far vibration of a note
Reaches to us and seems to bring us near ;
Causing our face to glow with braver cheer,
 Making the serried mist to stand afloat,
 Subduing languor with an antidote,
And strengthening love almost to cast out fear :
Till for one moment golden city walls
 Rise looming on us, golden walls of home,
Light of our eyes until the darkness falls ;
 Then thro' the outer darkness burdensome
I hear again the tender voice that calls,
 " Follow me hither, follow, rise, and come."

## CHILD'S TALK IN APRIL.

I WISH you were a pleasant wren,
    And I your small accepted mate;
How we'd look down on toilsome men!
    We'd rise and go to bed at eight
    Or it may be not quite so late.

Then you should see the nest I'd build,
    The wondrous nest for you and me;
The outside rough perhaps, but filled
    With wool and down; ah, you should see
    The cosy nest that it would be.

We'd have our change of hope and fear,
    Small quarrels, reconcilements sweet:
I'd perch by you to chirp and cheer,
    Or hop about on active feet,
    And fetch you dainty bits to eat.

We'd be so happy by the day,
    So safe and happy through the night,
We both should feel, and I should say,
    It's all one season of delight,
And we'll make merry whilst we may,

Perhaps some day there'd be an egg
   When spring had blossomed from the snow :
I'd stand triumphant on one leg ;
   Like chanticleer I'd almost crow
   To let our little neighbours know.

Next you should sit and I would sing
Through lengthening days of sunny spring ;
   Till, if you wearied of the task,
I'd sit ; and you should spread your wing
   From bough to bough ; I'd sit and bask.

Fancy the breaking of the shell,
   The chirp, the chickens wet and bare,
The untried proud paternal swell ;
   And you with housewife-matron air
   Enacting choicer bills of fare.

Fancy the embryo coats of down,
   The gradual feathers soft and sleek ;
Till clothed and strong from tail to crown,
   With virgin warblings in their beak,
   They too go forth to soar and seek.

So would it last an April through
And early summer fresh with dew,
   Then should we part and live as twain :
Love-time would bring me back to you
   And build our happy nest again.

## A GREEN CORNFIELD.

" And singing still dost soar and soaring ever singest."

THE earth was green, the sky was blue :
 I saw and heard one sunny morn
A skylark hang between the two,
 A singing speck above the corn ;

A stage below, in gay accord,
 White butterflies danced on the wing,
And still the singing skylark soared
 And silent sank and soared to sing.

The cornfield stretched a tender green
 To right and left beside my walks ;
I knew he had a nest unseen
 Somewhere among the million stalks :

And as I paused to hear his song
 While swift the sunny moments slid,
Perhaps his mate sat listening long,
 And listened longer than I did.

## THE LAMBS OF GRASMERE, 1860.

THE upland flocks grew starved and thinned:
  Their shepherds scarce could feed the lambs
Whose milkless mothers butted them,
  Or who were orphaned of their dams.
The lambs athirst for mother's milk
  Filled all the place with piteous sounds:
Their mothers' bones made white for miles
  The pastureless wet pasture grounds.

Day after day, night after night,
  From lamb to lamb the shepherds went,
With teapots for the bleating mouths,
  Instead of nature's nourishment.
The little shivering gaping things
  Soon knew the step that brought them aid,
And fondled the protecting hand,
  And rubbed it with a woolly head.

Then, as the days waxed on to weeks,
  It was a pretty sight to see
These lambs with frisky heads and tails
  Skipping and leaping on the lea,
Bleating in tender trustful tones,
  Resting on rocky crag or mound,
And following the beloved feet
  That once had sought for them and found.

These very shepherds of their flocks,
   These loving lambs so meek to please,
Are worthy of recording words
   And honour in their due degrees :
So 1 might live a hundred years,
   And roam from strand to foreign strand,
Yet not forget this flooded spring
   And scarce-saved lambs of Westmoreland.


## A BIRTHDAY.

MY heart is like a singing bird
   Whose nest is in a watered shoot ;
My heart is like an apple-tree
   Whose boughs are bent with thickset fruit
My heart is like a rainbow shell
   That paddles in a halcyon sea ;
My heart is gladder than all these
   Because my love is come to me.

Raise me a dais of silk and down ;
   Hang it with vair and purple dyes ;
Carve it in doves and pomegranates,
   And peacocks with a hundred eyes ;
Work it in gold and silver grapes,
   In leaves and silver fleurs-de-lys ;
Because the birthday of my life
   Is come, my love is come to me.

## A BRIDE SONG

THROUGH the vales to my love!
    To the happy small nest of home
Green from basement to roof;
    Where the honey-bees come
To the window-sill flowers,
    And dive from above,
Safe from the spider that weaves
    Her warp and her woof
In some outermost leaves.

Through the vales to my love!
    In sweet April hours
    All rainbows and showers,
While dove answers dove,—
    In beautiful May,
When the orchards are tender
    And frothing with flowers,—
    In opulent June,
When the wheat stands up slender
    By sweet-smelling hay,
And half the sun's splendour
    Descends to the moon.

Through the vales to my love!
    Where the turf is so soft to the feet
    And the thyme makes it sweet,
And the stately foxglove

Hangs silent its exquisite bells ;
   And where water wells
The greenness grows greener,
   And bulrushes stand
Round a lily to screen her.

Nevertheless, if this land,
   Like a garden to smell and to sight,
Were turned to a desert of sand ;
   Stripped bare of delight,
   All its best gone to worst,
For my feet no repose,
   No water to comfort my thirst,
And heaven like a furnace above,—
   The desert would be
   As gushing of waters to me,
The wilderness be as a rose,
   If it led me to thee,
   O my love.

## CONFLUENTS.

As rivers seek the sea,
   Much more deep than they,
So my soul seeks thee
      Far away :
As running rivers moan
On their course alone,
   So I moan
   Left alone.

As the delicate rose
　　To the sun's sweet strength
Doth herself unclose,
　　Breadth and length ;
So spreads my heart to thee
Unveiled utterly,
　　I to thee
　　Utterly.

As morning dew exhales
　　Sunwards pure and free,
So my spirit fails
　　After thee :
As dew leaves not a trace
On the green earth's face ;
　　I, no trace
　　On thy face.

Its goal the river knows,
　　Dewdrops find a way,
Sunlight cheers the rose
　　In her day :
Shall I, lone sorrow past,
Find thee at the last ?
　　Sorrow past,
　　Thee at last ?

## REMEMBER.

### SONNET.

REMEMBER me when I am gone away,
  Gone far away into the silent land ;
  When you can no more hold me by the hand,
Nor I half turn to go yet turning stay.
Remember me when no more day by day
  You tell me of our future that you planned :
  Only remember me ; you understand
It will be late to counsel then or pray.
Yet if you should forget me for a while
  And afterwards remember, do not grieve :
  For if the darkness and corruption leave
  A vestige of the thoughts that once I had,
Better by far you should forget and smile
  Than that you should remember and be sad.

## AFTER DEATH.

### SONNET.

THE curtains were half drawn, the floor was swept
    And strewn with rushes, rosemary and may
  Lay thick upon the bed on which I lay,
Where through the lattice ivy-shadows crept.
He leaned above me, thinking that I slept
    And could not hear him; but I heard him say:
    " Poor child, poor child:" and as he turned away
Came a deep silence, and I knew he wept.
He did not touch the shroud, or raise the fold
    That hid my face, or take my hand in his,
        Or ruffle the smooth pillows for my head:
        He did not love me living; but once dead
    He pitied me; and very sweet it is
To know he still is warm though I am cold.

## THE LOWEST ROOM.

LIKE flowers sequestered from the sun
   And wind of summer, day by day
I dwindled paler, whilst my hair
    Showed the first tinge of grey.

" Oh what is life, that we should live ?
   Or what is death, that we must die ?
A bursting bubble is our life
    I also, what am I ?"

" What is your grief ? now tell me, sweet,
   That I may grieve," my sister said ;
And stayed a white embroidering hand
    And raised a golden head :

Her tresses showed a richer mass,
   Her eyes looked softer than my own,
Her figure had a statelier height,
    Her voice a tenderer tone.

" Some must be second and not first ;
   All cannot be the first of all :
Is not this, too, but vanity ?
    I stumble like to fall.

" So yesterday I read the acts
    Of Hector and each clangorous king
With wrathful great Æacides :—
    Old Homer leaves a sting."


The comely face looked up again,
    The deft hand lingered on the thread :
" Sweet, tell me what is Homer's sting,
    Old Homer's sting?" she said.


" He stirs my sluggish pulse like wine,
    He melts me like the wind of spice,
Strong as strong Ajax' red right hand,
    And grand like Juno's eyes.


" I cannot melt the sons of men,
    I cannot fire and tempest-toss :—
Besides, those days were golden days,
    Whilst these are days of dross."


She laughed a feminine low laugh,
    Yet did not stay her dexterous hand :
" Now tell me of those days," she said,
    " When time ran golden sand."


" Then men were men of might and right,
    Sheer might, at least, and weighty swords
Then men in open blood and fire
    Bore witness to their words,

" Crest-rearing kings with whistling spears
    But if these shivered in the shock
They wrenched up hundred-rooted trees,
    Or hurled the effacing rock.

" Then hand to hand, then foot to foot,
    Stern to the death-grip grappling then,
Who ever thought of gunpowder
    Amongst these men of men ?

" They knew whose hand struck home the death,
    They knew who broke but would not bend,
Could venerate an equal foe
    And scorn a laggard friend.

" Calm in the utmost stress of doom,
    Devout toward adverse powers above,
They hated with intenser hate
    And loved with fuller love.

" Then heavenly beauty could allay
    As heavenly beauty stirred the strife :
By them a slave was worshipped more
    Than is by us a wife."

She laughed again, my sister laughed ;
    Made answer o'er the laboured cloth :
" I rather would be one of us
    Than wife, or slave, or both."

" Oh better then be slave or wife
　　Than fritter now blank life away :
Then night had holiness of night,
　　And day was sacred day.

" The princess laboured at her loom,
　　Mistress and handmaiden alike ;
Beneath their needles grew the field
　　With warriors armed to strike.

" Or, look again, dim Dian's face
　　Gleamed perfect through the attendant night :
Were such not better than those holes
　　Amid that waste of white ?

" A shame it is, our aimless life ;
　　I rather from my heart would feed
From silver dish in gilded stall
　　With wheat and wine the steed—

" The faithful steed that bore my lord
　　In safety through the hostile land,
The faithful steed that arched his neck
　　To fondle with my hand."

Her needle erred ; a moment's pause,
　　A moment's patience, all was well.
Then she : " But just suppose the horse.
　　Suppose the rider fell ?

" Then captive in an alien house,
  Hungering on exile's bitter bread,—
They happy, they who won the lot
  Of sacrifice," she said.


Speaking she faltered, while her look
  Showed forth her passion like a glass :
With hand suspended, kindling eye,
  Flushed cheek, how fair she was !


" Ah well, be those the days of dross ;
  This, if you will, the age of gold :
Yet had those days a spark of warmth,
  While these are somewhat cold—


" Are somewhat mean and cold and slow,
  Are stunted from heroic growth :
We gain but little when we prove
  The worthlessness of both."


" But life is in our hands," she said :
  " In our own hands for gain or loss :
Shall not the Sevenfold Sacred Fire
  Suffice to purge our dross ?


" Too short a century of dreams,
  One day of work sufficient length :
Why should not you, why should not I
  Attain heroic strength ?

" Our life is given us as a blank ;
    Ourselves must make it blest or curst :
Who dooms me I shall only be
     The second, not the first ?


" Learn from old Homer, if you will,
    Such wisdom as his books have said :
In one the acts of Ajax shine,
     In one of Diomed.


" Honoured all heroes whose high deeds
    Through life, through death, enlarge their span
Only Achilles in his rage
     And sloth is less than man."


" Achilles only less than man ?
    He less than man who, half a god,
Discomfited all Greece with rest,
     Cowed Ilion with a nod ?


" He offered vengeance, lifelong grief
    To one dear ghost, uncounted price :
Beasts, Trojans, adverse gods, himself,
     Heaped up the sacrifice.


" Self-immolated to his friend,
    Shrined in world's wonder, Homer's page,
Is this the man, the less than men
     Of this degenerate age ? "

" Gross from his acorns, tusky boar
   Does memorable acts like his ;
So for her snared offended young
    Bleeds the swart lioness."

But here she paused ; our eyes had met,
   And I was whitening with the jeer ;
She rose ; " I went too far," she said ;
    Spoke low ; " Forgive me, dear.

" To me our days seem pleasant days,
   Our home a haven of pure content ;
Forgive me if I said too much,
    So much more than I meant.

" Homer, though greater than his gods,
   With rough-hewn virtues was sufficed
And rough-hewn men : but what are such
    To us who learn of Christ ? "

The much-moved pathos of her voice,
   Her almost tearful eyes, her cheek
Grown pale, confessed the strength of love
    Which only made her speak :

For mild she was, of few soft words,
   Most gentle, easy to be led,
Content to listen when I spoke
    And reverence what I said ;

I elder sister by six years ;
 Not half so glad, or wise, or good :
Her words rebuked my secret self
 And shamed me where I stood.

She never guessed her words reproved
 A silent envy nursed within,
A selfish, souring discontent
 Pride-born, the devil's sin.

I smiled, half bitter, half in jest :
 " The wisest man of all the wise
Left for his summary of life
 ' Vanity of vanities.'

" Beneath the sun there's nothing new :
 Men flow, men ebb, mankind flows on
If I am wearied of my life,
 Why so was Solomon.

" Vanity of vanities he preached
 Of all he found, of all he sought :
Vanity of vanities, the gist
 Of all the words he taught.

" This in the wisdom of the world,
 In Homer's page, in all, we find :
As the sea is not filled, so yearns
 Man's universal mind.

" This Homer felt, who gave his men
    With glory but a transient state :
His very Jove could not reverse
    Irrevocable fate.


" Uncertain all their lot save this—
    Who wins must lose, who lives must die :
All trodden out into the dark
    Alike, all vanity."


She scarcely answered when I paused
    But rather to herself said : " One
Is here," low-voiced and loving, " Yea,
    Greater than Solomon."


So both were silent, she and I :
    She laid her work aside, and went
Into the garden-walks, like spring,
    All gracious with content ;


A little graver than her wont,
    Because her words had fretted me ;
Not warbling quite her merriest tune
    Bird-like from tree to tree.


I chose a book to read and dream :
    Yet half the while with furtive eyes
Marked how she made her choice of flowers
    Intuitively wise,

And ranged them with instinctive taste
    Which all my books had failed to teach ;
Fresh rose herself, and daintier
    Than blossom of the peach.

By birthright higher than myself,
    Though nestling of the self-same nest :
No fault of hers, no fault of mine,
    But stubborn to digest.

I watched her, till my book unmarked
    Slid noiseless to the velvet floor ;
Till all the opulent summer-world
    Looked poorer than before.

Just then her busy fingers ceased,
    Her fluttered colour went and came :
I knew whose step was on the walk,
    Whose voice would name her name.

\*    \*    \*    \*    \*

Well, twenty years have passed since then :
    My sister now, a stately wife
Still fair, looks back in peace and sees
    The longer half of life—

The longer half of prosperous life,
    With little grief, or fear, or fret :
She, loved and loving long ago,
    Is loved and loving yet.

A husband honourable, brave,
　　Is her main wealth in all the world :
And next to him one like herself,
　　One daughter golden-curled ;

Fair image of her own fair youth,
　　As beautiful and as serene,
With almost such another love
　　As her own love has been.

Yet, though of world-wide charity,
　　And in her home most tender dove,
Her treasure and her heart are stored
　　In the home-land of love :

She thrives, God's blessed husbandry ;
　　Most like a vine which full of fruit
Doth cling and lean and climb toward heaven,
　　While earth still binds its root.

I sit and watch my sister's face :
　　How little altered since the hours
When she, a kind, light-hearted girl,
　　Gathered her garden flowers ;

Her song just mellowed by regret
　　For having teased me with her talk ;
Then all-forgetful as she heard
　　One step upon the walk.

While I ?    I sat alone and watched
    My lot in life, to live alone
In mine own world of interests,
        Much felt but little shown.


Not to be first : how hard to learn
    That lifelong lesson of the past ;
Line graven on line and stroke on stroke
        But, thank God, learned at last.


So now in patience I possess
    My soul year after tedious year,
Content to take the lowest place,
        The place assigned me here.


Yet sometimes, when I feel my strength
    Most weak, and life most burdensome
I lift mine eyes up to the hills
        From whence my help shall come :


Yea, sometimes still I lift my heart
    To the Archangelic trumpet-burst,
When all deep secrets shall be shown,
        And many last be first.

## DREAM-LOVE.

YOUNG LOVE lies sleeping
    In May-time of the year,
Among the lilies,
    Lapped in the tender light :
White lambs come grazing,
    White doves come building there ;
And round about him
    The May-bushes are white.

Soft moss the pillow
    For oh, a softer cheek ;
Broad leaves cast shadow
    Upon the heavy eyes :
There winds and waters
    Grow lulled and scarcely speak ;
There twilight lingers
    The longest in the skies.

Young Love lies dreaming ;
    But who shall tell the dream ?
A perfect sunlight
    On rustling forest tips ;
Or perfect moonlight
    Upon a rippling stream ;
Or perfect silence,
    Or song of cherished lips.

Burn odours round him
  To fill the drowsy air ;
Weave silent dances
  Around him to and fro ;
For oh, in waking
  The sights are not so fair,
And song and silence
  Are not like these below.

Young Love lies dreaming
  Till summer days are gone,
Dreaming and drowsing
  Away to perfect sleep :
He sees the beauty
  Sun hath not looked upon,
And tastes the fountain
  Unutterably deep.

Him perfect music
  Doth hush unto his rest,
And through the pauses
  The perfect silence calms
Oh, poor the voices
  Of earth from east to west,
And poor earth's stillness
  Between her stately palms.

Young Love lies drowsing
  Away to poppied death ;
Cool shadows deepen
  Across the sleeping face :

So fails the summer
　　With warm, delicious breath ;
And what hath autumn
　　To give us in its place ?

Draw close the curtains
　　Of branched evergreen ;
Change cannot touch them
　　With fading fingers sere :
Here the first violets
　　Perhaps will bud unseen,
And a dove, may be,
　　Return to nestle here.


## AN END.

L OVE, strong as Death, is dead,
　　Come, let us make his bed
Among the dying flowers :
A green turf at his head ;
And a stone at his feet,
Whereon we may sit
In the quiet evening hours.

He was born in the spring,
And died before the harvesting :
On the last warm summer day
He left us ; he would not stay

For autumn twilight cold and grey.
Sit we by his grave, and sing
He is gone away.

To few chords and sad and low
Sing we so :
Be our eyes fixed on the grass
Shadow-veiled as the years pass,
While we think of all that was
In the long ago.

## DEAD HOPE.

HOPE new born one pleasant morn
    Died at even ;
Hope dead lives nevermore,
    No, not in heaven.

If his shroud were but a cloud
    To weep itself away ;
Or were he buried underground
    To sprout some day !
But dead and gone is dead and gone
    Vainly wept upon.

Nought we place above his face
    To mark the spot,
But it shows a barren place
    In our lot.

Hope has birth no more on earth
    Morn or even ;
Hope dead lives nevermore,
    No, not in heaven.


## TWICE.

I TOOK my heart in my hand
    (O my love, O my love),
I said : Let me fall or stand,
    Let me live or die,
But this once hear me speak—
    (O my love, O my love)—
Yet a woman's words are weak ;
    You should speak, not I.

You took my heart in your hand
    With a friendly smile,
With a critical eye you scanned.
    Then set it down,
And said : It is still unripe,
    Better wait awhile ;
Wait while the skylarks pipe,
    Till the corn grows brown.

As you set it down it broke—
    Broke, but I did not wince ;
I smiled at the speech you spoke,
    At your judgment that I heard :

But I have not often smiled
　　Since then, nor questioned since,
Nor cared for corn-flowers wild,
　　Nor sung with the singing bird.

I take my heart in my hand,
　　O my God, O my God,
My broken heart in my hand :
　　Thou hast seen, judge Thou.
My hope was written on sand,
　　O my God, O my God :
Now let Thy judgment stand—
　　Yea, judge me now.

This contemned of a man,
　　This marred one heedless day,
This heart take Thou to scan
　　Both within and without :
Refine with fire its gold,
　　Purge Thou its dross away—
Yea, hold it in Thy hold,
　　Whence none can pluck it out.

I take my heart in my hand—
　　I shall not die, but live—
Before Thy face I stand ;
　　I, for Thou callest such :
All that I have I bring,
　　All that I am I give,
Smile Thou and I shall sing,
　　But shall not question much

## MY DREAM.

HEAR now a curious dream I dreamed last night,
  Each word whereof is weighed and sifted truth

I stood beside Euphrates while it swelled
Like overflowing Jordan in its youth :
It waxed and coloured sensibly to sight,
Till out of myriad pregnant waves there welled
Young crocodiles, a gaunt blunt-featured crew,
Fresh-hatched perhaps and daubed with birthday dew.
The rest if I should tell, I fear my friend,
My closest friend, would deem the facts untrue ;
And therefore it were wisely left untold ;
Yet if you will, why, hear it to the end.

Each crocodile was girt with massive gold
And polished stones that with their wearers grew :
But one there was who waxed beyond the rest,
Wore kinglier girdle and a kingly crown,
Whilst crowns and orbs and sceptres starred his breast
All gleamed compact and green with scale on scale,
But special burnishment adorned his mail
And special terror weighed upon his frown ;
His punier brethren quaked before his tail,
Broad as a rafter, potent as a flail.

So he grew lord and master of his kin :
But who shall tell the tale of all their woes ?
An execrable appetite arose,
He battened on them, crunched, and sucked them in.
He knew no law, he feared no binding law,
But ground them with inexorable jaw :
The luscious fat distilled upon his chin,
Exuded from his nostrils and his eyes,
While still like hungry death he fed his maw ;
Till every minor crocodile being dead
And buried too, himself gorged to the full.
He slept with breath oppressed and unstrung claw.
Oh marvel passing strange which next I saw :
In sleep he dwindled to the common size,
And all the empire faded from his coat.
Then from far off a wingèd vessel came,
Swift as a swallow, subtle as a flame :
I know not what it bore of freight or host,
But white it was as an avenging ghost.
It levelled strong Euphrates in its course ;
Supreme yet weightless as an idle mote
It seemed to tame the waters without force
Till not a murmur swelled or billow beat :
Lo, as the purple shadow swept the sands,
The prudent crocodile rose on his feet
And shed appropriate tears and wrung his hands.

What can it mean ? you ask.  I answer not
For meaning, but myself must echo, What ?
And tell it as I saw it on the spot.

## SONGS IN A CORNFIELD.

A SONG in a cornfield
　　Where corn begins to fall,
Where reapers are reaping,
　　Reaping one, reaping all.
Sing pretty Lettice,
　　Sing Rachel, sing May;
Only Marian cannot sing
　　While her sweetheart's away

Where is he gone to
　　And why does he stay?
He came across the green sea
　　But for a day,
Across the deep green sea
　　To help with the hay.
His hair was curly yellow
　　And his eyes were grey,
He laughed a merry laugh
　　And said a sweet say.
Where is he gone to
　　That he comes not home?
To-day or to-morrow
　　He surely will come.
Let him haste to joy
　　Lest he lag for sorrow
For one weeps to-day
　　Who'll not weep to-morrow

To-day she must weep
   For gnawing sorrow,
To-night she may sleep
   And not wake to-morrow.

May sang with Rachel
   In the waxing warm weather,
Lettice sang with them,
   They sang all together :—

" Take the wheat in your arm
   Whilst day is broad above,
Take the wheat to your bosom
   But not a false false love
   Out in the fields
     Summer heat gloweth,
   Out in the fields
     Summer wind bloweth,
   Out in the fields
     Summer friend showeth,
   Out in the fields
     Summer wheat groweth ;
But in the winter
   When summer heat is dead
And summer wind has veered
   And summer friend has fled,
Only summer wheat remaineth,
   White cakes and bread.
Take the wheat, clasp the wheat
   That's food for maid and dove
Take the wheat to your bosom,
   But not a false false love."

A silence of full noontide heat
    Grew on them at their toil :
The farmer's dog woke up from sleep,
    The green snake hid her coil
Where grass stood thickest ; bird and beast
    Sought shadows as they could,
The reaping men and women paused
    And sat down where they stood ;
They ate and drank and were refreshed,
    For rest from toil is good.

While the reapers took their ease,
    Their sickles lying by,
Rachel sang a second strain,
    And singing seemed to sigh :—

  " There goes the swallow—
  Could we but follow !
    Hasty swallow stay,
    Point us out the way ;
Look back swallow, turn back swallow, stop swallow.

  " There went the swallow—
  Too late to follow :
    Lost our note of way,
    Lost our chance to-day ;
Good bye swallow, sunny swallow, wise swallow.

  " After the swallow
  All sweet things follow :

All things go their way,
Only we must stay,
Must not follow ; good bye swallow, good swallow."

Then listless Marian raised her head
Among the nodding sheaves ;
Her voice was sweeter than that voice ;
She sang like one who grieves :
Her voice was sweeter than its wont
Among the nodding sheaves ;
All wondered while they heard her sing
Like one who hopes and grieves :—

" Deeper than the hail can smite,
Deeper than the frost can bite,
Deep asleep through day and night,
      Our delight.

" Now thy sleep no pang can break,
No to-morrow bid thee wake,
Not our sobs who sit and ache
      For thy sake.

" Is it dark or light below?
Oh, but is it cold like snow?
Dost thou feel the green things grow
      Fast or slow?

" Is it warm or cold beneath,
Oh, but it is cold like death?

Cold like death, without a breath,
  Cold like death?"

If he comes to-day
  He will find her weeping;
If he comes to-morrow
  He will find her sleeping;
If he comes the next day,
  He'll not find her at all,
He may tear his curling hair,
  Beat his breast and call.

## ON THE WING.

### SONNET.

ONCE in a dream (for once I dreamed of you)
    We stood together in an open field;
  Above our heads two swift-winged pigeons wheeled,
Sporting at ease and courting full in view.
When loftier still a broadening darkness flew,
    Down-swooping, and a ravenous hawk revealed;
    Too weak to fight, too fond to fly, they yield;
So farewell life and love and pleasures new.
Then as their plumes fell fluttering to the ground,
    Their snow-white plumage flecked with crimson drops,
      I wept, and thought I turned towards you to weep:
    But you were gone; while rustling hedgerow tops
Bent in a wind which bore to me a sound
      Of far-off piteous bleat of lambs and sheep.

## L. E. L.

" Whose heart was breaking for a little love."

DOWNSTAIRS I laugh, I sport and jest with all
    But in my solitary room above
I turn my face in silence to the wall ;
    My heart is breaking for a little love.
        Though winter frosts are done,
        And birds pair every one,
And leaves peep out, for springtide is begun.

I feel no spring, while spring is well-nigh blown,
    I find no nest, while nests are in the grove :
Woe's me for mine own heart that dwells alone,
    My heart that breaketh for a little love.
        While golden in the sun
        Rivulets rise and run,
While lilies bud, for springtide is begun.

All love, are loved, save only I ; their hearts
    Beat warm with love and joy, beat full thereof
They cannot guess, who play the pleasant parts,
    My heart is breaking for a little love.
        While bee-hives wake and whirr,
        And rabbit thins his fur,
In living spring that sets the world astir.

I deck myself with silks and jewelry,
  I plume myself like any mated dove :
They praise my rustling show, and never see
    My heart is breaking for a little love.
      While sprouts green lavender
      With rosemary and myrrh,
For in quick spring the sap is all astir.

Perhaps some saints in glory guess the truth,
  Perhaps some angels read it as they move,
And cry one to another full of ruth,
    " Her heart is breaking for a little love."
      Though other things have birth,
      And leap and sing for mirth,
When spring-time wakes and clothes and feeds the
  earth.

Yet saith a saint: "Take patience for thy scathe;"
  Yet saith an angel : " Wait, for thou shalt prove
True best is last, true life is born of death,
    O thou, heart-broken for a little love.
      Then love shall fill thy girth,
      And love make fat thy dearth,
When new spring builds new heaven and clean
  new earth."

## SONG.

OH roses for the flush of youth,
   And laurel for the perfect prime;
But pluck an ivy branch for me
   Grown old before my time.

Oh violets for the grave of youth,
   And bay for those dead in their prime,
Give me the withered leaves I chose
   Before in the old time.

## THE HOUR AND THE GHOST.

### BRIDE.

O LOVE, love, hold me fast,
   He draws me away from thee;
I cannot stem the blast,
Nor the cold strong sea:
Far away a light shines
Beyond the hills and pines;
It is lit for me.

### BRIDEGROOM.

I have thee close, my dear,
No terror can come near;
Only far off the northern light shines clear.

GHOST.

Come with me, fair and false,
To our home, come home.
It is my voice that calls :
Once thou wast not afraid
When I woo'd, and said,
" Come, our nest is newly made "—
Now cross the tossing foam.

BRIDE.

Hold me one moment longer,
He taunts me with the past,
His clutch is waxing stronger,
Hold me fast, hold me fast.
He draws me from thy heart,
And I cannot withhold :
He bids my spirit depart
With him into the cold :—
Oh bitter vows of old !

BRIDEGROOM.

Lean on me, hide thine eyes :
Only ourselves, earth and skies,
Are present here : be wise.

GHOST.

Lean on me, come away,
I will guide and steady :
Come, for I will not stay :
Come, for house and bed are ready

Ah, sure bed and house,
For better and worse, for life and death
Goal won with shortened breath :
Come, crown our vows.

BRIDE.

One moment, one more word,
While my heart beats still,
While my breath is stirred
By my fainting will.
O friend forsake me not,
Forget not as I forgot :
But keep thy heart for me,
Keep thy faith true and bright ;
Through the lone cold winter night
Perhaps I may come to thee.

BRIDEGROOM.

Nay peace, my darling, peace :
Let these dreams and terrors cease :
Who spoke of death or change or aught but ease

GHOST.

O fair frail sin,
O poor harvest gathered in !
Thou shalt visit him again
To watch his heart grow cold :
To know the gnawing pain
I knew of old ;

To see one much more fair
Fill up the vacant chair,
Fill his heart, his children bear
While thou and I together,
In the outcast weather,
Toss and howl and spin.


## SHALL I FORGET?

SHALL I forget on this side of the grave?
  I promise nothing : you must wait and see
    Patient and brave.
(O my soul, watch with him and he with me.)

Shall I forget in peace of Paradise?
I promise nothing : follow, friend, and see
    Faithful and wise.
(O my soul, lead the way he walks with me.)


## LIFE AND DEATH.

LIFE is not sweet. One day it will be sweet
  To shut our eyes and die :
Nor feel the wild flowers blow, nor birds dart by
  With flitting butterfly,
Nor grass grow long above our heads and feet,
Nor hear the happy lark that soars sky high,

Nor sigh that spring is fleet and summer fleet,
  Nor mark the waxing wheat,
Nor know who sits in our accustomed seat.

Life is not good.   One day it will be good
  To die, then live again ;
To sleep meanwhile : so not to feel the wane
Of shrunk leaves dropping in the wood,
Nor hear the foamy lashing of the main,
Nor mark the blackened bean-fields, nor where stood
  Rich ranks of golden grain
Only dead refuse stubble clothe the plain :
Asleep from risk, asleep from pain.

## A SUMMER WISH.

LIVE all thy sweet life through,
  Sweet Rose, dew-sprent,
Drop down thine evening dew
To gather it anew
When day is bright :
  I fancy thou wast meant
Chiefly to give delight.

Sing in the silent sky,
  Glad soaring bird ;

Sing out thy notes on high
To sunbeam straying by
Or passing cloud ;
   Heedless if thou art heard
Sing thy full song aloud.

Oh that it were with me
   As with the flower;
Blooming on its own tree
For butterfly and bee
Its summer morns :
   That I might bloom mine hour
A rose in spite of thorns.

Oh that my work were done
   As birds' that soar
Rejoicing in the sun :
That when my time is run
And daylight too,
   I so might rest once more
Cool with refreshing dew.

## A YEAR'S WINDFALLS.

ON the wind of January
        Down flits the snow,
Travelling from the frozen North
        As cold as it can blow.
Poor robin redbreast,
        Look where he comes;
Let him in to feel your fire,
        And toss him of your crumbs.

On the wind in February
        Snowflakes float still,
Half inclined to turn to rain,
        Nipping, dripping, chill.
Then the thaws swell the streams,
        And swollen rivers swell the sea :—
If the winter ever ends
        How pleasant it will be

In the wind of windy March
        The catkins drop down,
Curly, caterpillar-like,
        Curious green and brown.
With concourse of nest-building birds
        And leaf-buds by the way,
We begin to think of flowers
        And life and nuts some day.

With the gusts of April
  Rich fruit-tree blossoms fall,
On the hedged-in orchard-green,
  From the southern wall.
Apple-trees and pear-trees
  Shed petals white or pink,
Plum-trees and peach-trees ;
  While sharp showers sink and sink.

Little brings the May breeze
  Beside pure scent of flowers,
While all things wax and nothing wanes
  In lengthening daylight hours.
Across the hyacinth beds
  The wind lags warm and sweet,
Across the hawthorn tops,
  Across the blades of wheat.

In the wind of sunny June
  Thrives the red rose crop,
Every day fresh blossoms blow
  While the first leaves drop ;
White rose and yellow rose
  And moss rose choice to find,
And the cottage cabbage-rose
  Not one whit behind.

On the blast of scorched July
  Drives the pelting hail,
From thunderous lightning-clouds, that blot
  Blue heaven grown lurid-pale.

Weedy waves are tossed ashore,
  Sea-things strange to sight
Gasp upon the barren shore
  And fade away in light.

In the parching August wind
  Corn-fields bow the head,
Sheltered in round valley depths,
  On low hills outspread.
Early leaves drop loitering down
  Weightless on the breeze,
First fruits of the year's decay
  From the withering trees.

In brisk wind of September
  The heavy-headed fruits
Shake upon their bending boughs
  And drop from the shoots ;
Some glow golden in the sun,
  Some show green and streaked,
Some set forth a purple bloom,
  Some blush rosy-cheeked.

In strong blast of October
  At the equinox,
Stirred up in his hollow bed
  Broad ocean rocks ;
Plunge the ships on his bosom,
  Leaps and plunges the foam, —
It's oh ! for mothers' sons at sea,
  That they were safe at home.

In slack wind of November
    The fog forms and shifts ;
All the world comes out again
    When the fog lifts.
Loosened from their sapless twigs
    Leaves drop with every gust ;
Drifting, rustling, out of sight
    In the damp or dust.

Last of all, December,
    The year's sands nearly run,
Speeds on the shortest day,
    Curtails the sun ;
With its bleak raw wind
    Lays the last leaves low,
Brings back the nightly frosts,
    Brings back the snow.


## AN APPLE GATHERING.

I PLUCKED pink blossoms from mine apple-tree
    And wore them all that evening in my hair :
Then in due season when I went to see
    I found no apples there.

With dangling basket all along the grass
    As I had come I went the selfsame track :
My neighbours mocked me while they saw me pass
    So empty-handed back.

Lilian and Lilias smiled in trudging by,
   Their heaped-up basket teazed me like a jeer;
Sweet-voiced they sang beneath the sunset sky,
    Their mother's home was near.

Plump Gertrude passed me with her basket full,
   A stronger hand than hers helped it along;
A voice talked with her through the shadows cool
    More sweet to me than song.

Ah Willie, Willie, was my love less worth
   Than apples with their green leaves piled above?
I counted rosiest apples on the earth
    Of far less worth than love.

So once it was with me you stooped to talk
   Laughing and listening in this very lane;
To think that by this way we used to walk
    We shall not walk again!

I let my neighbours pass me, ones and twos
   And groups; the latest said the night grew chill
And hastened: but I loitered, while the dews
    Fell fast I loitered still.

## SONG.

TWO doves upon the selfsame branch,
    Two lilies on a single stem,
Two butterflies upon one flower :—
    Oh happy they who look on them.

Who look upon them hand in hand
    Flushed in the rosy summer light ;
Who look upon them hand in hand
    And never give a thought to night.

## MAUDE CLARE.

OUT of the church she followed then.
    With a lofty step and mien :
His bride was like a village maid,
    Maude Clare was like a queen.

" Son Thomas," his lady mother said,
    With smiles, almost with tears :
" May Nell and you but live as true
    As we have done for years ;

" Your father thirty years ago
    Had just your tale to tell ;
But he was not so pale as you,
    Nor I so pale as Nell."

My lord was pale with inward strife,
    And Nell was pale with pride ;
My lord gazed long on pale Maude Clare
    Or ever he kissed the bride.

" Lo, I have brought my gift, my lord,
    Have brought my gift," she said :
" To bless the hearth, to bless the board,
    To bless the marriage-bed.

" Here's my half of the golden chain
    You wore about your neck,
That day we waded ankle-deep
    For lilies in the beck :

" Here's my half of the faded leaves
    We plucked from budding bough,
With feet amongst the lily leaves,—
    The lilies are budding now."

He strove to match her scorn with scorn,
    He faltered in his place :
" Lady," he said,—" Maude Clare," he said,—
    " Maude Clare :"—and hid his face.

She turn'd to Nell : " My Lady Nell,
    I have a gift for you ;
Though, were it fruit, the bloom were gone.
    Or, were it flowers, the dew.

" Take my share of a fickle heart,
   Mine of a paltry love :
Take it or leave it as you will,
   I wash my hands thereof."

" And what you leave," said Nell, " I'll take,
   And what you spurn, I'll wear ;
For he's my lord for better and worse,
   And him I love, Maude Clare.

" Yea, though you're taller by the head,
   More wise, and much more fair ;
I'll love him till he loves me best,
   Me best of all, Maude Clare."

## ECHO.

COME to me in the silence of the night ;
   Come in the speaking silence of a dream ;
Come with soft rounded cheeks and eyes as bright
   As sunlight on a stream ;
    Come back in tears,
O memory, hope, love of finished years.

O dream how sweet, too sweet, too bitter sweet,
   Whose wakening should have been in Paradise,
Where souls brimfull of love abide and meet ;
   Where thirsting longing eyes
    Watch the slow door
That opening, letting in, lets out no more.

Yet come to me in dreams, that I may live
  My very life again though cold in death :
Come back to me in dreams, that I may give
  Pulse for pulse, breath for breath :
    Speak low, lean low,
As long ago, my love, how long ago.

## ANOTHER SPRING.

IF I might see another Spring
    I'd not plant summer flowers and wait :
I'd have my crocuses at once,
My leafless pink mezereons,
    My chill-veined snow-drops, choicer yet
    My white or azure violet,
Leaf-nested primrose ; anything
    To blow at once, not late.


If I might see another Spring
    I'd listen to the daylight birds
That build their nests and pair and sing,
Nor wait for mateless nightingale ;
    I'd listen to the lusty herds,
    The ewes with lambs as white as snow,
I'd find out music in the hail
    And all the winds that blow.

If I might see another Spring—
   Oh stinging comment on my past
That all my past results in " if "—
   If I might see another Spring
I'd laugh to-day, to-day is brief;
I would not wait for anything :
   I'd use to-day that cannot last,
   Be glad to-day and sing.


## BIRD OR BEAST?

DID any bird come flying
   After Adam and Eve,
When the door was shut against them
   And they sat down to grieve?

I think not Eve's peacock
   Splendid to see,
And I think not Adam's eagle ;
   But a dove may be.

Did any beast come pushing
   Through the thorny hedge
Into the thorny thistly world,
   Out from Eden's edge?

I think not a lion,
   Though his strength is such ;
But an innocent loving lamb
   May have done as much.

If the dove preached from her bough,
 And the lamb from his sod;
The lamb and the dove
 Were preachers sent from God.


### EVE.

" WHILE I sit at the door,
  Sick to gaze within,
Mine eye weepeth sore
For sorrow and sin:
As a tree my sin stands
To darken all lands;
Death is the fruit it bore.

"How have Eden bowers grown
Without Adam to bend them!
How have Eden flowers blown,
Squandering their sweet breath,
Without me to tend them!
The Tree of Life was ours,
Tree twelvefold-fruited,
Most lofty tree that flowers,
Most deeply rooted:
I chose the Tree of Death.

"Hadst thou but said me nay,
Adam, my brother,
I might have pined away;
I, but none other:

God might have let thee stay
Safe in our garden,
By putting me away
Beyond all pardon.

" I, Eve, sad mother
Of all who must live,
I, not another,
Plucked bitterest fruit to give
My friend, husband, lover.
O wanton eyes run over ;
Who but I should grieve ?—
Cain hath slain his brother :
Of all who must die mother,
Miserable Eve !"

Thus she sat weeping,
Thus Eve our mother,
Where one lay sleeping
Slain by his brother.
Greatest and least
Each piteous beast
To hear her voice
Forgot his joys
And set aside his feast.

The mouse paused in his walk
And dropped his wheaten stalk ;
Grave cattle wagged their heads
In rumination ;

The eagle gave a cry
From his cloud station :
Larks on thyme beds
Forbore to mount or sing ;
Bees drooped upon the wing ;
The raven perched on high
Forgot his ration ;
The conies in their rock,
A feeble nation,
Quaked sympathetical ;
The mocking-bird left off to mock ;
Huge camels knelt as if
In deprecation ;
The kind hart's tears were falling ;
Chattered the wistful stork ;
Dove-voices with a dying fall
Cooed desolation
Answering grief by grief.

Only the serpent in the dust,
Wriggling and crawling,
Grinned an evil grin and thrust
His tongue out with its fork.

## A DAUGHTER OF EVE.

A FOOL I was to sleep at noon,
   And wake when night is chilly
Beneath the comfortless cold moon ;
A fool to pluck my rose too soon,
   A fool to snap my lily.

My garden-plot I have not kept ;
   Faded and all-forsaken,
I weep as I have never wept :
Oh it was summer when I slept,
   It's winter now I waken.

Talk what you please of future Spring
   And sun-warmed sweet to-morrow :—
Stripped bare of hope and everything,
No more to laugh, no more to sing,
   I sit alone with sorrow.

## A PEAL OF BELLS.

STRIKE the bells wantonly,
   Tinkle tinkle well ;
Bring me wine, bring me flowers,
   Ring the silver bell.

All my lamps burn scented oil,
　　Hung on laden orange-trees,
Whose shadowed foliage is the foil
　　To golden lamps and oranges.
Heap my golden plates with fruit,
　　Golden fruit, fresh-plucked and ripe;
　　Strike the bells and breathe the pipe;
Shut out showers from summer hours—
Silence that complaining lute—
Shut out thinking, shut out pain,
From hours that cannot come again.

Strike the bells solemnly,
　　Ding dong deep:
My friend is passing to his bed,
　　Fast asleep;
There's plaited linen round his head,
　　While foremost go his feet—
His feet that cannot carry him.
My feast's a show, my lights are dim;
　　Be still, your music is not sweet,—
There is no music more for him:
　　His lights are out, his feast is done:
His bowl that sparkled to the brim
Is drained, is broken, cannot hold;
My blood is chill, his blood is cold;
　　His death is full, and mine begun.

## THE BOURNE.

UNDERNEATH the growing grass,
　　Underneath the living flowers,
Deeper than the sound of showers :
There we shall not count the hours
By the shadows as they pass.

Youth and health will be but vain,
　　Beauty reckoned of no worth :
There a very little girth
Can hold round what once the earth
Seemed too narrow to contain.

## SONG.

OH what comes over the sea,
　　Shoals and quicksands past ;
And what comes home to me,
　　Sailing slow, sailing fast ?

A wind comes over the sea
　　With a moan in its blast ;
But nothing comes home to me,
　　Sailing slow, sailing fast.

Let me be, let me be,
　　For my lot is cast :
Land or sea all's one to me,
　　And sail it slow or fast.

## VENUS'S LOOKING-GLASS.

I MARKED where lovely Venus and her court
   With song and dance and merry laugh went by;
   Weightless, their wingless feet seemed made to fly,
Bound from the ground and in mid air to sport.
Left far behind I heard the dolphins snort,
   Tracking their goddess with a wistful eye,
   Around whose head white doves rose, wheeling high
Or low, and cooed after their tender sort.
All this I saw in Spring.   Through Summer heat
   I saw the lovely Queen of Love no more.
   But when flushed Autumn through the woodlands
      went
I spied sweet Venus walk amid the wheat:
   Whom seeing, every harvester gave o'er
   His toil, and laughed and hoped and was content.

## LOVE LIES BLEEDING.

L OVE that is dead and buried, yesterday
   Out of his grave rose up before my face;
   No recognition in his look, no trace
Of memory in his eyes dust-dimmed and grey.
While I, remembering, found no word to say,
   But felt my quickened heart leap in its place;
   Caught afterglow thrown back from long set days,

Caught echoes of all music passed away.
Was this indeed to meet?—I mind me yet
  In youth we met when hope and love were quick,
    We parted with hope dead, but love alive :
  I mind me how we parted then heart sick,
    Remembering, loving, hopeless, weak to strive:—
Was this to meet?   Not so, we have not met.


## BIRD RAPTURES.

THE sunrise wakes the lark to sing,
    The moonrise wakes the nightingale.
Come darkness, moonrise, everything
    That is so silent, sweet, and pale,
    Come, so ye wake the nightingale.


Make haste to mount, thou wistful moon,
    Make haste to wake the nightingale :
Let silence set the world in tune
    To hearken to that wordless tale
    Which warbles from the nightingale.


O herald skylark, stay thy flight
    One moment, for a nightingale
Floods us with sorrow and delight.
    To-morrow thou shalt hoist the sail ;
    Leave us to-night the nightingale.

## THE QUEEN OF HEARTS.

HOW comes it, Flora, that, whenever we
    Play cards together, you invariably,
      However the pack parts,
      Still hold the Queen of Hearts?

I've scanned you with a scrutinising gaze,
Resolved to fathom these your secret ways:
      But, sift them as I will,
      Your ways are secret still.

I cut and shuffle; shuffle, cut, again;
But all my cutting, shuffling, proves in vain:
      Vain hope, vain forethought too;
      That Queen still falls to you.

I dropped her once, prepense; but, ere the deal
Was dealt, your instinct seemed her loss to feel:
      "There should be one card more,"
      You said, and searched the floor.

I cheated once; I made a private notch
In Heart-Queen's back, and kept a lynx-eyed watch;
      Yet such another back
      Deceived me in the pack:

The Queen of Clubs assumed by arts unknown
An imitative dint that seemed my own;

> This notch, not of my doing,
>   Misled me to my ruin.
>
> It baffles me to puzzle out the clue,
> Which must be skill, or craft, or luck in you:
>     Unless, indeed, it be
>     Natural affinity.

## "NO, THANK YOU, JOHN."

I NEVER said I loved you, John:
    Why will you tease me day by day,
And wax a weariness to think upon
    With always "do" and "pray"?

You know I never loved you, John;
    No fault of mine made me your toast:
Why will you haunt me with a face as wan
    As shows an hour-old ghost?

I dare say Meg or Moll would take
    Pity upon you, if you'd ask:
And pray don't remain single for my sake
    Who can't perform that task.

I have no heart?—Perhaps I have not;
    But then you're mad to take offence
That I don't give you what I have not got:
    Use your own common sense.

Let bygones be bygones :
   Don't call me false, who owed not to be true
I'd rather answer " No," to fifty Johns
   Than answer " Yes," to you.

Let's mar our pleasant days no more,
   Song-birds of passage, days of youth :
Catch at to-day, forget the days before :
   I'll wink at your untruth.

Let us strike hands as hearty friends ;
   No more, no less ; and friendship's good :
Only don't keep in view ulterior ends,
   And points not understood

In open treaty.   Rise above
   Quibbles and shuffling off and on :
Here's friendship for you if you like ; but love,—
   No, thank you, John.

## BEAUTY IS VAIN.

WHILE roses are so red,
   While lilies are so white
Shall a woman exalt her face
   Because it gives delight ?
She's not so sweet as a rose,
   A lily's straighter than she,
And if she were as red or white
   She'd be but one of three.

Whether she flush in love's summer
Or in its winter grow pale,
Whether she flaunt her beauty
Or hide it away in a veil,
Be she red or white,
And stand she erect or bowed,
Time will win the race he runs with her
And hide her away in a shroud.

## MAY.

I CANNOT tell you how it was;
But this I know: it came to pass
Upon a bright and breezy day
When May was young; ah, pleasant May
As yet the poppies were not born
Between the blades of tender corn;
The last eggs had not hatched as yet,
Nor any bird forgone its mate.

I cannot tell you what it was;
But this I know: it did but pass.
It passed away with sunny May,
With all sweet things it passed away,
And left me old, and cold, and grey.

## A PAUSE OF THOUGHT.

I LOOKED for that which is not, nor can be,
  And hope deferred made my heart sick in truth
But years must pass before a hope of youth
  Is resigned utterly.

I watched and waited with a steadfast will :
  And though the object seemed to flee away
  That I so longed for, ever day by day
  I watched and waited still.

Sometimes I said : This thing shall be no more ,
  My expectation wearies and shall cease ;
  I will resign it now and be at peace :
  Yet never gave it o'er.

Sometimes I said : It is an empty name
  I long for ; to a name why should I give
  The peace of all the days I have to live ?—
  Yet gave it all the same.

Alas, thou foolish one ! alike unfit
  For healthy joy and salutary pain :
  Thou knowest the chase useless, and again
  Turnest to follow it.

## TWILIGHT CALM.

OH, pleasant eventide!
  Clouds on the western side
Grow grey and greyer, hiding the warm sun:
The bees and birds, their happy labours done,
  Seek their close nests and bide.

Screened in the leafy wood
  The stock-doves sit and brood:
The very squirrel leaps from bough to bough
But lazily; pauses; and settles now
  Where once he stored his food.

One by one the flowers close,
  Lily and dewy rose
Shutting their tender petals from the moon:
The grasshoppers are still; but not so soon
  Are still the noisy crows.

The dormouse squats and eats
  Choice little dainty bits
Beneath the spreading roots of a broad lime;
Nibbling his fill he stops from time to time
  And listens where he sits.

From far the lowings come
  Of cattle driven home:

From farther still the wind brings fitfully
The vast continual murmur of the sea,
    Now loud, now almost dumb.

    The gnats whirl in the air,
    The evening gnats ; and there
The owl opes broad his eyes and wings to sail
For prey ; the bat wakes ; and the shell-less snail
    Comes forth, clammy and bare.

    Hark ! that's the nightingale,
    Telling the self-same tale
Her song told when this ancient earth was young:
So echoes answered when her song was sung
    In the first wooded vale.

    We call it love and pain
    The passion of her strain ;
And yet we little understand or know :
Why should it not be rather joy that so
    Throbs in each throbbing vein ?

    In separate herds the deer
    Lie ; here the bucks, and here
The does, and by its mother sleeps the fawn :
Through all the hours of night until the dawn
    They sleep, forgetting fear.

    The hare sleeps where it lies,
    With wary half-closed eyes ;

The cock has ceased to crow, the hen to cluck :
Only the fox is out, some heedless luck
    Or chicken to surprise.

    Remote, each single star
    Comes out, till there they are
All shining brightly : how the dews fall damp !
While close at hand the glow-worm lights her lamp,
    Or twinkles from afar.

    But evening now is done
    As much as if the sun
Day-giving had arisen in the East .
For night has come ; and the great calm has ceased,
    The quiet sands have run.


## WIFE TO HUSBAND.

PARDON the faults in me,
    For the love of years ago :
      Good-bye.
I must drift across the sea,
    I must sink into the snow,
      I must die.

You can bask in this sun,
    You can drink wine, and eat :
      Good-bye.

I must gird myself and run,
　Though with unready feet :
　　I must die.

Blank sea to sail upon,
　Cold bed to sleep in :
　　Good-bye.
While you clasp, I must be gone
　For all your weeping :
　　I must die.

A kiss for one friend,
　And a word for two,—
　　Good-bye :—
A lock that you must send,
　A kindness you must do :
　　I must die.

Not a word for you,
　Not a lock or kiss,
　　Good-bye.
We, one, must part in two ,
　Verily death is this :
　　I must die.

## THREE SEASONS.

" A CUP for hope ! " she said,
  In springtime ere the bloom was old
The crimson wine was poor and cold
  By her mouth's richer red.

" A cup for love ! " how low,
How soft the words ; and all the while
Her blush was rippling with a smile
  Like summer after snow.

" A cup for memory ! "
Cold cup that one must drain alone :
While autumn winds are up and moan
  Across the barren sea.

Hope, memory, love :
Hope for fair morn, and love for day,
And memory for the evening grey
  And solitary dove.


## MIRAGE.

THE hope I dreamed of was a dream,
  Was but a dream ; and now I wake
Exceeding comfortless, and worn, and old,
  For a dream's sake.

I hang my harp upon a tree,
　A weeping willow in a lake;
I hang my silenced harp there, wrung and snapt
　For a dream's sake.

Lie still, lie still, my breaking heart;
　My silent heart, lie still and break:
Life, and the world, and mine own self, are changed
　For a dream's sake.


## A ROYAL PRINCESS.

I A PRINCESS, king-descended, decked with
　　jewels, gilded, drest,
Would rather be a peasant with her baby at her breast,
For all I shine so like the sun, and am purple like the
　　west.

Two and two my guards behind, two and two before,
Two and two on either hand, they guard me evermore;
Me, poor dove that must not coo—eagle that must
　　not soar.

All my fountains cast up perfumes, all my gardens
　　grow
Scented woods and foreign spices, with all flowers in
　　blow
That are costly, out of season as the seasons go.

All my walls are lost in mirrors, whereupon I trace
Self to right hand, self to left hand, self in every place,
Self-same solitary figure, self-same seeking face.

Then I have an ivory chair high to sit upon,
Almost like my father's chair, which is an ivory throne;
There I sit uplift and upright, there I sit alone.

Alone by day, alone by night, alone days without end ;
My father and my mother give me treasures, search
    and spend—
O my father ! O my mother ! have you ne'er a friend ?

As I am a lofty princess, so my father is
A lofty king, accomplished in all kingly subtilties,
Holding in his strong right hand world-kingdoms'
    balances.

He has quarrelled with his neighbours, he has
    scourged his foes ;
Vassal counts and princes follow where his pennon
    goes,
Long-descended valiant lords whom the vulture knows,

On whose track the vulture swoops, when they ride
    in state
To break the strength of armies and topple down the
    great :
Each of these my courteous servant, none of these my
    mate.

My father counting up his strength sets down with
    equal pen
So many head of cattle, head of horses, head of men ;
These for slaughter, these for labour, with the how
    and when.

Some to work on roads, canals ; some to man his
    ships ;
Some to smart in mines beneath sharp overseers'
    whips ;
Some to trap fur-beasts in lands where utmost winter
    nips.

Once it came into my heart, and whelmed me like a
    flood,
That these too are men and women, human flesh and
    blood ;
Men with hearts and men with souls, though trodden
    down like mud.

Our feasting was not glad that night, our music was
    not gay :
On my mother's graceful head I marked a thread of
    grey,
My father frowning at the fare seemed every dish to
    weigh.

I sat beside them sole princess in my exalted place,
My ladies and my gentlemen stood by me on the dais :
A mirror showed me I look old and haggard in the
    face ;

It showed me that my ladies all are fair to gaze upon
Plump, plenteous-haired, to every one love's secret
    lore is known,
They laugh by day, they sleep by night ; ah me, what
    is a throne ?

The singing men and women sang that night as usual,
The dancers danced in pairs and sets, but music had
    a fall,
A melancholy windy fall as at a funeral.

Amid the toss of torches to my chamber back we
    swept ;
My ladies loosed my golden chain ; meantime I could
    have wept
To think of some in galling chains whether they
    waked or slept.

I took my bath of scented milk, delicately waited on,
They burned sweet things for my delight, cedar and
    cinnamon,
They lit my shaded silver lamp, and left me there
    alone.

A day went by, a week went by. One day I heard it
    said :
" Men are clamouring, women, children, clamouring
    to be fed ;
Men like famished dogs are howling in the streets for
    bread."

So two whispered by my door, not thinking I could
hear,
Vulgar naked truth, ungarnished for a royal ear ;
Fit for cooping in the background, not to stalk so near.

But I strained my utmost sense to catch this truth,
and mark :
" There are families out grazing, like cattle in the
park."
" A pair of peasants must be saved, even if we build
an ark."

A merry jest, a merry laugh, each strolled upon his
way ;
One was my page, a lad I reared and bore with day
by day ;
One was my youngest maid, as sweet and white as
cream in May.

Other footsteps followed softly with a weightier tramp;
Voices said : " Picked soldiers have been summoned
from the camp,
To quell these base-born ruffians who make free to
howl and stamp."

" Howl and stamp ? " one answered : " They made
free to hurl a stone
At the minister's state coach, well aimed and stoutly
thrown."
" There's work then for the soldiers, for this rank crop
must be mown."

One I saw, a poor old fool with ashes on his head,
Whimpering because a girl had snatched his crust of
    bread :
Then he dropped ; when some one raised him, it
    turned out he was dead."

" After us the deluge," was retorted with a laugh :
" If bread's the staff of life they must walk without a
    staff."
" While I've a loaf they're welcome to my blessing and
    the chaff."

These passed. " The king : " stand up. Said my
    father with a smile :
" Daughter mine, your mother comes to sit with you
    awhile,
She's sad to-day, and who but you her sadness can
    beguile ? "

He too left me. Shall I touch my harp now while I
    wait,—
 I hear them doubling guard below before our palace
    gate)—
Or shall I work the last gold stitch into my veil of
    state ;

Or shall my woman stand and read some unimpas
    sioned scene,
There's music of a lulling sort in words that pause
    between ;
Or shall she merely fan me while I wait here for the
    queen ?

Again I caught my father's voice in sharp word of
    command :
" Charge " a clash of steel : " Charge again, the rebels
    stand.
Smite and spare not, hand to hand ; smite and spare
    not, hand to hand."

There swelled a tumult at the gate, high voices wax-
    ing higher ;
A flash of red reflected light lit the cathedral spire ;
I heard a cry for faggots, then I heard a yell for fire.

" Sit and roast there with your meat, sit and bake
    there with your bread,
You who sat to see us starve," one shrieking woman
    said :
" Sit on your throne and roast with your crown upon
    your head."

Nay, this thing will I do, while my mother tarrieth,
I will take my fine spun gold, but not to sew there-
    with,
I will take my gold and gems, and rainbow fan and
    wreath ;

With a ransom in my lap, a king's ransom in my
    hand,
I will go down to this people, will stand face to face,
    will stand
Where they curse king, queen, and princess of this
    cursed land.

They shall take all to buy them bread, take all I have
    to give ;
I, if I perish, perish ; they to-day shall eat and live ;
I, if I perish, perish ; that's the goal I half conceive :

Once to speak before the world, rend bare my heart
    and show
The lesson I have learned, which is death, is life, to
    know.
I, if I perish, perish ; in the name of God I go.


## MY FRIEND.

TWO days ago with dancing glancing hair,
    With living lips and eyes ;
  Now pale, dumb, blind, she lies ;
So pale, yet still so fair.

We have not left her yet, not yet alone ;
    But soon must leave her where
  She will not miss our care,
Bone of our bone.

Weep not ; O friends, we should not weep :
    Our friend of friends lies full of rest ;
  No sorrow rankles in her breast,
Fallen fast asleep.

She sleeps below,
　　She wakes and laughs above ;
　　To-day, as she walked, let us walk in love :
To-morrow follow so.


## SHUT OUT.

THE door was shut.   I looked between
　　Its iron bars ; and saw it lie,
　My garden, mine, beneath the sky,
Pied with all flowers bedewed and green :

From bough to bough the song-birds crossed
　　From flower to flower the moths and bees
　　With all its nests and stately trees
It had been mine, and it was lost.

A shadowless spirit kept the gate,
　　Blank and unchanging like the grave.
　　I, peering through, said ; " Let me have
Some buds to cheer my outcast state."

He answered not.   " Or give me, then,
　　But one small twig from shrub or tree ;
　　And bid my home remember me
Until I come to it again."

The spirit was silent; but he took
   Mortar and stone to build a wall;
   He left no loophole great or small
Through which my straining eyes might look:

So now I sit here quite alone
   Blinded with tears; nor grieve for that,
   For nought is left worth looking at
Since my delightful land is gone.

A violet bed is budding near,
   Wherein a lark has made her nest:
   And good they are, but not the best,
And dear they are, but not so dear.

## SOUND SLEEP.

SOME are laughing, some are weeping;
   She is sleeping, only sleeping.
Round her rest wild flowers are creeping,
There the wind is heaping, heaping
Sweetest sweets of Summer's keeping,
By the corn-fields ripe for reaping.

There are lilies, and there blushes
The deep rose, and there the thrushes
Sing till latest sunlight flushes
In the west; a fresh wind brushes
Through the leaves while evening hushes

N

There by day the lark is singing
And the grass and weeds are springing ;
There by night the bat is winging ;
There for ever winds are bringing
Far-off chimes of church-bells ringing.

Night and morning, noon and even,
Their sound fills her dreams with Heaven :
The long strife at length is striven :
'Till her grave-bands shall be riven,
Such is the good portion given
To her soul at rest and shriven.

## SONG.

SHE sat and sang alway
    By the green margin of a stream,
Watching the fishes leap and play
    Beneath the glad sunbeam.

I sat and wept alway
    Beneath the moon's most shadowy beam,
Watching the blossoms of the May
    Weep leaves into the stream.

I wept for memory ;
    She sang for hope that is so fair ;
My tears were swallowed by the sea ;
    Her songs died on the air.

## SONG.

WHEN I am dead, my dearest,
　　Sing no sad songs for me ;
Plant thou no roses at my head,
　　Nor shady cypress tree :
Be the green grass above me
　　With showers and dewdrops wet
And if thou wilt, remember,
　　And if thou wilt, forget.

I shall not see the shadows,
　　I shall not feel the rain ;
I shall not hear the nightingale
　　Sing on, as if in pain :
And dreaming through the twilight
　　That doth not rise nor set,
Haply I may remember,
　　And haply may forget

## DEAD BEFORE DEATH.

### SONNET.

A H ! changed and cold, how changed and very cold
  With stiffened smiling lips and cold calm eyes
 Changed, yet the same ; much knowing, little wise
*This* was the promise of the days of old !
Grown hard and stubborn in the ancient mould,
 Grown rigid in the sham of lifelong lies :
 We hoped for better things as years would rise,
But it is over as a tale once told.
All fallen the blossom that no fruitage bore,
 All lost the present and the future time,
All lost, all lost, the lapse that went before :
So lost till death shut to the opened door,
 So lost from chime to everlasting chime,
So cold and lost for ever evermore.


### TWILIGHT NIGHT.

#### I.

W E met, hand to hand,
  We clasped hands close and fast,
As close as oak and ivy stand ;
  But it is past :
  Come day, come night, day comes at last.

We loosed hand from hand,
  We parted face from face

Each went his way to his own land
  At his own pace,
  Each went to fill his separate place

If we should meet one day,
  If both should not forget,
We shall clasp hands the accustomed way,
  As when we met,
  So long ago, as I remember yet.

## II.

Where my heart is (wherever that may be)
  Might I but follow!
If you fly thither over heath and lea,
O honey-seeking bee,
  O careless swallow,
Bid some for whom I watch keep watch for me.

Alas! that we must dwell, my heart and I,
  So far asunder.
Hours wax to days, and days and days creep by;
I watch with wistful eye,
  I wait and wonder:
When will that day draw nigh—that hour draw nigh?

Not yesterday, and not I think to-day;
  Perhaps to-morrow.
Day after day "to-morrow," thus I say:
I watched so yesterday
  In hope and sorrow,
Again to-day I watch the accustomed way.

## BITTER FOR SWEET

SUMMER is gone with all its roses,
　　Its sun and perfumes and sweet flowers,
　Its warm air and refreshing showers :
　　And even Autumn closes.

Yea, Autumn's chilly self is going,
　　And winter comes which is yet colder ;
　Each day the hoar-frost waxes bolder ,
　　And the last buds cease blowing.

## WHAT WOULD I GIVE?

WHAT would I give for a heart of flesh to warm
　　me through,
Instead of this heart of stone ice-cold whatever I do ;
Hard and cold and small, of all hearts the worst of all.

What would I give for words, if only words would
　　come ;
But now in its misery my spirit has fallen dumb :
Oh, merry friends, go your way, I have never a word
　　to say.

What would I give for tears, not smiles but scalding
　　tears,
To wash the black mark clean, and to thaw the frost
　　of years,
To wash the stain ingrain, and to make me clean again.

## THE FIRST SPRING DAY.

I WONDER if the sap is stirring yet,
  If wintry birds are dreaming of a mate,
If frozen snowdrops feel as yet the sun
And crocus fires are kindling one by one :
    Sing, robin, sing ;
I still am sore in doubt concerning Spring.

I wonder if the springtide of this year
Will bring another Spring both lost and dear :
If heart and spirit will find out their Spring,
Or if the world alone will bud and sing :
    Sing, hope, to me ;
Sweet notes, my hope, soft notes for memory.

The sap will surely quicken soon or late,
The tardiest bird will twitter to a mate ;
So Spring must dawn again with warmth and bloom,
Or in this world, or in the world to come :
    Sing, voice of Spring,
Till I too blossom and rejoice and sing.

## A BIRD SONG.

IT'S a year almost that I have not seen her :
   Oh last summer green things were greener
Brambles fewer, the blue sky bluer.

It's surely summer, for there's a swallow :
Come one swallow, his mate will follow,
The bird race quicken and wheel and thicken.

Oh happy swallow whose mate will follow
O'er height, o'er hollow !  I'd be a swallow,
To build this weather one nest together.

## A SMILE AND A SIGH.

A SMILE because the nights are short !
   And every morning brings such pleasure
Of sweet love-making, harmless sport :
   Love that makes and finds its treasure ;
   Love, treasure without measure.

A sigh because the days are long !
   Long long these days that pass in sighing,
A burden saddens every song :
   While time lags which should be flying,
   We live who would be dying

## ONE DAY.

I WILL tell you when they met:
In the limpid days of Spring;
Elder boughs were budding yet,
Oaken boughs looked wintry still,
But primrose and veined violet
In the mossful turf were set,
While meeting birds made haste to sing
And build with right good will.

I will tell you when they parted.
When plenteous Autumn sheaves were brown
Then they parted heavy-hearted;
The full rejoicing sun looked down
As grand as in the days before;
Only they had lost a crown;
Only to them those days of yore
Could come back nevermore.

When shall they meet? I cannot tell,
Indeed, when they shall meet again,
Except some day in Paradise:
For this they wait, one waits in pain.
Beyond the sea of death love lies
For ever, yesterday, to-day;
Angels shall ask them, " Is it well?"
And they shall answer " Yea."

## REST.

### SONNET.

O EARTH, lie heavily upon her eyes ;
　　Seal her sweet eyes weary of watching, Earth :
Lie close around her ; leave no room for mirth
With its harsh laughter, nor for sound of sighs.
She hath no questions, she hath no replies,
　　Hushed in and curtained with a blessed dearth
　　Of all that irked her from the hour of birth ;
With stillness that is almost Paradise.
Darkness more clear than noonday holdeth her,
　　Silence more musical than any song ;
Even her very heart has ceased to stir :
Until the morning of Eternity
Her rest shall not begin nor end, but be ;
　　And when she wakes she will not think it long.

## THE CONVENT THRESHOLD.

THERE'S blood between us, love, my love.
　　There's father's blood, there's brother's blood ;
And blood's a bar I cannot pass :
I choose the stairs that mount above,
Stair after golden skyward stair,
To city and to sea of glass.

My lily feet are soiled with mud,
With scarlet mud which tells a tale
Of hope that was, of guilt that was,
Of love that shall not yet avail ;
Alas, my heart, if I could bare
My heart, this selfsame stain is there :
I seek the sea of glass and fire
To wash the spot, to burn the snare ;
Lo, stairs are meant to lift us higher :
Mount with me, mount the kindled stair.

Your eyes look earthward, mine look up.
I see the far-off city grand,
Beyond the hills a watered land,
Beyond the gulf a gleaming strand
Of mansions where the righteous sup ;
Who sleep at ease among their trees,
Or wake to sing a cadenced hymn
With Cherubim and Seraphim ;
They bore the Cross, they drained the cup,
Racked, roasted, crushed, wrenched limb from limb
They the offscouring of the world :
The heaven of starry heavens unfurled,
The sun before their face is dim.

You looking earthward, what see you ?
Milk-white, wine-flushed among the vines,
Up and down leaping, to and fro,
Most glad, most full, made strong with wines,

Blooming as peaches pearled with dew,
Their golden windy hair afloat,
Love-music warbling in their throat,
Young men and women come and go.

You linger, yet the time is short :
Flee for your life, gird up your strength
To flee ; the shadows stretched at length
Show that day wanes, that night draws nigh ;
Flee to the mountain, tarry not.
Is this a time for smile and sigh,
For songs among the secret trees
Where sudden blue birds nest and sport?
The time is short and yet you stay :
To-day, while it is called to-day,
Kneel, wrestle, knock, do violence, pray ;
To-day is short, to-morrow nigh :
Why will you die ? why will you die ?

You sinned with me a pleasant sin :
Repent with me, for I repent.
Woe's me the lore I must unlearn !
Woe's me that easy way we went,
So rugged when I would return !
How long until my sleep begin,
How long shall stretch these nights and days ?
Surely, clean Angels cry, she prays ;
She laves her soul with tedious tears :
How long must stretch these years and years ?

I turn from you my cheeks and eyes,
My hair which you shall see no more—
Alas for joy that went before,
For joy that dies, for love that dies.
Only my lips still turn to you,
My livid lips that cry, Repent
O weary life, O weary Lent,
O weary time whose stars are few.

How should I rest in Paradise,
Or sit on steps of heaven alone
If Saints and Angels spoke of love
Should I not answer from my throne
Have pity upon me, ye my friends,
For I have heard the sound thereof:
Should I not turn with yearning eyes,
Turn earthwards with a pitiful pang?
Oh save me from a pang in heaven.
By all the gifts we took and gave,
Repent, repent, and be forgiven:
This life is long, but yet it ends;
Repent and purge your soul and save:
No gladder song the morning stars
Upon their birthday morning sang
Than Angels sing when one repents.

I tell you what I dreamed last night:
A spirit with transfigured face
Fire-footed clomb an infinite space.

I heard his hundred pinions clang,
Heaven-bells rejoicing rang and rang,
Heaven-air was thrilled with subtle scents,
Worlds spun upon their rushing cars :
He mounted shrieking : " Give me light."
Still light was poured on him, more light ;
Angels, Archangels he outstripped
Exultant in exceeding might,
And trod the skirts of Cherubim.
Still " Give me light," he shrieked ; and dipped
His thirsty face, and drank a sea,
Athirst with thirst it could not slake.
I saw him, drunk with knowledge, take
From aching brows the aureole crown—
His locks writhed like a cloven snake—
He left his throne to grovel down
And lick the dust of Seraphs' feet :
For what is knowledge duly weighed ?
Knowledge is strong, but love is sweet ;
Yea all the progress he had made
Was but to learn that all is small
Save love, for love is all in all.

I tell you what I dreamed last night :
It was not dark, it was not light,
Cold dews had drenched my plenteous hair
Through clay ; you came to seek me there.
And " Do you dream of me ? " you said.
My heart was dust that used to leap

To you ; I answered half asleep :
" My pillow is damp, my sheets are red,
There's a leaden tester to my bed :
Find you a warmer playfellow,
A warmer pillow for your head,
A kinder love to love than mine."
You wrung your hands ; while I, like lead,
Crushed downwards through the sodden earth
You smote your hands but not in mirth,
And reeled but were not drunk with wine.


For all night long I dreamed of you :
I woke and prayed against my will,
Then slept to dream of you again.
At length I rose and knelt and prayed :
I cannot write the words I said,
My words were slow, my tears were few ;
But through the dark my silence spoke
Like thunder.   When this morning broke
My face was pinched, my hair was grey,
And frozen blood was on the sill
Where stifling in my struggle I lay.


If now you saw me you would say :
Where is the face I used to love ?
And I would answer : Gone before ;
It tarries veiled in Paradise.
When once the morning star shall rise
When earth with shadow flees away

And we stand safe within the door,
Then you shall lift the veil thereof.
Look up, rise up : for far above
Our palms are grown, our place is set ;
There we shall meet as once we met,
And love with old familiar love.


## AMOR MUNDI.

" O WHERE are you going with your love-locks
    flowing,
 On the west wind blowing along this valley track ? "
" The downhill path is easy, come with me an it
        please ye,
    We shall escape the uphill by never turning back."


So they two went together in glowing August weather,
    The honey-breathing heather lay to their left and
        right ;
And dear she was to doat on, her swift feet seemed
        to float on
    The air like soft twin pigeons too sportive to alight.


' Oh, what is that in heaven where grey cloud-flakes
        are seven,
    Where blackest clouds hang riven just at the rainy
        skirt ? "

' Oh, that's a meteor sent us, a message dumb,
portentous,
An undeciphered solemn signal of help or hurt."

" Oh, what is that glides quickly where velvet flowers
grow thickly,
Their scent comes rich and sickly?" "A scaled
and hooded worm."
" Oh, what's that in the hollow, so pale I quake to
follow?"
" Oh, that's a thin dead body which waits the
eternal term."

" Turn again, O my sweetest,—turn again, false and
fleetest:
This beaten way thou beatest, I fear is hell's own
track."
" Nay, too steep for hill mounting; nay, too late for
cost counting:
This downhill path is easy, but there's no turning
back."

## UP-HILL.

DOES the road wind up-hill all the way?
　　Yes, to the very end.
Will the day's journey take the whole long day?
　　From morn to night, my friend.

But is there for the night a resting-place?
　　A roof for when the slow dark hours begin.
May not the darkness hide it from my face?
　　You cannot miss that inn.

Shall I meet other wayfarers at night?
　　Those who have gone before.
Then must I knock, or call when just in sight?
　　They will not keep you standing at that door

Shall I find comfort, travel-sore and weak?
　　Of labour you shall find the sum.
Will there be beds for me and all who seek?
　　Yea, beds for all who come.

## "THE INIQUITY OF THE FATHERS UPON THE CHILDREN."

OH the rose of keenest thorn!
  One hidden summer morn
Under the rose I was born.

I do not guess his name
Who wrought my Mother's shame,
And gave me life forlorn,
But my Mother, Mother, Mother,
I know her from all other.
My Mother pale and mild,
Fair as ever was seen,
She was but scarce sixteen,
Little more than a child,
When I was born
To work her scorn.
With secret bitter throes,
In a passion of secret woes,
She bore me under the rose.

One who my Mother nursed
Took me from the first :—
" O nurse, let me look upon
This babe that costs so dear ;
To-morrow she will be gone :

Other mothers may keep
Their babes awake and asleep,
But I must not keep her here."—
Whether I know or guess,
I know this not the less.

So I was sent away
That none might spy the truth:
And my childhood waxed to youth
And I left off childish play.
I never cared to play
With the village boys and girls;
And I think they thought me proud,
I found so little to say
And kept so from the crowd:
But I had the longest curls
And I had the largest eyes,
And my teeth were small like pearls
The girls might flout and scout me,
But the boys would hang about me,
In sheepish mooning wise.

Our one-street village stood
A long mile from the town,
A mile of windy down
And bleak one-sided wood,
With not a single house.
Our town itself was small,
With just the common shops,
And throve in its small way.

Our neighbouring gentry reared
The good old-fashioned crops,
And made old-fashioned boasts
Of what John Bull would do
If Frenchman Frog appeared,
And drank old-fashioned toasts,
And made old-fashioned bows
To my Lady at the Hall.

My Lady at the Hall
Is grander than they all :
Hers is the oldest name
In all the neighbourhood ;
But the race must die with her
Though she's a lofty dame,
For she's unmarried still.
Poor people say she's good
And has an open hand
As any in the land,
And she's the comforter
Of many sick and sad ;
My nurse once said to me
That everything she had
Came of my Lady's bounty :
" Though she's greatest in the county
She's humble to the poor,
No beggar seeks her door
But finds help presently.
I pray both night and day
For her, and you must pray :

But she'll never feel distress
If needy folk can bless."

I was a little maid
When here we came to live
From somewhere by the sea.
Men spoke a foreign tongue
There where we used to be
When I was merry and young,
Too young to feel afraid ;
The fisher folk would give
A kind strange word to me,
There by the foreign sea :
I don't know where it was,
But I remember still
Our cottage on a hill,
And fields of flowering grass
On that fair foreign shore.

I liked my old home best,
But this was pleasant too :
So here we made our nest
And here I grew.
And now and then my Lady
In riding past our door
Would nod to Nurse and speak,
Or stoop and pat my cheek
And I was always ready
To hold the field-gate wide
For my Lady to go through ;

My Lady in her veil
So seldom put aside,
My Lady grave and pale.


I often sat to wonder
Who might my parents be,
For I knew of something under
My simple-seeming state.
Nurse never talked to me
Of mother or of father,
But watched me early and late
With kind suspicious cares :
Or not suspicious, rather
Anxious, as if she knew
Some secret I might gather
And smart for unawares.
Thus I grew.


But Nurse waxed old and grey
Bent and weak with years.
There came a certain day
That she lay upon her bed
Shaking her palsied head,
With words she gasped to say
Which had to stay unsaid.
Then with a jerking hand
Held out so piteously
She gave a ring to me
Of gold wrought curiously

A ring which she had worn
Since the day that I was born,
She once had said to me :
I slipped it on my finger ;
Her eyes were keen to linger
On my hand that slipped it on ;
Then she sighed one rattling sigh
And stared on with sightless eye :—
The one who loved me was gone.

How long I stayed alone
With the corpse I never knew,
For I fainted dead as stone :
When I came to life once more
I was down upon the floor,
With neighbours making ado
To bring me back to life.
I heard the sexton's wife
Say : " Up, my lad, and run
To tell it at the Hall ;
She was my Lady's nurse,
And done can't be undone
I'll watch by this poor lamb.
I guess my Lady's purse
Is always open to such :
I'd run up on my crutch
A cripple as I am,"
(For cramps had vexed her much)
" Rather than this dear heart
Lack one to take her part."

For days day after day
On my weary bed I lay
Wishing the time would pass;
Oh, so wishing that I was
Likely to pass away:
For the one friend whom I knew
Was dead, I knew no other,
Neither father nor mother;
And I, what should I do?

One day the sexton's wife
Said: "Rouse yourself, my dear:
My Lady has driven down
From the Hall into the town,
And we think she's coming here.
Cheer up, for life is life."

But I would not look or speak,
Would not cheer up at all.
My tears were like to fall,
So I turned round to the wall
And hid my hollow cheek
Making as if I slept,
As silent as a stone,
And no one knew I wept.
What was my Lady to me,
The grand lady from the Hall?
She might come, or stay away,
I was sick at heart that day:
The whole world seemed to be

Nothing, just nothing to me,
For aught that I could see.

Yet I listened where I lay :
A bustle came below,
A clear voice said : " I know :
I will see her first alone,
It may be less of a shock
If she's so weak to-day :"—
A light hand turned the lock,
A light step crossed the floor,
One sat beside my bed :
But never a word she said.

For me, my shyness grew
Each moment more and more :
So I said never a word
And neither looked nor stirred ;
I think she must have heard
My heart go pit-a-pat :
Thus I lay, my Lady sat,
More than a mortal hour—
(I counted one and two
By the house-clock while I lay) :
I seemed to have no power
To think of a thing to say,
Or do what I ought to do,
Or rouse myself to a choice.

At last she said : " Margaret,
Won't you even look at me ? "

A something in her voice
Forced my tears to fall at last,
Forced sobs from me thick and fast;
Something not of the past,
Yet stirring memory;
A something new, and yet
Not new, too sweet to last,
Which I never can forget.

I turned and stared at her:
Her cheek showed hollow-pale;
Her hair like mine was fair,
A wonderful fall of hair
That screened her like a veil;
But her height was statelier,
Her eyes had depth more deep:
I think they must have had
Always a something sad,
Unless they were asleep.

While I stared, my Lady took
My hand in her spare hand
Jewelled and soft and grand,
And looked with a long long look
Of hunger in my face;
As if she tried to trace
Features she ought to know,
And half hoped, half feared, to find.
Whatever was in her mind
She heaved a sigh at last,
And began to talk to me.

"Your nurse was my dear nurse,
And her nursling's dear," said she:
"No one told me a word
Of her getting worse and worse,
Till her poor life was past"
(Here my Lady's tears dropped fast);
"I might have been with her,
I might have promised and heard,
But she had no comforter.
She might have told me much
Which now I shall never know,
Never never shall know."
She sat by me sobbing so,
And seemed so woe-begone,
That I laid one hand upon
Hers with a timid touch,
Scarce thinking what I did,
Not knowing what to say:
That moment her face was hid
In the pillow close by mine,
Her arm was flung over me,
She hugged me, sobbing so
As if her heart would break,
And kissed me where I lay.

After this she often came
To bring me fruit or wine,
Or sometimes hothouse flowers.
And at nights I lay awake
Often and often thinking
What to do for her sake.

Wet or dry it was the same :
She would come in at all hours,
Set me eating and drinking
And say I must grow strong ;
At last the day seemed long
And home seemed scarcely home
If she did not come.

Well, I grew strong again :
In time of primroses,
I went to pluck them in the lane ;
In time of nestling birds,
I heard them chirping round the house ;
And all the herds
Were out at grass when I grew strong,
And days were waxen long.
And there was work for bees
Among the May-bush boughs,
And I had shot up tall,
And life felt after all
Pleasant, and not so long
When I grew strong.

I was going to the Hall
To be my Lady's maid :
" Her little friend," she said to me,
" Almost her child,"
She said and smiled,
Sighing painfully ;
Blushing, with a second flush
As if she blushed to blush.

Friend, servant, child : just this
My standing at the Hall ;
The other servants call me " Miss,"
My Lady calls me " Margaret,"
With her clear voice musical.
She never chides when I forget
This or that ; she never chides.
Except when people come to stay
(And that's not often) at the Hall,
I sit with her all day
And ride out when she rides.
She sings to me and makes me sing ;
Sometimes I read to her,
Sometimes we merely sit and talk.
She noticed once my ring
And made me tell its history :
That evening in our garden walk
She said she should infer
The ring had been my father's first,
Then my mother's, given for me
To the nurse who nursed
My mother in her misery,
That so quite certainly
Some one might know me, who . . .
Then she was silent, and I too.

I hate when people come :
The women speak and stare
And mean to be so civil.
This one will stroke my hair,

That one will pat my cheek
And praise my Lady's kindness,
Expecting me to speak ;
I like the proud ones best
Who sit as struck with blindness,
As if I wasn't there.
But if any gentleman
Is staying at the Hall
('Though few come prying here),
My Lady seems to fear
Some downright dreadful evil,
And makes me keep my room
As closely as she can :
So I hate when people come,
It is so troublesome.
In spite of all her care,
Sometimes to keep alive
I sometimes do contrive
To get out in the grounds
For a whiff of wholesome air,
Under the rose you know :
It's charming to break bounds,
Stolen waters are sweet,
And what's the good of feet
If for days they mustn't go ?
Give me a longer tether,
Or I may break from it.

Now I have eyes and ears,
And just some little wit :

" Almost my Lady's child ; "
I recollect she smiled,
Sighed and blushed together ;
Then her story of the ring
Sounds not improbable,
She told it me so well
It seemed the actual thing :—
Oh, keep your counsel close,
But I guess under the rose,
In long past summer weather
When the world was blossoming,
And the rose upon its thorn :
I guess not who he was
Flawed honour like a glass,
And made my life forlorn,
But my Mother, Mother, Mother,
Oh, I know her from all other.

My Lady, you might trust
Your daughter with your fame.
Trust me, I would not shame
Our honourable name,
For I have noble blood
Though I was bred in dust
And brought up in the mud.
I will not press my claim,
Just leave me where you will :
But you might trust your daughter,
For blood is thicker than water
And you're my mother still.

So my Lady holds her own
With condescending grace,
And fills her lofty place
With an untroubled face
As a queen may fill a throne.
While I could hint a tale—
(But then I am her child)—
Would make her quail ;
Would set her in the dust,
Lorn with no comforter,
Her glorious hair defiled
And ashes on her cheek :
The decent world would thrust
Its finger out at her,
Not much displeased I think
To make a nine days' stir ;
The decent world would sink
Its voice to speak of her

Now this is what I mean
To do, no more, no less :
Never to speak, or show
Bare sign of what I know.
Let the blot pass unseen ;
Yea, let her never guess
I hold the tangled clue
She huddles out of view.
Friend, servant, almost child,
So be it and nothing more
On this side of the grave.

Mother, in Paradise,
You'll see with clearer eyes;
Perhaps in this world even
When you are like to die
And face to face with Heaven
You'll drop for once the lie:
But you must drop the mask, not I

My Lady promises
Two hundred pounds with me
Whenever I may wed
A man she can approve:
And since besides her bounty
I'm fairest in the county
(For so I've heard it said,
Though I don't vouch for this),
Her promised pounds may move
Some honest man to see
My virtues and my beauties;
Perhaps the rising grazier,
Or temperance publican,
May claim my wifely duties.
Meanwhile I wait their leisure
And grace-bestowing pleasure,
I wait the happy man;
But if I hold my head
And pitch my expectations
Just higher than their level,
They must fall back on patience
I may not mean to wed,
Yet I'll be civil.

Now sometimes in a dream
My heart goes out of me
To build and scheme,
Till I sob after things that seem
So pleasant in a dream :
A home such as I see
My blessed neighbours live in
With father and with mother,
All proud of one another,
Named by one common name
From baby in the bud
To full-blown workman Father ;
It's little short of Heaven.
I'd give my gentle blood
To wash my special shame
And drown my private grudge ;
I'd toil and moil much rather
The dingiest cottage drudge
Whose mother need not blush,
Than live here like a lady
And see my Mother flush
And hear her voice unsteady
Sometimes, yet never dare
Ask to share her care.


Of course the servants sneer
Behind my back at me ;
Of course the village girls,
Who envy me my curls

And gowns and idleness,
Take comfort in a jeer;
Of course the ladies guess
Just so much of my history
As points the emphatic stress
With which they laud my Lady;
The gentlemen who catch
A casual glimpse of me
And turn again to see,
Their valets on the watch
To speak a word with me,
All know and sting me wild;
Till I am almost ready
To wish that I were dead,
No faces more to see,
No more words to be said,
My Mother safe at last
Disburdened of her child,
And the past past.


" All equal before God "—
Our Rector has it so,
And sundry sleepers nod:
It may be so; I know
All are not equal here,
And when the sleepers wake
They make a difference.
" All equal in the grave "—
That shows an obvious sense.

Yet something which I crave
Not death itself brings near;
How should death half atone
For all my past; or make
The name I bear my own?

I love my dear old Nurse
Who loved me without gains;
I love my mistress even,
Friend, Mother, what you will:
But I could almost curse
My Father for his pains;
And sometimes at my prayer
Kneeling in sight of Heaven
I almost curse him still:
Why did he set his snare
To catch at unaware
My Mother's foolish youth;
Load me with shame that's hers,
And her with something worse,
A lifelong lie for truth?

I think my mind is fixed
On one point and made up:
To accept my lot unmixed;
Never to drug the cup
But drink it by myself.
I'll not be wooed for pelf;
I'll not blot out my shame
With any man's good name;

But nameless as I stand,
My hand is my own hand,
And nameless as I came
I go to the dark land.

"All equal in the grave"—
I bide my time till then :
"All equal before God"—
To-day I feel His rod,
To-morrow He may save :
              Amen.


## IN THE ROUND TOWER AT JHANSI.

### June 8, 1857.

A HUNDRED, a thousand to one ; even so ;
   Not a hope in the world remained :
The swarming howling wretches below
   Gained and gained and gained.

Skene looked at his pale young wife :—
   "Is the time come?"—"The time is come!"—
Young, strong, and so full of life :
   The agony struck them dumb.

Close his arm about her now,
   Close her cheek to his,
Close the pistol to her brow—
   God forgive them this !

"Will it hurt much?"—"No, mine own:
    I wish I could bear the pang for both."
"I wish I could bear the pang alone:
    Courage, dear, I am not loth."

Kiss and kiss: "It is not pain
    Thus to kiss and die.
One kiss more."—"And yet one again."—
    "Good-bye."—"Good-bye."

\*\*\* I retain this little poem, not as historically accurate, but as written and published before I heard the supposed facts of its first verse contradicted.

## THE GERMAN-FRENCH CAMPAIGN.

### 1870-1871.

These two pieces, written during the suspense of a great nation's agony, aim at expressing human sympathy, not political bias.

### I.

## "THY BROTHER'S BLOOD CRIETH."

ALL her corn-fields rippled in the sunshine,
    All her lovely vines, sweets-laden, bowed;
Yet some weeks to harvest and to vintage:
    When, as one man's hand, a cloud
Rose and spread, and, blackening, burst asunder
    In rain and fire and thunder.

Is there nought to reap in the day of harvest?
　　Hath the vine in her day no fruit to yield?
Yea, men tread the press, but not for sweetness,
　　And they reap a red crop from the field.
Build barns, ye reapers, garner all aright,
　　　　Though your souls be called to-night.

A cry of tears goes up from blackened homesteads,
　　A cry of blood goes up from reeking earth :
Tears and blood have a cry that pierces Heaven
　　Through all its Hallelujah swells of mirth ;
God hears their cry, and though He tarry, yet
　　　　He doth not forget.

Mournful Mother, prone in dust and weeping
　　Who shall comfort thee for those who are not?
As thou didst, men do to thee ; and heap the measure
　　And heat the furnace sevenfold hot :
As thou once, now these to thee—who pitieth thee
　　　　From sea to sea?

O thou King, terrible in strength, and building
　　Thy strong future on thy past !
Though he drink the last, the King of Sheshach,
　　Yet he shall drink at the last.
Art thou greater than great Babylon,
　　　　Which lies overthrown?

Take heed, ye unwise among the people ;
　　O ye fools, when will ye understand?---

He that planted the ear shall He not hear,
  Nor He smite who formed the hand?
" Vengeance is Mine, is Mine," thus saith the Lord : —
  O Man, put up thy sword.


2.

## "TO-DAY FOR ME."

SHE sitteth still who used to dance,
    She weepeth sore and more and more :—
Let us sit with thee weeping sore,
    O fair France.

She trembleth as the days advance
Who used to be so light of heart :—
We in thy trembling bear a part,
    Sister France.

Her eyes shine tearful as they glance :
" Who shall give back my slaughtered sons?
" Bind up," she saith, " my wounded ones."—
    Alas, France !

She struggles in a deathly trance,
As in a dream her pulses stir,
She hears the nations calling her,
    " France, France, France."

Thou people of the lifted lance,
Forbear her tears, forbear her blood :
Roll back, roll back, thy whelming flood,
      Back from France.

Eye not her loveliness askance,
Forge not for her a galling chain ;
Leave her at peace to bloom again,
      Vine-clad France.

A time there is for change and chance,
A time for passing of the cup :
And One abides can yet bind up
      Broken France.

A time there is for change and chance
Who next shall drink the trembling cup,
Wring out its dregs and suck them up
      After France ?

# DEVOTIONAL PIECES.

## A CHRISTMAS CAROL.

IN the bleak mid-winter
     Frosty wind made moan,
Earth stood hard as iron,
     Water like a stone ;
Snow had fallen, snow on snow,
     Snow on snow,
In the bleak mid-winter
     Long ago.

Our God, Heaven cannot hold Him,
     Nor earth sustain ;
Heaven and earth shall flee away
     When He comes to reign :
In the bleak mid-winter
     A stable-place sufficed
The Lord God Almighty
     Jesus Christ.

Enough for Him whom cherubim
     Worship night and day,
A breastful of milk
     And a mangerful of hay ;
Enough for Him whom angels
     Fall down before,
The ox and ass and camel
     Which adore.

> Angels and archangels
>  May have gathered there.
> Cherubim and seraphim
>  Throng'd the air,
> But only His mother
>  In her maiden bliss
> Worshipped the Beloved
>  With a kiss.
>
> What can I give Him,
>  Poor as I am?
> If I were a shepherd
>  I would bring a lamb,
> If I were a wise man
>  I would do my part,—
> Yet what I can I give Him,
>  Give my heart.

## "THE LOVE OF CHRIST WHICH PASSETH KNOWLEDGE."

I BORE with thee long weary days and nights,
 Through many pangs of heart, through many tears;
I bore with thee, thy hardness, coldness, slights,
 For three-and-thirty years.

Who else had dared for thee what I have dared?
 I plunged the depth most deep from bliss above;
I not My flesh, I not My spirit spared:
 Give thou Me love for love.

For thee I thirsted in the daily drouth,
  For thee I trembled in the nightly frost :
Much sweeter thou than honey to My mouth :
    Why wilt thou still be lost ?

I bore thee on My shoulders and rejoiced :
  Men only marked upon My shoulders borne
The branding cross ; and shouted hungry-voiced,
    Or wagged their heads in scorn.

Thee did nails grave upon My hands, thy name
  Did thorns for frontlets stamp between Mine eyes :
I, Holy One, put on thy guilt and shame ;
    I, God, Priest, Sacrifice.

A thief upon My right hand and My left ;
  Six hours alone, athirst, in misery :
At length in death one smote My heart and cleft
    A hiding-place for thee.

Nailed to the racking cross, than bed of down
  More dear, whereon to stretch Myself and sleep :
So did I win a kingdom,—share My crown ;
    A harvest.—come and reap.

## "A BRUISED REED SHALL HE NOT BREAK."

I WILL accept thy will to do and be,
  Thy hatred and intolerance of sin,
Thy will at least to love, that burns within
  And thirsteth after Me:
So will I render fruitful, blessing still,
  The germs and small beginnings in thy heart,
  Because thy will cleaves to the better part.—
    Alas, I cannot will.

Dost not thou will, poor soul? Yet I receive
  The inner unseen longings of the soul,
  I guide them turning towards Me; I control
    And charm hearts till they grieve:
If thou desire, it yet shall come to pass,
  Though thou but wish indeed to choose My love;
  For I have power in earth and heaven above.—
    I cannot wish, alas!

What, neither choose nor wish to choose? and yet
  I still must strive to win thee and constrain:
  For thee I hung upon the cross in pain,
    How then can I forget?
If thou as yet dost neither love, nor hate,
  Nor choose, nor wish,—resign thyself, be still
  Till I infuse love, hatred, longing, will.—
    I do not deprecate.

## LONG BARREN.

THOU who didst hang upon a barren **tree**,
  My God, for me ;
   Though I till now be barren, now at **length**,
   Lord, give me strength
To bring forth fruit to Thee.


Thou who didst bear for me the crown of thorn,
Spitting and scorn ;
   Though I till now have put forth thorns, yet now
   Strengthen me Thou
That better fruit be borne.


Thou Rose of Sharon, Cedar of broad **roots**
Vine of sweet fruits,
   Thou Lily of the vale with fadeless **leaf**,
   Of thousands Chief,
Feed Thou my feeble shoots.

## DESPISED AND REJECTED.

MY sun has set, I dwell
    In darkness as a dead man out of sight;
And none remains, not one, that I should tell
To him mine evil plight
This bitter night.
I will make fast my door
That hollow friends may trouble me no more.

"Friend, open to Me."—Who is this that calls?
Nay, I am deaf as are my walls:
Cease crying, for I will not hear
Thy cry of hope or fear.
Others were dear,
Others forsook me: what art thou indeed
That I should heed
Thy lamentable need?
Hungry should feed,
Or stranger lodge thee here?

"Friend, My Feet bleed.
Open thy door to Me and comfort Me."
I will not open, trouble me no more.
Go on thy way footsore,
I will not rise and open unto thee.

" Then is it nothing to thee ?   Open, see
Who stands to plead with thee.
Open, lest I should pass thee by, and thou
One day entreat my Face
And howl for grace,
And I be deaf as thou art now.
Open to Me."

Then I cried out upon him : **Cease,**
Leave me in peace :
Fear not that I should crave
Aught thou mayst have.
Leave me in peace, yea trouble me no more,
Lest I arise and chase thee from my door.
What, shall I not be let
Alone, that thou dost vex me yet ?

But all night long that voice spake urgently :
" Open to Me."
Still harping in mine ears :
" Rise, let Me in."
Pleading with tears :
" Open to Me, that I may come to thee."
While the dew dropped, while the dark hours were
    cold :
" My Feet bleed, see My Face,
See My Hands bleed that bring thee grace,
My Heart doth bleed for thee,
Open to Me."

So till the break of day:
Then died away
That voice, in silence as of sorrow;
Then footsteps echoing like a sigh
Passed me by,
Lingering footsteps slow to pass.
On the morrow
I saw upon the grass
Each footprint marked in blood, and on my door
The mark of blood for evermore.


## A BETTER RESURRECTION.

I HAVE no wit, no words, no tears;
   My heart within me like a stone
Is numbed too much for hopes or fears
   Look right, look left, I dwell alone;
I lift mine eyes, but dimned with grief
   No everlasting hills I see;
My life is in the falling leaf:
   O Jesus, quicken me.

My life is like a faded leaf,
   My harvest dwindled to a husk:
Truly my life is void and brief
   And tedious in the barren dusk;
My life is like a frozen thing,
   No bud nor greenness can I see:
Yet rise it shall—the sap of Spring;
   O Jesus, rise in me.

My life is like a broken bowl,
   A broken bowl that cannot hold
One drop of water for my soul
   Or cordial in the searching cold ;
Cast in the fire the perished thing ;
   Melt and remould it, till it be
A royal cup for Him, my King :
   O Jesus, drink of me.


## IF ONLY.

IF ONLY I might love my God and die
   But now He bids me love Him and live on,
   Now when the bloom of all my life is gone,
The pleasant half of life has quite gone by.
My tree of hope is lopped that spread so high ;
   And I forget how summer glowed and shone,
   While autumn grips me with its fingers wan
And frets me with its fitful windy sigh.
When autumn passes then must winter numb,
   And winter may not pass a weary while,
     But when it passes spring shall flower again :
And in that spring who weepeth now shall smile,
     Yea, they shall wax who now are on the wane,
Yea, they shall sing for love when Christ shall come.

## ADVENT.

THIS Advent moon shines cold and clear,
　　These Advent nights are long;
Our lamps have burned year after year
　　And still their flame is strong.
"Watchman, what of the night?" we cry
　　Heart-sick with hope deferred:
"No speaking signs are in the sky,"
　　Is still the watchman's word.

The Porter watches at the gate,
　　The servants watch within;
The watch is long betimes and late,
　　The prize is slow to win.
"Watchman, what of the night?" but still
　　His answer sounds the same:
"No daybreak tops the utmost hill,
　　Nor pale our lamps of flame."

One to another hear them speak
　　The patient virgins wise:
"Surely He is not far to seek"—
　　All night we watch and rise."
"The days are evil looking back,
　　The coming days are dim;
Yet count we not His promise slack
　　But watch and wait for Him."

One with another, soul with soul,
   They kindle fire from fire:
" Friends watch us who have touched the goal."
   " They urge us, come up higher."
" With them shall rest our waysore feet,
   With them is built our home,
With Christ."—" They sweet, but He most sweet,
   Sweeter than honeycomb."


There no more parting, no more pain,
   The distant ones brought near,
The lost so long are found again,
   Long lost but longer dear:
Eye hath not seen, ear hath not heard,
   Nor heart conceived that rest,
With them our good things long deferred,
   With Jesus Christ our Best.


We weep because the night is long,
   We laugh for day shall rise,
We sing a slow contented song
   And knock at Paradise.
Weeping we hold Him fast, Who wept
   For us, we hold Him fast;
And will not let Him go except
   He bless us first or last.


Weeping we hold Him fast to-night;
   We will not let Him go

Till daybreak smite our wearied sight
  And summer smite the snow :
Then figs shall bud, and dove with dove
  Shall coo the livelong day ;
Then He shall say, " Arise, My love,
  My fair one, come away."


## THE THREE ENEMIES.

### THE FLESH.

" S WEET, thou art pale."
                " More pale to see,
Christ hung upon the cruel tree
And bore His Father's wrath for me."

" Sweet, thou art sad."
                " Beneath a rod
More heavy, Christ for my sake trod
The winepress of the wrath of God."

" Sweet, thou art weary."
                " Not so Christ :
Whose mighty love of me sufficed
For Strength, Salvation, Eucharist."

" Sweet, thou art footsore."
                " If I bleed,
His feet have bled ; yea in my need.
His Heart once bled for mine indeed."

### THE WORLD.

' Sweet, thou art young."
                    " So He was young
Who for my sake in silence hung
Upon the Cross with Passion wrung."

" Look, thou art fair.
                    " He was more fair
Than men, Who deigned for me to wear
A visage marred beyond compare."

" And thou hast riches."
                    " Daily bread :
All else is His : Who, living, dead,
For me lacked where to lay His Head."

" And life is sweet."
                    " It was not so
To Him, Whose Cup did overflow
With mine unutterable woe."

### THE DEVIL.

" Thou drinkest deep."
                    " When Christ would sup
He drained the dregs from out my cup :
So how should I be lifted up?"

" Thou shalt win Glory."

　　　　　　　　　" In the skies,
Lord Jesus, cover up mine eyes
Lest they should look on vanities."

" Thou shalt have Knowledge."

　　　　　　　　　" Helpless dust !
In thee, O Lord, I put my trust :
Answer Thou for me, Wise and Just."

" And Might."—

　　　　　　　　" Get thee behind me.　Lord,
Who hast redeemed and not abhorred
My soul, oh keep it by Thy Word."

## CONSIDER.

Consider
The lilies of the field whose bloom is brief ;--
　　　We are as they ;
　　　Like them we fade away,
As doth a leaf.

　　　Consider
The sparrows of the air of small account :
　　　Our God doth view
Whether they fall or mount,—
　　　He guards us too.

Consider
The lilies that do neither spin nor toil,
    Yet are most fair :—
    What profits all this care
And all this coil ?


    Consider
The birds that have no barn nor harvest-weeks ;
    God gives them food :—
Much more our Father seeks
    To do us good.


## DOST THOU NOT CARE?

I LOVE and love not : Lord, it breaks my heart
    To love and not to love.
Thou veiled within Thy glory, gone apart
    Into Thy shrine, which is above,
Dost thou not love me, Lord, or care
    For this mine ill ?—
*I love thee here or there,*
    *I will accept thy broken heart, lie still.*


Lord, it was well with me in time gone by
    That cometh not again,
When I was fresh and cheerful, who but I ?
    I fresh, I cheerful : worn with pain

Now, out of sight and out of heart ;
　　O Lord, how long?—
*I watch thee as thou art,*
　　*I will accept thy fainting heart, be strong.*


" Lie still," " be strong," to-day ; but, Lord, to-morrow
　　What of to-morrow, Lord ?
Shall there be rest from toil, be truce from sorrow,
　　Be living green upon the sward
Now but a barren grave to me,
　　Be joy for sorrow ?—
*Did I not die for thee ?*
　　*Do I not live for thee ? leave Me to-morrow.*


## WEARY IN WELL-DOING.

I WOULD have gone ; God bade me stay :
　　I would have worked ; God bade me rest.
He broke my will from day to day,
　　He read my yearnings unexpressed
　　　And said them nay.


Now I would stay ; God bids me go :
　　Now I would rest ; God bids me work.
He breaks my heart tossed to and fro,
　　My soul is wrung with doubts that lurk
　　　And vex it so.

I go, Lord, where Thou sendest me;
Day after day I plod and moil:
But, Christ my God, when will it be
That I may let alone my toil
And rest with Thee?

## ONE CERTAINTY.

### SONNET.

VANITY of vanities, the Preacher saith,
All things are vanity.  The eye and ear
Cannot be filled with what they see and hear
Like early dew, or like the sudden breath
Of wind, or like the grass that withereth,
Is man, tossed to and fro by hope and fear:
So little joy hath he, so little cheer,
Till all things end in the long dust of death.
To-day is still the same as yesterday,
To-morrow also even as one of them;
And there is nothing new under the sun:
Until the ancient race of Time be run,
The old thorns shall grow out of the old stem,
And morning shall be cold and twilight grey.

## BY THE WATERS OF BABYLON.

### B.C. 570.

HERE, where I dwell, I waste to skin and bone;
  The curse is come upon me, and I waste
In penal torment powerless to atone.
The curse is come on me, which makes no haste
  And doth not tarry, crushing both the proud
  Hard man and him the sinner double-faced.
Look not upon me, for my soul is bowed
  Within me, as my body in this mire;
  My soul crawls dumb-struck, sore bestead and cowed
As Sodom and Gomorrah scourged by fire,
  As Jericho before God's trumpet-peal,
  So we the elect ones perish in His ire.
Vainly we gird on sackcloth, vainly kneel
  With famished faces toward Jerusalem:
  His heart is shut against us not to feel,
His ears against our cry He shutteth them,
  His hand He shorteneth that He will not save,
  His law is loud against us to condemn:
And we, as unclean bodies in the grave
  Inheriting corruption and the dark,
  Are outcast from His presence which we crave.
Our Mercy hath departed from His Ark,
  Our Glory hath departed from His rest,
  Our Shield hath left us naked as a mark
Unto all pitiless eyes made manifest.

Our very Father hath forsaken us,
Our God hath cast us from Him : we oppress'd
Unto our foes are even marvellous,
A hissing and a butt for pointing hands,
Whilst God Almighty hunts and grinds us thus ;
For He hath scattered us in alien lands,
Our priests, our princes, our anointed king,
And bound us hand and foot with brazen bands.
Here while I sit my painful heart takes wing
Home to the home-land I may see no more,
Where milk and honey flow, where waters spring
And fail not, where I dwelt in days of yore
Under my fig-tree and my fruitful vine,
There where my parents dwelt at ease before :
Now strangers press the olives that are mine,
Reap all the corners of my harvest-field,
And make their fat hearts wanton with my wine
To them my trees, to them my gardens yield
Their sweets and spices and their tender green,
O'er them in noontide heat outspread their shield.
Yet these are they whose fathers had not been
Housed with my dogs, whom hip and thigh we smote
And with their blood washed their pollutions clean,
Purging the land which spewed them from its throat ;
Their daughters took we for a pleasant prey,
Choice tender ones on whom the fathers doat.
Now they in turn have led our own away ;
Our daughters and our sisters and our wives
Sore weeping as they weep who curse the day,
To live, remote from help, dishonoured lives,

Soothing their drunken masters with a song,
Or dancing in their golden tinkling gyves :
Accurst if they remember through the long
Estrangement of their exile, twice accursed
If they forget and join the accursèd throng.
How doth my heart that is so wrung not burst
When I remember that my way was plain,
And that God's candle lit me at the first,
Whilst now I grope in darkness, grope in vain,
Desiring but to find Him Who is lost,
To find Him once again, but once again !
His wrath came on us to the uttermost,
His covenanted and most righteous wrath :
Yet this is He of Whom we made our boast,
Who lit the Fiery Pillar in our path,
Who swept the Red Sea dry before our feet,
Who in His jealousy smote kings, and hath
Sworn once to David : One shall fill thy seat
Born of thy body, as the sun and moon
'Stablished for aye in sovereignty complete.
O Lord, remember David, and that soon.
The Glory hath departed, Ichabod !
Yet now, before our sun grow dark at noon,
Before we come to nought beneath Thy rod,
Before we go down quick into the pit,
Remember us for good, O God, our God :—
Thy Name will I remember, praising it,
Though Thou forget me, though Thou hide Thy
face,
And blot me from the Book which Thou hast writ

Thy Name will I remember in my praise
And call to mind Thy faithfulness of old,
Though as a weaver Thou cut off my days
And end me as a tale ends that is told.

## CHRISTIAN AND JEW.

### A DIALOGUE.

" OH happy happy land !
    Angels like rushes stand
About the wells of light."—
" Alas, I have not eyes for this fair sight :
Hold fast my hand."—

" As in a soft wind, they
Bend all one blessed way,
    Each bowed in his own glory, star with star."—
" I cannot see so far,
Here shadows are."—

"White-winged the cherubim,
Yet whiter seraphim,
    Glow white with intense fire of love."—
" Mine eyes are dim :
    I look in vain above,
And miss their hymn."—

" Angels, Archangels cry
One to other ceaselessly
(I hear them sing)
One ' Holy, Holy, Holy ' to their King."—
" I do not hear them, I."—

" Joy to thee, Paradise,—
    Garden and goal and nest !
Made green for wearied eyes ;
    Much softer than the breast
Of mother-dove clad in a rainbow's dyes.

" All precious souls are there
    Most safe, elect by grace,
    All tears are wiped for ever from their face :
Untired in prayer
    They wait and praise
    Hidden for a little space.

" Boughs of the Living Vine
They spread in summer shine
    Green leaf with leaf :
Sap of the Royal Vine it stirs like wine
    In all both less and chief.

" Sing to the Lord,
    All spirits of all flesh, sing ;
For He hath not abhorred
    Our low estate nor scorn'd our offering :
    Shout to our King."—

" But Zion said :
  My Lord forgetteth me.
Lo, she hath made her bed
  In dust ; forsaken weepeth she
  Where alien rivers swell the sea.

" She laid her body as the ground,
  Her tender body as the ground to those
Who passed ; her harpstrings cannot sound
In a strange land ; discrowned
  She sits, and drunk with woes."—

" O drunken not with wine,
  Whose sins and sorrows have fulfilled the sum,—
  Be not afraid, arise, be no more dumb ;
Arise, shine,
  For thy light is come."—

" Can these bones live ? "—
                  " God knows:
  The prophet saw such clothed with flesh and skin;
  A wind blew on them, and life entered in ;
They shook and rose.
  Hasten the time, O Lord, blot out their sin,
  Let life begin."

## GOOD FRIDAY.

AM I a stone, and not a sheep,
　That I can stand, O Christ, beneath Thy cross,
　To number drop by drop Thy Blood's slow loss,
And yet not weep?

Not so those women loved
　Who with exceeding grief lamented Thee;
　Not so fallen Peter weeping bitterly;
Not so the thief was moved;

Not so the Sun and Moon
　Which hid their faces in a starless sky,
　A horror of great darkness at broad noon—
I, only I.

Yet give not o'er,
　But seek Thy sheep, true Shepherd of the flock;
　Greater than Moses, turn and look once more
And smite a rock.

## SWEET DEATH.

THE sweetest blossoms die.
    And so it was that, going day by day
  Unto the Church to praise and pray,
And crossing the green churchyard thoughtfully,
    I saw how on the graves the flowers
    Shed their fresh leaves in showers,
And how their perfume rose up to the sky
  Before it passed away.

The youngest blossoms die.
    They die and fall and nourish the rich earth
  From which they lately had their birth ;
Sweet life, but sweeter death that passeth by
    And is as though it had not been :—
    All colours turn to green ;
The bright hues vanish, and the odours fly,
  The grass hath lasting worth.

And youth and beauty die.
    So be it, O my God, Thou God of Truth :
  Better than beauty and than youth
Are Saints and Angels, a glad company ;
    And Thou, O Lord, our Rest and Ease,
    Art better far than these.
Why should we shrink from our full harvest ? why
  Prefer to glean with Ruth ?

## SYMBOLS.

I WATCHED a rosebud very long
   Brought on by dew and sun and shower,
  Waiting to see the perfect flower :
Then, when I thought it should be strong,
   It opened at the matin hour
And fell at evensong.

I watched a nest from day to day,
   A green nest full of pleasant shade,
  Wherein three speckled eggs were laid :
But when they should have hatched in May,
   The two old birds had grown afraid
Or tired, and flew away.

Then in my wrath I broke the bough
   That I had tended so with care,
  Hoping its scent should fill the air ;
I crushed the eggs, not heeding how
   Their ancient promise had been fair :
I would have vengeance now.

But the dead branch spoke from the sod,
   And the eggs answered me again :
  Because we failed dost thou complain ?
Is thy wrath just ?   And what if God,
   Who waiteth for thy fruits in vain,
Should also take the rod ?

## 'CONSIDER THE LILIES OF THE FIELD.'

FLOWERS preach to us if we will hear :—
    The rose saith in the dewy morn:
I am most fair ;
Yet all my loveliness is born
Upon a thorn.
The poppy saith amid the corn:
Let but my scarlet head appear
And I am held in scorn ;
Yet juice of subtle virtue lies
Within my cup of curious dyes.
The lilies say : Behold how we
Preach without words of purity.
The violets whisper from the shade
Which their own leaves have made :
Men scent our fragrance on the air,
Yet take no heed
Of humble lessons we would read.

But not alone the fairest flowers:
The merest grass
Along the roadside where we pass,
Lichen and moss and sturdy weed,
Tell of His love who sends the dew,
The rain and sunshine too,
To nourish one small seed.

## THE WORLD.

### SONNET.

BY day she woos me, soft, exceeding fair :
　　But all night as the moon so changeth she ;
　Loathsome and foul with hideous leprosy
And subtle serpents gliding in her hair.
By day she woos me to the outer air,
　　Ripe fruits, sweet flowers, and full satiety :
But through the night a beast she grins at me,
A very monster void of love and prayer.
By day she stands a lie : by night she stands
　　In all the naked horror of the truth
With pushing horns and clawed and clutching hands
Is this a friend indeed ; that I should sell
　　My soul to her, give her my life and youth,
Till my feet, cloven too, take hold on hell ?

## A TESTIMONY.

I SAID of laughter : it is vain.
　　Of mirth I said : what profits it ?
　Therefore I found a book, and writ
Therein how ease and also pain,
How health and sickness, every one
Is vanity beneath the sun.

Man walks in a vain shadow; he
   Disquieteth himself in vain.
   The things that were shall be again;
The rivers do not fill the sea,
But turn back to their secret source;
The winds too turn upon their course.

Our treasures moth and rust corrupt,
   Or thieves break through and steal, or they
   Make themselves wings and fly away.
One man made merry as he supped,
Nor guessed how when that night grew dim
His soul would be required of him.

We build our houses on the sand
   Comely withoutside and within;
   But when the winds and rains begin
To beat on them, they cannot stand:
They perish, quickly overthrown,
Loose from the very basement stone.

All things are vanity, I said:
   Yea vanity of vanities.
   The rich man dies; and the poor dies:
The worm feeds sweetly on the dead.
Whate'er thou lackest, keep this trust:
All in the end shall have but dust:

The one inheritance, which best
   And worst alike shall find and share:
   The wicked cease from troubling there,

And there the weary be at rest ;
There all the wisdom of the wise
Is vanity of vanities.

Man flourishes as a green leaf,
   And as a leaf doth pass away ;
   Or as a shade that cannot stay
And leaves no track, his course is brief :
Yet man doth hope and fear and plan
Till he is dead :—oh foolish man !

Our eyes cannot be satisfied
   With seeing, nor our ears be filled
   With hearing : yet we plant and build
And buy and make our borders wide ;
We gather wealth, we gather care,
But know not who shall be our heir.

Why should we hasten to arise
   So early, and so late take rest ?
   Our labour is not good ; our best
Hopes fade ; our heart is stayed on lies
Verily, we sow wind ; and we
Shall reap the whirlwind, verily.

He who hath little shall not lack ;
   He who hath plenty shall decay :
   Our fathers went ; we pass away ;
Our children follow on our track :
So generations fail, and so
They are renewed and come and go.

The earth is fattened with our dead ;
  She swallows more and doth not cease :
  Therefore her wine and oil increase
And her sheaves are not numberèd ;
Therefore her plants are green, and all
Her pleasant trees lusty and tall.

Therefore the maidens cease to sing,
  And the young men are very sad ;
  Therefore the sowing is not glad,
And mournful is the harvesting.
Of high and low, of great and small,
Vanity is the lot of all.

A King dwelt in Jerusalem ;
  He was the wisest man on earth ;
  He had all riches from his birth,
And pleasures till he tired of them :
Then, having tested all things, he
Witnessed that all are vanity.

## PARADISE.

ONCE in a dream I saw the flowers
      That bud and bloom in Paradise ;
   More fair they are than waking eyes
Have seen in all this world of ours.
And faint the perfume-bearing rose,
      And faint the lily on its stem,
And faint the perfect violet
      Compared with them.

I heard the songs of Paradise :
      Each bird sat singing in his place ;
   A tender song so full of grace
It soared like incense to the skies.
Each bird sat singing to his mate
      Soft cooing notes among the trees :
The nightingale herself were cold
      To such as these.

I saw the fourfold River flow,
      And deep it was, with golden sand ;
   It flowed between a mossy land
With murmured music grave and low.
It hath refreshment for all thirst,
      For fainting spirits strength and rest ;
Earth holds not such a draught as this
      From east to west.

The Tree of Life stood budding there,
  Abundant with its twelvefold fruits ;
  Eternal sap sustains its roots,
Its shadowing branches fill the air.
Its leaves are healing for the world,
  Its fruit the hungry world can feed,
Sweeter than honey to the taste
    And balm indeed.

I saw the gate called Beautiful ;
  And looked, but scarce could look within ;
  I saw the golden streets begin,
And outskirts of the glassy pool.
Oh harps, oh crowns of plenteous stars,
  Oh green palm branches many-leaved—
Eye hath not seen, nor ear hath heard,
    Nor heart conceived.

I hope to see these things again,
  But not as once in dreams by night ;
  To see them with my very sight,
And touch and handle and attain :
To have all Heaven beneath my feet
  For narrow way that once they trod ;
To have my part with all the saints.
    And with my God.

## SLEEP AT SEA.

SOUND the deep waters :—
   Who shall sound that deep ?—
Too short the plummet,
   And the watchmen sleep.
Some dream of effort
   Up a toilsome steep ;
Some dream of pasture grounds
   For harmless sheep.

White shapes flit to and fro
   From mast to mast ;
They feel the distant tempest
   That nears them fast :
Great rocks are straight ahead,
   Great shoals not past ;
They shout to one another
   Upon the blast.

Oh, soft the streams drop music
   Between the hills,
And musical the birds' nests
   Beside those rills
The nests are types of home
   Love-hidden from ills,
The nests are types of spirits
   Love-music fills.

So dream the sleepers,
　　Each man in his place;
The lightning shows the smile
　　Upon each face:
The ship is driving,—driving,—
　　It drives apace:
And sleepers smile, and spirits
　　Bewail their case.

The lightning glares and reddens
　　Across the skies;
It seems but sunset
　　To those sleeping eyes.
When did the sun go down
　　On such a wise?
From such a sunset
　　When shall day arise?

" Wake," call the spirits:
　　But to heedless ears:
They have forgotten sorrows
　　And hopes and fears;
They have forgotten perils
　　And smiles and tears;
Their dream has held them long
　　Long years and years.

" Wake," call the spirits again ·
　　But it would take
A louder summons
　　To bid them awake.

Some dream of pleasure
   For another's sake :
Some dream, forgetful
   Of a lifelong ache.

One by one slowly,
   Ah, how sad and slow !
Wailing and praying
   The spirits rise and go :
Clear stainless spirits
   White, as white as snow ,
Pale spirits, wailing
   For an overthrow.

One by one flitting,
   Like a mournful bird
Whose song is tired at last
   For no mate heard.
The loving voice is silent,
   The useless word ;
One by one flitting
   Sick with hope deferred.

Driving and driving,
   The ship drives amain :
While swift from mast to mast
   Shapes flit again,
Flit silent as the silence
   Where men lie slain ;
Their shadow cast upon the sails
   Is like a stain.

No voice to call the sleepers,
  No hand to raise :
They sleep to death in dreaming
  Of length of days.
Vanity of vanities,
  The Preacher says :
Vanity is the end
  Of all their ways.


## MOTHER COUNTRY

OH what is that country
    And where can it be,
Not mine own country,
    But dearer far to me ?
Yet mine own country,
    If I one day may see
Its spices and cedars,
    Its gold and ivory.

As I lie dreaming
    It rises, that land ;
There rises before me
    Its green golden strand,
With the bowing cedars
    And the shining sand ;
It sparkles and flashes
    Like a shaken brand.

Do angels lean nearer
  While I lie and long?
1 see their soft plumage
  And catch their windy song,
Like the rise of a high tide
  Sweeping full and strong;
I mark the outskirts
  Of their reverend throng.

Oh what is a king here,
  Or what is a boor?
Here all starve together,
  All dwarfed and poor:
Here Death's hand knocketh
  At door after door,
He thins the dancers
  From the festal floor.

Oh what is a handmaid,
  Or what is a queen?
All must lie down together
  Where the turf is green,
The foulest face hidden,
  The fairest not seen;
Gone as if never,
  They had breathed or been.

Gone from sweet sunshine
  Underneath the sod,
Turned from warm flesh and blood
  To senseless clod,

Gone as if never
  They had toiled or trod,
Gone out of sight of all
  Except our God.

Shut into silence
  From the accustomed song,
Shut into solitude
  From all earth's throng,
Run down though swift of foot,
  Thrust down though strong :
Life made an end of,
  Seemed it short or long.

Life made an end of,
  Life but just begun ;
Life finished yesterday,
  Its last sand run ;
Life new-born with the morrow,
  Fresh as the sun :
While done is done for ever ;
  Undone, undone.

And if that life is life,
  This is but a breath,
The passage of a dream
  And the shadow of death :
But a vain shadow
  If one considereth ;
Vanity of vanities,
  As the Preacher saith.

## "I WILL LIFT UP MINE EYES UNTO THE HILLS."

I AM pale with sick desire,
  For my heart is far away
From this world's fitful fire
  And this world's waning day ,
In a dream it overleaps
  A world of tedious ills
To where the sunshine sleeps
  On the everlasting hills. —
    Say the Saints : There Angels ease us
      Glorified and white.
    They say : We rest in Jesus,
      Where is not day or night.

My soul saith : I have sought
  For a home that is not gained,
I have spent yet nothing bought,
  Have laboured but not attained ;
My pride strove to mount and grow,
  And hath but dwindled down ;
My love sought love, and lo !
  Hath not attained its crown. —
    Say the Saints : Fresh souls increase us,
      None languish or recede.
    They say : We love our Jesus,
      And He loves us indeed.

I cannot rise above,
   I cannot rest beneath,
I cannot find out love,
   Or escape from death ;
Dear hopes and joys gone by
   Still mock me with a name ;
My best beloved die,
   And I cannot die with them.——
   Say the Saints : No deaths decrease us,
     Where our rest is glorious.
   They say : We live in Jesus,
     Who once died for us.


O my soul, she beats her wings
   And pants to fly away
Up to immortal things
   In the heavenly day :
Yet she flags and almost faints ;
   Can such be meant for me ?——
Come and see, say the Saints
   Saith Jesus : Come and see.
   Say the Saints : His pleasures please us
     Before God and the Lamb.
   Come and taste My sweets, saith Jesus :
     Be with Me where I am.

## "THE MASTER IS COME, AND CALLETH FOR THEE."

WHO calleth?—Thy Father calleth,
    Run, O Daughter, to wait on Him :
He Who chasteneth but for a season
    Trims thy lamp that it burn not dim.

Who calleth?—Thy Master calleth,
    Sit, Disciple, and learn of Him :
He Who teacheth wisdom of Angels
    Makes thee wise as the Cherubim.

Who calleth?—Thy Monarch calleth,
    Rise, O Subject, and follow Him :
He is stronger than Death or Devil,
    Fear not thou if the foe be grim.

Who calleth?—Thy Lord God calleth,
    Fall, O Creature, adoring Him :
He is jealous, thy God Almighty,
    Count not dear to thee life or limb.

Who calleth?—Thy Bridegroom calleth,
    Soar, O Bride, with the Seraphim :
He Who loves thee as no man loveth,
    Bids thee give up thy heart to Him.

## WHO SHALL DELIVER ME?

GOD strengthen me to bear myself,
That heaviest weight of all to bear,
Inalienable weight of care.

All others are outside myself;
I lock my door and bar them out,
The turmoil, tedium, gad-about.

I lock my door upon myself,
And bar them out; but who shall wall
Self from myself, most loathed of all?

If I could once lay down myself,
And start self-purged upon the race
That all must run!   Death runs apace.

If I could set aside myself,
And start with lightened heart upon
The road by all men overgone!

God harden me against myself,
This coward with pathetic voice
Who craves for ease, and rest, and joys:

Myself, arch-traitor to myself;
My hollowest friend, my deadliest foe,
My clog whatever road I go.

Yet One there is can curb myself,
Can roll the strangling load from me,
Break off the yoke and set me free.

## "WHEN MY HEART IS VEXED, I WILL COMPLAIN."

"O LORD, how canst Thou say Thou lovest me
    Me whom thou settest in a barren land,
Hungry and thirsty on the burning sand,
Hungry and thirsty where no waters be
Nor shadows of date-bearing tree :—
O Lord, how canst Thou say Thou lovest me?"

" I came from Edom by as parched a track,
    As rough a track beneath My bleeding feet.
    I came from Edom seeking thee, and sweet
I counted bitterness ; I turned not back
But counted life as death, and trod
The winepress all alone : and I am God."

" Yet, Lord, how canst Thou say Thou lovest me ?
    For Thou art strong to comfort : and could I
    But comfort one I love, who, like to die,
Lifts feeble hands and eyes that fail to see
In one last prayer for comfort—nay,
I could not stand aside or turn away."

" Alas ! thou knowest that for thee I died,
    For thee I thirsted with the dying thirst ;
    I, Blessed, for thy sake was counted cursed,
In sight of men and angels crucified :
All this and more I bore to prove
My love, and wilt thou yet mistrust My love ? "

" Lord, I am fain to think Thou lovest me,
    For Thou art all in all and I am Thine,
    And lo ! Thy love is better than new wine,
And I am sick of love in loving Thee.
But dost Thou love me ? speak and save,
For jealousy is cruel as the grave."

" Nay, if thy love is not an empty breath
    My love is as thine own, deep answers deep.
    Peace, peace : I give to my beloved sleep,
Not death but sleep, for love is strong as death
Take patience ; sweet thy sleep shall be,
Yea, thou shalt wake in Paradise with Me."

## AFTER COMMUNION.

WHY should I call Thee Lord, Who art my God?
   Why should I call Thee Friend, Who art my
      Love?
   Or King, Who art my very Spouse above?
Or call Thy Sceptre on my heart Thy rod?
   Lo, now Thy banner over me is love,
All heaven flies open to me at Thy nod:
For Thou hast lit Thy flame in me a clod,
   Made me a nest for dwelling of Thy Dove.
   What wilt Thou call me in our home above,
Who now hast called me friend? how will it be
      When Thou for good wine settest forth the best?
Now Thou dost bid me come and sup with Thee,
   Now Thou dost make me lean upon Thy breast:
   How will it be with me in time of love?


## MARTYRS' SONG.

WE meet in joy, though we part in sorrow;
      We part to-night, but we meet to-morrow.
Be it flood or blood the path that's trod,
All the same it leads home to God:
Be it furnace-fire voluminous,
One like God's Son will walk with us.

What are these that glow from afar,
These that lean over the golden bar,
Strong as the lion, pure as the dove,
With open arms and hearts of love?
They the blessed ones gone before,
They the blessed for evermore.
Out of great tribulation they went
Home to their home of Heaven-content;
Through flood, or blood, or furnace-fire,
To the rest that fulfils desire.

What are these that fly as a cloud,
With flashing heads and faces bowed,
In their mouths a victorious psalm,
In their hands a robe and a palm?
Welcoming angels these that shine,
Your own angel, and yours, and mine;
Who have hedged us both day and night
On the left hand and on the right,
Who have watched us both night and day
Because the devil keeps watch to slay.

Light above light, and Bliss beyond bliss,
Whom words cannot utter, lo, Who is This?
As a King with many crowns He stands,
And our names are graven upon His hands;
As a Priest, with God-uplifted eyes,
He offers for us His Sacrifice;
As the Lamb of God for sinners slain,
That we too may live He lives again;
As our Champion behold Him stand,
Strong to save us, at God's Right Hand.

God the Father give us grace
To walk in the light of Jesus' Face.
God the Son give us a part
In the hiding-place of Jesus' Heart :
God the Spirit so hold us up,
That we may drink of Jesus' cup.

Death is short, and life is long ;
Satan is strong, but Christ more strong.
At His Word, Who hath led us hither,
The Red Sea must part hither and thither
At His Word, Who goes before us too,
Jordan must cleave to let us through.

Yet one pang searching and sore,
And then Heaven for evermore :
Yet one moment awful and dark,
Then safety within the Veil and the Ark
Yet one effort by Christ His grace,
Then Christ for ever face to face.

God the Father we will adore,
In Jesus' Name, now and evermore :
God the Son we will love and thank
In this flood and on the farther bank :
God the Holy Ghost we will praise,
In Jesus' Name through endless days :
God Almighty, God Three in One,
God Almighty, God alone.

## AFTER THIS THE JUDGMENT.

A S eager homebound traveller to the goal,
 Or steadfast seeker on an unsearched main,
Or martyr panting for an aureole,
 My fellow-pilgrims pass me, and attain
That hidden mansion of perpetual peace
 Where keen desire and hope dwell free from pain
That gate stands open of perennial ease ;
 I view the glory till I partly long,
Yet lack the fire of love which quickens these.
 O passing Angel, speed me with a song,
A melody of heaven to reach my heart
 And rouse me to the race and make me strong ;
Till in such music I take up my part
 Swelling those Hallelujahs full of rest,
One, tenfold, hundredfold, with heavenly art,
 Fulfilling north and south and east and west,
Thousand, ten thousandfold, innumerable,
 All blent in one yet each one manifest ;
Each one distinguished and beloved as well
 As if no second voice in earth or heaven
Were lifted up the Love of God to tell.
 Ah, Love of God, which thine own Self hast given
To me most poor, and made me rich in love.
 Love that dost pass the tenfold seven times seven,
Draw Thou mine eyes, draw Thou my heart above,
 My treasure and my heart store Thou in Thee.

Brood over me with yearnings of a dove ;
   Be Husband, Brother, closest Friend to me ;
Love me as very mother loves her son,
   Her sucking firstborn fondled on her knee :
Yea, more than mother loves her little one ;
   For, earthly, even a mother may forget
And feel no pity for its piteous moan ;
   But thou, O Love of God, remember yet,
Through the dry desert, through the waterflood
   (Life, death), until the Great White Throne is set
If now I am sick in chewing the bitter cud
   Of sweet past sin, though solaced by Thy grace
And ofttimes strengthened by Thy Flesh and Blood,
   How shall I then stand up before Thy face
When from Thine eyes repentance shall be hid
   And utmost Justice stand in Mercy's place :
When every sin I thought or spoke or did
   Shall meet me at the inexorable bar,
And there be no man standing in the mid
   To plead for me ; while star fallen after star
With heaven and earth are like a ripened shock,
   And all time's mighty works and wonders are
Consumed as in a moment ; when no rock
   Remains to fall on me, no tree to hide,
But I stand all creation's gazing-stock
   Exposed and comfortless on every side,
Placed trembling in the final balances
   Whose poise this hour, this moment, must be tried?—
Ah Love of God, if greater love than this
   Hath no man, that a man die for his friend,

And if such love of love Thine own Love is,
   Plead with Thyself, with me, before the end ;
Redeem me from the irrevocable past ;
   Pitch Thou Thy Presence round me to defend ;
Yea seek with piercèd feet, yea hold me fast
   With piercèd hands whose wounds were made by
      love ;
Not what I am, remember what Thou wast
   When darkness hid from Thee Thy heavens above,
And sin Thy Father's Face, while thou didst drink
   The bitter cup of death, didst taste thereof
For every man ; while Thou wast nigh to sink
   Beneath the intense intolerable rod,
Grown sick of love ; not what I am, but think
   Thy Life then ransomed mine, my God, my God !


## SAINTS AND ANGELS.

IT'S oh in Paradise that I fain would be,
   Away from earth and weariness and all beside :
Earth is too full of loss with its dividing sea,
   But Paradise upbuilds the bower for the bride.

Where flowers are yet in bud while the boughs are
      green,
   I would get quit of earth and get robed for heaven ;
Putting on my raiment white within the screen,
   Putting on my crown of gold whose gems are seven

Fair is the fourfold river that maketh no moan,
  Fair are the trees fruit-bearing of the wood,
Fair are the gold and bdellium and the onyx stone,
  And I know the gold of that land is good.

O my love, my dove, lift up your eyes
  Toward the eastern gate like an opening rose;
You and I who parted will meet in Paradise,
  Pass within and sing when the gates unclose.

This life is but the passage of a day,
  This life is but a pang and all is over,
But in the life to come which fades not away
  Every love shall abide and every lover.

He who wore out pleasure and mastered all lore,
  Solomon wrote " Vanity of vanities : "
Down to death, of all that went before
  In his mighty long life, the record is this.

With loves by the hundred, wealth beyond measure,
  Is this he who wrote " Vanity of vanities " ?
Yea, " Vanity of vanities " he saith of pleasure,
  And of all he learned set his seal to this.

Yet we love and faint not, for our love is one,
  And we hope and flag not, for our hope is sure.
Although there be nothing new beneath the sun
  And no help for life and for death no cure.

The road to death is life, the gate of life is death,
　We who wake shall sleep, we shall wax who wane ;
Let us not vex our souls for stoppage of a breath,
　The fall of a river that turneth not again.

Be the road short, and be the gate near,—
　Shall a short road tire, a strait gate appal ?
The loves that meet in Paradise shall cast out fear,
　And Paradise hath room for you and me and all.

## A ROSE PLANT IN JERICHO.

AT morn I plucked a rose and gave it Thee,
　A rose of joy and happy love and peace,
　　A rose with scarce a thorn :
　　But in the chillness of a second morn
　My rose bush drooped, and all its gay increase
Was but one thorn that wounded me.

I plucked the thorn and offered it to Thee
　And for my thorn Thou gavest love and peace,
　　Not joy this mortal morn :
　　If Thou hast given much treasure for a thorn,
　Wilt Thou not give me for my rose increase
Of gladness, and all sweets to me?

My thorny rose, my love and pain, to Thee
　I offer ; and I set my heart in peace,

And rest upon my thorn :
For verily I think to-morrow morn
Shall bring me Paradise, my gift's increase,
Yea, give Thy very Self to me.


# FROM HOUSE TO HOME.

THE first was like a dream through summer heat,
　The second like a tedious numbing swoon,
While the half-frozen pulses lagged to beat
　Beneath a winter moon.

" But," says my friend, " what was this thing and
　　　where ? "
　It was a pleasure-place within my soul ;
An earthly paradise supremely fair
　That lured me from the goal.

The first part was a tissue of hugged lies ;
　The second was its ruin fraught with pain :
Why raise the fair delusion to the skies
　But to be dashed again ?

My castle stood of white transparent glass
　Glittering and frail with many a fretted spire,
But when the summer sunset came to pass
　It kindled into fire.

My pleasaunce was an undulating green,
    Stately with trees whose shadows slept below,
With glimpses of smooth garden-beds between
    Like flame or sky or snow.

Swift squirrels on the pastures took their ease,
    With leaping lambs safe from the unfeared knife ;
All singing-birds rejoicing in those trees
    Fulfilled their careless life.

Woodpigeons cooed there, stockdoves nestled there ;
    My trees were full of songs and flowers and fruit,
Their branches spread a city to the air
    And mice lodged in their root.

My heath lay farther off, where lizards lived
    In strange metallic mail, just spied and gone ;
Like darted lightnings here and there perceived
    But nowhere dwelt upon.

Frogs and fat toads were there to hop or plod
    And propagate in peace, an uncouth crew,
Where velvet-headed rushes rustling nod
    And spill the morning dew.

All caterpillars throve beneath my rule,
    With snails and slugs in corners out of sight ;
I never marred the curious sudden stool
    That perfects in a night.

Safe in his excavated gallery
  The burrowing mole groped on from year to year;
No harmless hedgehog curled because of me
  His prickly back for fear.

Ofttimes one like an angel walked with me,
  With spirit-discerning eyes like flames of fire,
But deep as the unfathomed endless sea
  Fulfilling my desire:

And sometimes like a snowdrift he was fair,
  And sometimes like a sunset glorious red,
And sometimes he had wings to scale the air
  With aureole round his head.

We sang our songs together by the way,
  Calls and recalls and echoes of delight;
So communed we together all the day,
  And so in dreams by night.

I have no words to tell what way we walked,
  What unforgotten path now closed and sealed:
I have no words to tell all things we talked,
  All things that he revealed:

This only can I tell: that hour by hour
  I waxed more feastful, lifted up and glad
I felt no thorn-prick when I plucked a flower
  Felt not my friend was sad.

" To-morrow," once I said to him with smiles :
   " To-night," he answered gravely and was dumb,
But pointed out the stones that numbered miles
      And miles and miles to come.

" Not so," I said : " to-morrow shall be sweet :
   To-night is not so sweet as coming days."
Then first I saw that he had turned his feet,
      Had turned from me his face :

Running and flying miles and miles he went,
   But once looked back to beckon with his hand
And cry : " Come home, O love, from banishment :
      Come to the distant land."

That night destroyed me like an avalanche ;
   One night turned all my summer back to snow :
Next morning not a bird upon my branch,
      Not a lamb woke below,—

No bird, no lamb, no living breathing thing ;
   No squirrel scampered on my breezy lawn,
No mouse lodged by his hoard : all joys took wing
      And fled before that dawn.

Azure and sun were starved from heaven above,
   No dew had fallen, but biting frost lay hoar :
O love, I knew that I should meet my love,
      Should find my love no more.

" My love no more," I muttered, stunned with pain :
　I shed no tear, I wrung no passionate hand,
Till something whispered : " You shall meet again,
　Meet in a distant land."

Then with a cry like famine I arose,
　I lit my candle, searched from room to room,
Searched up and down ; a war of winds that froze
　Swept through the blank of gloom.

I searched day after day, night after night ;
　Scant change there came to me of night or day :
" No more," I wailed, " no more :" and trimmed my
　　light.
　And gnashed but did not pray.

Until my heart broke and my spirit broke :
　Upon the frost-bound floor I stumbled, fell,
And moaned : " It is enough : withhold the stroke.
　Farewell, O love, farewell."

Then life swooned from me.　And I heard the song
　Of spheres and spirits rejoicing over me :
One cried : " Our sister, she hath suffered long."—
　One answered : " Make her see."—

One cried : " Oh blessèd she who no more pain,
　Who no more disappointment shall receive."—·
One answered : " Not so : she must live again :
　Strengthen thou her to live."

So while I lay entranced a curtain seemed
　　To shrivel with crackling from before my face·
Across mine eyes a waxing radiance beamed
　　And showed a certain place.

I saw a vision of a woman, where
　　Night and new morning strive for domination ;
Incomparably pale, and almost fair,
　　And sad beyond expression.

Her eyes were like some fire-enshrining gem,
　　Were stately like the stars, and yet were tender ;
Her figure charmed me like a windy stem
　　Quivering and drooped and slender.

I stood upon the outer barren ground,
　　She stood on inner ground that budded flowers ;
While circling in their never-slackening round
　　Danced by the mystic hours.

But every flower was lifted on a thorn,
　　And every thorn shot upright from its sands
To gall her feet ; hoarse laughter pealed in scorn
　　With cruel clapping hands.

She bled and wept, yet did not shrink ; her strength
　　Was strung up until daybreak of delight :
She measured measureless sorrow toward its length.
　　And breadth, and depth, and height.

Then marked I how a chain sustained her form,
  A chain of living links not made nor riven:
It stretched sheer up through lightning, wind and storm
  And anchored fast in heaven.

One cried: " How long? yet founded on the Rock
  ·She shall do battle, suffer, and attain."—
One answered: " Faith quakes in the tempest shock
  Strengthen her soul again."

I saw a cup sent down and come to her
  Brimfull of loathing and of bitterness:
She drank with livid lips that seemed to stir
  The depth, not make it less.

But as she drank I spied a hand distil
  New wine and virgin honey; making it
First bitter-sweet, then sweet indeed, until
  She tasted only sweet.

Her lips and cheeks waxed rosy-fresh and young;
  Drinking she sang: " My soul shall nothing want ;'
And drank anew: while soft a song was sung,
  A mystical slow chant.

One cried: " The wounds are faithful of a friend:
  The wilderness shall blossom as a rose."—
One answered: " Rend the veil, declare the end,
  Strengthen her ere she goes."

Then earth and heaven were rolled up like a scroll ;
　Time and space, change and death, had passed away ;
Weight, number, measure, each had reached its whole :
　The day had come, that day.

Multitudes—multitudes—stood up in bliss,
　Made equal to the angels, glorious, fair ;
With harps, palms, wedding-garments, kiss of peace,
　And crowned and haloed hair.

They sang a song, a new song in the height,
　Harping with harps to Him Who is Strong and True :
They drank new wine, their eyes saw with new light,
　Lo, all things were made new.

Tier beyond tier they rose and rose and rose
　So high that it was dreadful, flames with flames :
No man could number them, no tongue disclose
　Their secret sacred names.

As though one pulse stirred all, one rush of blood
　Fed all, one breath swept through them myriad
　　　　voiced, 　　　　　　　　　　　　[stood
They struck their harps, cast down their crowns, they
　And worshipped and rejoiced.

Each face looked one way like a moon new-lit,
　Each face looked one way towards its Sun of Love ;
Drank love and bathed in love and mirrored it
　And knew no end thereof.

Glory touched glory on each blessèd head,
   Hands locked dear hands never to sunder more:
These were the new-begotten from the dead
   Whom the great birthday bore.

Heart answered heart, soul answered soul at rest,
   Double against each other, filled, sufficed:
All loving, loved of all; but loving best
   And best beloved of Christ.

I saw that one who lost her love in pain,
   Who trod on thorns, who drank the loathsome cup
The lost in night, in day was found again;
   The fallen was lifted up.

They stood together in the blessèd noon,
   They sang together through the length of days;
Each loving face bent Sunwards like a moon
   New-lit with love and praise.

Therefore, O friend, I would not if I might
   Rebuild my house of lies, wherein I joyed
One time to dwell: my soul shall walk in white,
   Cast down but not destroyed.

Therefore in patience I possess my soul;
   Yea, therefore as a flint I set my face,
To pluck down, to build up again the whole--
   But in a distant place.

These thorns are sharp, yet I can tread on them;
   This cup is loathsome, yet He makes it sweet:
My face is steadfast toward Jerusalem,
   My heart remembers it.

I lift the hanging hands, the feeble knees—
   I, precious more than seven times molten gold—
Until the day when from His storehouses
   God shall bring new and old;

Beauty for ashes, oil of joy for grief,
   Garment of praise for spirit of heaviness:
Although to-day I fade as doth a leaf,
   I languish and grow less.

Although to-day He prunes my twigs with pain,
   Yet doth His blood nourish and warm my root
To-morrow I shall put forth buds again
   And clothe myself with fruit.

Although to-day I walk in tedious ways,
   To-day His staff is turned into a rod,
Yet will I wait for Him the appointed days
   And stay upon my God.

## OLD AND NEW YEAR DITTIES.

### 1.

NEW Year met me somewhat sad :
  Old Year leaves me tired,
Stripped of favourite things I had,
  Baulked of much desired :
Yet farther on my road to-day
God willing, farther on my way.

New Year coming on apace
  What have you to give me ?
Bring you scathe, or bring you grace,
Face me with an honest face ;
  You shall not deceive me :
Be it good or ill, be it what you will,
It needs shall help me on my road,
My rugged way to heaven, please God

### 2.

Watch with me, men, women, and children dear,
You whom I love, for whom I hope and fear,
Watch with me this last vigil of the year.
Some hug their business, some their pleasure scheme ;
Some seize the vacant hour to sleep or dream ;
Heart locked in heart some kneel and watch apart.

Watch with me, blessèd spirits, who delight
All through the holy night to walk in white,
Or take your ease after the long-drawn fight.

I know not if they watch with me: I know
They count this eve of resurrection slow,
And cry, " How long? " with urgent utterance strong

Watch with me, Jesus, in my loneliness :
Though others say me nay, yet say Thou yes ;
Though others pass me by, stop Thou to bless.
Yea, Thou dost stop with me this vigil night ;
To-night of pain, to-morrow of delight :
I, Love, am Thine ; Thou, Lord my God, art mine

3.

Passing away, saith the World, passing away :
Chances, beauty and youth sapped day by day .
Thy life never continueth in one stay.
Is the eye waxen dim, is the dark hair changing to grey
That hath won neither laurel nor bay ?
I shall clothe myself in Spring and bud in May :
Thou, root-stricken, shalt not rebuild thy decay
On my bosom for aye.
Then I answered : Yea.

Passing away, saith my Soul, passing away :
With its burden of fear and hope, of labour and play,
Hearken what the past doth witness and say :
Rust in thy gold, a moth is in thine array,
A canker is in thy bud, thy leaf must decay.
At midnight, at cockcrow, at morning, one certain day
Lo, the Bridegroom shall come and shall not delay :
Watch thou and pray.
Then I answered : Yea.

Passing away, saith my God, passing away :
Winter passeth after the long delay :
New grapes on the vine, new figs on the tender spray
Turtle calleth turtle in Heaven's May.
Though I tarry, wait for Me, trust Me, watch and pray.
Arise, come away, night is past and lo it is day,
My love, My sister, My spouse, thou shalt hear Me say
Then I answered : Yea.


## AMEN.

IT is over.   What is over?
    Nay, now much is over truly !—
Harvest days we toiled to sow for ;
    Now the sheaves are gathered newly
    Now the wheat is garnered duly.

It is finished.   What is finished?
    Much is finished known or unknown :
Lives are finished ; time diminished ;
    Was the fallow field left unsown?
    Will these buds be always unblown?

It suffices.   What suffices?
    All suffices reckoned rightly :
Spring shall bloom where now the ice is,
    Roses make the bramble sightly,
    And the quickening sun shine brightly
    And the latter wind blow lightly,
And my garden teem with spices.

## THE LOWEST PLACE.

GIVE me the lowest place : not that I dare
　　Ask for that lowest place, but Thou hast died
That I might live and share
　　Thy glory by Thy side.

Give me the lowest place : or if for me
　　That lowest place too high, make one more low
Where I may sit and see
　　My God and love Thee so.

**END OF THE FIRST SERIES.**

# THE SECOND SERIES

SONNETS are full of love, and this my tome
    Has many sonnets: so here now shall be
  One sonnet more, a love sonnet, from me
To her whose heart is my heart's quiet home,
    To my first Love, my Mother, on whose knee
I learnt love-lore that is not troublesome;
    Whose service is my special dignity,
And she my loadstar while I go and come.
And so because you love me, and because
    I love you, Mother, I have woven a wreath
        Of rhymes wherewith to crown your honoured
            name:
        In you not fourscore years can dim the flame
Of love, whose blessed glow transcends the laws
    Of time and change and mortal life and death.

# THE KEY-NOTE.

WHERE are the songs I used to know,
    Where are the notes I used to sing?
  I have forgotten everything
I used to know so long ago;
Summer has followed after Spring;
    Now Autumn is so shrunk and sere,
I scarcely think a sadder thing
    Can be the Winter of my year.

Yet Robin sings through Winter's rest,
    When bushes put their berries on;
    While they their ruddy jewels don,
He sings out of a ruddy breast;
The hips and haws and ruddy breast
    Make one spot warm where snowflakes lie,
They break and cheer the unlovely rest
    Of Winter's pause—and why not I?

# THE MONTHS:

## 𝔄 Pageant.

### PERSONIFICATIONS.

| *Boys.* | *Girls.* |
|---------|----------|
| JANUARY. | FEBRUARY. |
| MARCH. | APRIL. |
| JULY. | MAY. |
| AUGUST. | JUNE. |
| OCTOBER. | SEPTEMBER. |
| DECEMBER. | NOVEMBER. |

ROBIN REDBREASTS ; LAMBS AND SHEEP ; NIGHTINGALE AND NESTLINGS.

Various Flowers, Fruits, etc.

*Scene:* A COTTAGE WITH ITS GROUNDS.

[A room in a large comfortable cottage ; a fire burning on the hearth ; a table on which the breakfast things have been left standing. January discovered seated by the fire.]

### JANUARY.

COLD the day and cold the drifted snow,
Dim the day until the cold dark night.

[Stirs the fire.

Crackle, sparkle, faggot; embers glow:
Some one may be plodding through the snow
Longing for a light,
For the light that you and I can show.
If no one else should come,
Here Robin Redbreast's welcome to a crumb,
And never troublesome:
Robin, why don't you come and fetch your crumb?

Here's butter for my hunch of bread,
    And sugar for your crumb;
Here's room upon the hearthrug,
    If you'll only come.

In your scarlet waistcoat,
    With your keen bright eye,
Where are you loitering?
    Wings were made to fly!

Make haste to breakfast,
    Come and fetch your crumb,
For I'm as glad to see you
    As you are glad to come.

[Two Robin Redbreasts are seen tapping with their beaks at
the lattice, which January opens. The birds flutter in,
hop about the floor, and peck up the crumbs and sugar
thrown to them. They have scarcely finished their meal,
when a knock is heard at the door. January hangs a
guard in front of the fire, and opens to February, who
appears with a bunch of snowdrops in her hand.]

JANUARY.

Good-morrow, sister.

## February.

Brother, joy to you!
I've brought some snowdrops; only just a few,
But quite enough to prove the world awake,
Cheerful and hopeful in the frosty dew
And for the pale sun's sake.

[She hands a few of her snowdrops to January, who retires
into the background. While February stands arranging
the remaining snowdrops in a glass of water on the
window-sill, a soft butting and bleating are heard outside.
She opens the door, and sees one foremost lamb, with
other sheep and lambs bleating and crowding towards
her.]

## February.

O you, you little wonder, come—come in,
You wonderful, you woolly soft white lamb:
You panting mother ewe, come too,
And lead that tottering twin
Safe in:
Bring all your bleating kith and kin,
Except the horny ram.

[February opens a second door in the background, and the
little flock files through into a warm and sheltered com-
partment out of sight.]

The lambkin tottering in its walk
With just a fleece to wear;
The snowdrop drooping on its stalk
So slender,—
Snowdrop and lamb, a pretty pair,

Braving the cold for our delight,
        Both white,
        Both tender.

[A rattling of doors and windows; branches seen without, tossing violently to and fro.]

How the doors rattle, and the branches sway!
Here's brother March comes whirling on his way
With winds that eddy and sing :—

[She turns the handle of the door, which bursts open, and discloses March hastening up, both hands full of violets and anemones.]

### FEBRUARY.

Come, show me what you bring;
For I have said my say, fulfilled my day,
And must away.

### MARCH.

[Stopping short on the threshold.]

I blow an arouse
Through the world's wide house
To quicken the torpid earth :
    Grappling I fling
    Each feeble thing,
But bring strong life to the birth.
    I wrestle and frown,
    And topple down;
I wrench, I rend, I uproot;
    Yet the violet

Is born where I set
The sole of my flying foot,

[Hands violets and anemones to February, who retires into
the background.]

And in my wake
Frail wind-flowers quake,
And the catkins promise fruit.
I drive ocean ashore
With rush and roar,
And he cannot say me nay :
My harpstrings all
Are the forests tall,
Making music when I play.
And as others perforce,
So I on my course
Run and needs must run,
With sap on the mount
And buds past count
And rivers and clouds and sun,
With seasons and breath
And time and death
And all that has yet begun.

[Before March has done speaking, a voice is heard approach-
ing accompanied by a twittering of birds. April comes
along singing, and stands outside and out of sight to finish
her song.]

APRIL.

[Outside.]

Pretty little three
Sparrows in a tree,

    Light upon the wing;
    Though you cannot sing
        You can chirp of Spring:
    Chirp of Spring to me,
    Sparrows, from your tree.

    Never mind the showers,
    Chirp about the flowers
        While you build a nest:
        Straws from east and west,
        Feathers from your breast,
    Make the snuggest bowers
    In a world of flowers.

    You must dart away
    From the chosen spray,
        You intrusive third
        Extra little bird;
        Join the unwedded herd!
    These have done with play,
    And must work to-day.


        APRIL.

    [Appearing at the open door.]

Good-morrow and good-bye : if others fly,
Of all the flying months you're the most flying.


        MARCH.

You're hope and sweetness, April.

### APRIL.

Birth means dying,
As wings and wind mean flying;
So you and I and all things fly or die;
And sometimes I sit sighing to think of dying.
But meanwhile I've a rainbow in my showers,
And a lapful of flowers,
And these dear nestlings aged three hours;
And here's their mother sitting,
Their father's merely flitting
To find their breakfast somewhere in my bowers.

[As she speaks April shows March her apron full of flowers
and nest full of birds. March wanders away into the
grounds. April, without entering the cottage, hangs over
the hungry nestlings watching them.]

### APRIL.

What beaks you have, you funny things,
    What voices shrill and weak;
Who'd think that anything that sings
    Could sing through such a beak?
Yet you'll be nightingales one day,
    And charm the country side,
When I'm away and far away
    And May is queen and bride.

[May arrives unperceived by April, and gives her a kiss
April starts and looks round.]

### APRIL.

Ah May, good-morrow May, and so good-bye.

## MAY.

That's just your way, sweet April, smile and sigh :
Your sorrow's half in fun,
Begun and done
And turned to joy while twenty seconds run.
I've gathered flowers all as I came along,
At every step a flower
Fed by your last bright shower,—

[She divides an armful of all sorts of flowers with April, who
   strolls away through the garden.]

## MAY.

And gathering flowers I listened to the song
Of every bird in bower.

    The world and I are far too full of bliss
    To think or plan or toil or care ;
      The sun is waxing strong,
      The days are waxing long,
        And all that is,
        Is fair.

    Here are my buds of lily and of rose,
    And here's my namesake blossom may ;
      And from a watery spot
      See here forget-me-not,
        With all that blows
        To-day.

    Hark to my linnets from the hedges green,
    Blackbird and lark and thrush and dove,

And every nightingale
And cuckoo tells its tale,
And all they mean
Is love.

[June appears at the further end of the garden, coming slowly
towards May, who, seeing her, exclaims]

### MAY.

Surely you're come too early, sister June.

### JUNE.

Indeed I feel as if I came too soon
To round your young May moon
And set the world a-gasping at my noon.
Yet come I must. So here are strawberries
Sun-flushed and sweet, as many as you please ;
And here are full-blown roses by the score,
More roses, and yet more.

[May, eating strawberries, withdraws among the flower beds.]

### JUNE.

The sun does all my long day's work for me,
Raises and ripens everything ;
I need but sit beneath a leafy tree
And watch and sing.

[Seats herself in the shadow of a laburnum.

Or if I'm lulled by note of bird and bee,
Or lulled by noontide's silence deep,

I need but nestle down beneath my tree
    And drop asleep.

[June falls asleep ; and is not awakened by the voice of July,
   who behind the scenes is heard half singing, half calling.]

### JULY.

[Behind the scenes.]

Blue flags, yellow flags, flags all freckled,
Which will you take ? yellow, blue, speckled !
Take which you will, speckled, blue, yellow,
Each in its way has not a fellow.

[Enter July, a basket of many-coloured irises slung upon his
   shoulders, a bunch of ripe grass in one hand, and a plate
   piled full of peaches balanced upon the other.   He steals
   up to June, and tickles her with the grass.   She wakes.]

### JUNE.

What, here already ?

### JULY.

           Nay, my tryst is kept ;
The longest day slipped by you while you slept.
I've brought you one curved pyramid of bloom,

           [Hands her the plate.

Not flowers but peaches, gathered where the bees,
As downy, bask and boom
In sunshine and in gloom of trees.
But get you in, a storm is at my heels ;
The whirlwind whistles and wheels,

Lightning flashes and thunder peals,
Flying and following hard upon my heels.

[June takes shelter in a thickly-woven arbour.]


## JULY.

The roar of a storm sweeps up
   From the east to the lurid west,
The darkening sky, like a cup,
    Is filled with rain to the brink;
The sky is purple and fire,
   Blackness and noise and unrest;
The earth, parched with desire,
    Opens her mouth to drink.

Send forth thy thunder and fire,
   Turn over thy brimming cup,
O sky, appease the desire
    Of earth in her parched unrest;
Pour out drink to her thirst,
   Her famishing life lift up;
Make thyself fair as at first,
    With a rainbow for thy crest.

Have done with thunder and fire,
   O sky with the rainbow crest;
O earth, have done with desire,
    Drink, and drink deep, and rest.

[Enter August, carrying a sheaf made up of different kinds of
   grain.]

### July.

Hail, brother August, flushed and warm
And scatheless from my storm.
Your hands are full of corn, I see,
As full as hands can be:
And earth and air both smell as sweet as balm
In their recovered calm,
And that they owe to me.

[July retires into a shrubbery.]

### August.

Wheat sways heavy, oats are airy,
　　Barley bows a graceful head,
Short and small shoots up canary,
　　Each of these is some one's bread;
Bread for man or bread for beast,
　　　　Or at very least
　　　　A bird's savoury feast.

Men are brethren of each other,
　　One in flesh and one in food;
And a sort of foster brother
　　Is the litter, or the brood,
Of that folk in fur or feather,
　　　　Who, with men together,
　　　　Breast the wind and weather.

[August descries September toiling across the lawn.]

### August.

My harvest home is ended; and I spy
September drawing nigh

With the first thought of Autumn in her eye,
And the first sigh
Of Autumn wind among her locks that fly.

[September arrives, carrying upon her head a basket heaped
high with fruit.]

### SEPTEMBER.

Unload me, brother.    I have brought a few
Plums and these pears for you,
A dozen kinds of apples, one or two
Melons, some figs all bursting through
Their skins, and pearled with dew
These damsons violet-blue.

[While September is speaking, August lifts the basket to the
ground, selects various fruits, and withdraws slowly along
the gravel walk, eating a pear as he goes.]

### SEPTEMBER.

My song is half a sigh
Because my green leaves die ;
Sweet are my fruits, but all my leaves are dying ;
And well may Autumn sigh,
And well may I
Who watch the sere leaves flying.

My leaves that fade and fall,
I note you one and all ;
I call you, and the Autumn wind is calling,
Lamenting for your fall,

And for the pall
You spread on earth in falling.

And here's a song of flowers to suit such hours :
A song of the last lilies, the last flowers,
Amid my withering bowers.

In the sunny garden bed
Lilies look so pale,
Lilies droop the head
In the shady grassy vale ;
If all alike they pine
In shade and in shine,
If everywhere they grieve,
Where will lilies live ?

[October enters briskly, some leafy twigs bearing different
sorts of nuts in one hand, and a long ripe hop-bine trail-
ing after him from the other. A dahlia is stuck in his
buttonhole.]

### OCTOBER.

Nay, cheer up sister.   Life is not quite over,
Even if the year has done with corn and clover,
With flowers and leaves ; besides, in fact it's true,
Some leaves remain and some flowers too,
For me and you.
Now see my crops :

[Offering his produce to September.]
I've brought you nuts and hops ;
And when the leaf drops, why, the walnut drops.

[October wreaths the hop-bine about September's neck, and
gives her the nut twigs. They enter the cottage together,

but without shutting the door. She steps into the background : he advances to the hearth, removes the guard, stirs up the smouldering fire, and arranges several chestnuts ready to roast.]

### OCTOBER.

Crack your first nut and light your first fire,
  Roast your first chestnut crisp on the bar ;
Make the logs sparkle, stir the blaze higher,
  Logs are cheery as sun or as star,
  Logs we can find wherever we are.

Spring one soft day will open the leaves,
  Spring one bright day will lure back the flowers ;
Never fancy my whistling wind grieves,
  Never fancy I've tears in my showers ;
  Dance, nights and days ! and dance on, my hours !

[Sees November approaching.]

### OCTOBER.

Here comes my youngest sister, looking dim
And grim,
With dismal ways.
What cheer, November ?

### NOVEMBER.

[Entering and shutting the door.]

Nought have I to bring
Tramping a-chill and shivering,
Except these pine-cones for a blaze,—
Except a fog which follows,

And stuffs up all the hollows,—
Except a hoar frost here and there,—
Except some shooting stars
Which dart their luminous cars
Trackless and noiseless through the keen night air.

[October, shrugging his shoulders, withdraws into the background, while November throws her pine-cones on the fire, and sits down listlessly.]

### NOVEMBER.

The earth lies fast asleep, grown tired
   Of all that's high or deep;
There's nought desired and nought required
    Save a sleep.
I rock the cradle of the earth,
   I lull her with a sigh;
And know that she will wake to mirth
    By and by.

[Through the window December is seen running and leaping in the direction of the door. He knocks.]

### NOVEMBER.

Ah, here's my youngest brother come at last:

    [Calls out without rising.]

Come in, December.

[He opens the door and enters, loaded with evergreens in berry, etc.]

### NOVEMBER.

        Come, and shut the door,
For now it's snowing fast;
It snows, and will snow more and more;

Don't let it drift in on the floor.
But you, you're all aglow; how can you be
Rosy and warm and smiling in the cold?


### DECEMBER.

Nay, no closed doors for me,
But open doors and open hearts and glee
To welcome young and old.

Dimmest and brightest month am I;
My short days end, my lengthening days begin;
What matters more or less sun in the sky,
 When all is sun within?
     [He begins making a wreath as he sings.]
Ivy and privet dark as night,
I weave with hips and haws a cheerful show,
And holly for a beauty and delight,
 And milky mistletoe.

While high above them all I set
Yew twigs and Christmas roses pure and pale;
Then Spring her snowdrop and her violet
 May keep, so sweet and frail;

May keep each merry singing bird,
Of all her happy birds that singing build:
For I've a carol which some shepherds heard
 Once in a wintry field.

[While December concludes his song all the other Months
troop in from the garden, or advance out of the back-
ground. The Twelve join hands in a circle, and begin
dancing round to a stately measure as the Curtain falls.]

## PASTIME.

A BOAT amid the ripples, drifting, rocking,
　　Two idle people, without pause or aim ;
While in the ominous west there gathers darkness
　　Flushed with flame.

A haycock in a hayfield backing, lapping,
　　Two drowsy people pillowed round about ;
While in the ominous west across the darkness
　　Flame leaps out.

Better a wrecked life than a life so aimless,
　　Better a wrecked life than a life so soft ;
The ominous west glooms thundering, with its fire
　　Lit aloft.


## "ITALIA, IO TI SALUTO!"

TO come back from the sweet South, to the North
　　Where I was born, bred, look to die ;
Come back to do my day's work in its day,
　　　Play out my play—
　　Amen, amen, say I.

To see no more the country half my own,
　　Nor hear the half familiar speech,

Amen, I say; I turn to that bleak North
  Whence I came forth—
The South lies out of reach.

But when our swallows fly back to the South,
 To the sweet South, to the sweet South,
The tears may come again into my eyes
  On the old wise,
And the sweet name to my mouth.


## MIRRORS OF LIFE AND DEATH.

THE mystery of Life, the mystery
  Of Death, I see
Darkly as in a glass;
Their shadows pass,
And talk with me.

As the flush of a Morning Sky,
As a Morning Sky colourless—
Each yields its measure of light
To a wet world or a dry;
Each fares through day to night
With equal pace,
And then each one
Is done.

As the Sun with glory and grace
In his face,

Benignantly hot,
Graciously radiant and keen,
Ready to rise and to run,—
Not without spot,
Not even the Sun.

As the Moon
On the wax, on the wane,
With night for her noon ;
Vanishing soon,
To appear again.

As Roses that droop
Half warm, half chill, in the languid May,
And breathe out a scent
Sweet and faint ;
Till the wind gives one swoop
To scatter their beauty away.

As Lilies a multitude,
One dipping, one rising, one sinking,
On rippling waters, clear blue
And pure for their drinking ;
One new dead, and one opened anew,
And all good.

As a cankered pale Flower,
With death for a dower,
Each hour of its life half dead ;
With death for a crown

Weighing down
Its head.

As an Eagle, half strength and half grace,
Most potent to face
Unwinking the splendour of light;
Harrying the East and the West,
Soaring aloft from our sight;
Yet one day or one night dropped to rest,
On the low common earth
Of his birth.

As a Dove,
Not alone,
In a world of her own
Full of fluttering soft noises
And tender sweet voices
Of love.

As a Mouse
Keeping house
In the fork of a tree,
With nuts in a crevice,
And an acorn or two;
What cares he
For blossoming boughs,
Or the song-singing bevies
Of birds in their glee,
Scarlet, or golden, or blue?

As a Mole grubbing underground ;
When it comes to the light
It grubs its way back again,
Feeling no bias of fur
To hamper it in its stir,
Scant of pleasure and pain,
Sinking itself out of sight
Without sound.

As Waters that drop and drop,
Weariness without end,
That drop and never stop,
Wear that nothing can mend,
Till one day they drop—
Stop—
And there's an end,
And matters mend.

As Trees, beneath whose skin
We mark not the sap begin
To swell and rise,
Till the whole bursts out in green :
We mark the falling leaves
When the wide world grieves
And sighs.

As a Forest on fire,
Where maddened creatures desire
Wet mud or wings
Beyond all those things

Which could assuage desire
On this side the flaming fire.

As Wind with a sob and sigh
To which there comes no reply
But a rustle and shiver
From rushes of the river;
As Wind with a desolate moan,
Moaning on alone.

As a Desert all sand,
Blank, neither water nor land
For solace, or dwelling, or culture,
Where the storms and the wild creatures howl;
Given over to lion and vulture,
To ostrich, and jackal, and owl:
Yet somewhere an oasis lies;
There waters arise
To nourish one seedling of balm
Perhaps, or one palm.

As the Sea,
Murmuring, shifting, swaying;
One time sunnily playing,
One time wrecking and slaying;
In whichever mood it be,
Worst or best,
Never at rest.

As still Waters and deep,
As shallow Waters that brawl,

As rapid Waters that leap
To their fall.

As Music, as Colour, as Shape,
Keys of rapture and pain
Turning in vain
In a lock which turns not again,
While breaths and moments escape.

As Spring, all bloom and desire ;
As Summer, all gift and fire ;
As Autumn, a dying glow ;
As Winter, with nought to show :

Winter which lays its dead all out of sight,
All clothed in white,
All waiting for the long-awaited light.


## BIRCHINGTON CHURCHYARD.

A LOWLY hill which overlooks a flat,
    Half sea, half country side ;
    A flat-shored sea of low-voiced creeping tide
Over a chalky weedy mat.

A hill of hillocks, flowery and kept green
    Round Crosses raised for hope,
    With many-tinted sunsets where the slope
Faces the lingering western sheen.

A lowly hope, a height that is but low,
  While Time sets solemnly,
  While the tide rises of Eternity,
Silent and neither swift nor slow.


## A BALLAD OF BODING.

THERE are sleeping dreams and waking dreams;
  What seems is not always as it seems.

I looked out of my window in the sweet new morning,
And there I saw three barges of manifold adorning
Went sailing toward the East:
The first had sails like fire,
The next like glittering wire,
But sackcloth were the sails of the least;
And all the crews made music, and two had spread
    a feast.

The first choir breathed in flutes,
And fingered soft guitars;
The second won from lutes
Harmonious chords and jars,
With drums for stormy bars:
But the third was all of harpers and scarlet trumpeters;
Notes of triumph, then
An alarm again,
As for onset, as for victory, rallies, stirs,
Peace at last and glory to the vanquishers.

The first barge showed for figurehead a Love with
    wings ;
The second showed for figurehead a Worm with stings;
The third, a Lily tangled to a Rose which clings.
The first bore for freight gold and spice and down ;
The second bore a sword, a sceptre, and a crown ;
The third, a heap of earth gone to dust and brown.
Winged Love meseemed like Folly in the face ;
Stinged Worm meseemed loathly in his place ;
Lily and Rose were flowers of grace.

Merry went the revel of the fire-sailed crew,
Singing, feasting, dancing to and fro :
Pleasures ever changing, ever graceful, ever new ;
Sighs, but scarce of woe ;
All the sighing
Wooed such sweet replying ;
All the sighing, sweet and low,
Used to come and go
For more pleasure, merely so.
Yet at intervals some one grew tired
Of everything desired,
And sank, I knew not whither, in sorry plight,
Out of sight.

The second crew seemed ever
Wider-visioned, graver,
More distinct of purpose, more sustained of will ;
With heads erect and proud,
And voices sometimes loud ;
With endless tacking, counter-tacking,

All things grasping, all things lacking,
It would seem ;
Ever shifting helm, or sail, or shroud,
Drifting on as in a dream.
Hoarding to their utmost bent,
Feasting to their fill,
Yet gnawed by discontent,
Envy, hatred, malice, on their road they went.
Their freight was not a treasure,
Their music not a pleasure ;
The sword flashed, cleaving through their bands,
Sceptre and crown changed hands.

The third crew as they went
Seemed mostly different ;
They toiled in rowing, for to them the wind was contrary.
As all the world might see.
They laboured at the oar,
While on their heads they bore
The fiery stress of sunshine more and more.
They laboured at the oar hand-sore,
Till rain went splashing,
And spray went dashing,
Down on them, and up on them, more and more.
Their sails were patched and rent,
Their masts were bent,
In peril of their lives they worked and went.
For them no feast was spread,
No soft luxurious bed
Scented and white,

No crown or sceptre hung in sight;
In weariness and painfulness,
In thirst and sore distress,
They rowed and steered from left to right
With all their might.
Their trumpeters and harpers round about
Incessantly played out,
And sometimes they made answer with a shout;
But oftener they groaned or wept,
And seldom paused to eat, and seldom slept.
I wept for pity watching them, but more
I wept heart-sore
Once and again to see
Some weary man plunge overboard, and swim
To Love or Worm ship floating buoyantly:
And there all welcomed him.

The ships steered each apart and seemed to scorn
    each other,
Yet all the crews were interchangeable;
Now one man, now another,
—Like bloodless spectres some, some flushed by
    health,—
Changed openly, or changed by stealth,
Scaling a slippery side, and scaled it well.
The most left Love ship, hauling wealth
Up Worm ship's side;
While some few hollow-eyed
Left either for the sack-sailed boat;
But this, though not remote,

Was worst to mount, and whoso left it once
Scarce ever came again,
But seemed to loathe his erst companions,
And wish and work them bane.

Then I knew (I know not how) there lurked quick-
    sands full of dread,
Rocks and reefs and whirlpools in the water bed,
Whence a waterspout
Instantaneously leaped out,
Roaring as it reared its head.
Soon I spied a something dim,
Many-handed, grim,
That went flitting to and fro the first and second ship;
It puffed their sails full out
With puffs of smoky breath
From a smouldering lip,
And cleared the waterspout
Which reeled roaring round about
Threatening death.
With a horny hand it steered,
And a horn appeared
On its sneering head upreared
Haughty and high
Against the blackening lowering sky
With a hoof it swayed the waves;
They opened here and there,
Till I spied deep ocean graves
Full of skeletons
That were men and women once

Foul or fair ;
Full of things that creep
And fester in the deep
And never breathe the clean life-nurturing air.

The third bark held aloof
From the Monster with the hoof,
Despite his urgent beck,
And fraught with guile
Abominable his smile ;
Till I saw him take a flying leap on to that deck.
Then full of awe,
With these same eyes I saw
His head incredible retract its horn
Rounding like babe's new born,
While silvery phosphorescence played
About his dis-horned head.
The sneer smoothed from his lip,
He beamed blandly on the ship ;
All winds sank to a moan,
All waves to a monotone
(For all these seemed his realm),
While he laid a strong caressing hand upon the helm.

Then a cry well nigh of despair
Shrieked to heaven, a clamour of desperate prayer.
The harpers harped no more,
While the trumpeters sounded sore,
An alarm to wake the dead from their bed :
To the rescue, to the rescue, now or never,

To the rescue, O ye living, O ye dead,
Or no more help or hope for ever !—
The planks strained as though they must part asunder,
The masts bent as though they must dip under,
And the winds and the waves at length
Girt up their strength,
And the depths were laid bare,
And heaven flashed fire and volleyed thunder
Through the rain-choked air,
And sea and sky seemed to kiss
In the horror and the hiss
Of the whole world shuddering everywhere.

Lo ! a Flyer swooping down
With wings to span the globe,
And splendour for his robe
And splendour for his crown.
He lighted on the helm with a foot of fire,
And spun the Monster overboard :
And that monstrous thing abhorred,
Gnashing with balked desire,
Wriggled like a worm infirm
Up the Worm
Of the loathly figurehead.
There he crouched and gnashed ;
And his head re-horned, and gashed
From the other's grapple, dripped bloody red.

I saw that thing accurst
Wreak his worst

On the first and second crew :
Some with baited hook
He angled for and took,
Some dragged overboard in a net he threw,
Some he did to death
With hoof or horn or blasting breath.

I heard a voice of wailing
Where the ships went sailing,
A sorrowful voice prevailing
Above the sound of the sea,
Above the singers' voices,
And musical merry noises ;
All songs had turned to sighing,
The light was failing,
The day was dying—
Ah me,
That such a sorrow should be !

There was sorrow on the sea and sorrow on the land
When Love ship went down by the bottomless quick-
    sand
To its grave in the bitter wave.
There was sorrow on the sea and sorrow on the land
When Worm ship went to pieces on the rock-bound
    strand,
And the bitter wave was its grave.
But land and sea waxed hoary
In whiteness of a glory
Never told in story

Nor seen by mortal eye,
When the third ship crossed the bar
Where whirls and breakers are,
And steered into the splendours of the sky ;
That third bark and that least
Which had never seemed to feast,
Yet kept high festival above sun and moon and star.


# YET A LITTLE WHILE.

I DREAMED and did not seek : to-day I seek
Who can no longer dream ;
But now am all behindhand, waxen weak,
And dazed amid so many things that gleam
Yet are not what they seem.

I dreamed and did not work : to-day I work
Kept wide awake by care
And loss, and perils dimly guessed to lurk ;
I work and reap not, while my life goes bare
And void in wintry air.

I hope indeed ; but hope itself is fear
Viewed on the sunny side ;
I hope, and disregard the world that's here,
The prizes drawn, the sweet things that betide ;
I hope, and I abide.

## HE AND SHE.

" SHOULD one of us remember,
        And one of us forget,
I wish I knew what each will do—
    But who can tell as yet ?"

"Should one of us remember,
        And one of us forget,
I promise you what I will do—
    And I'm content to wait for you,
    And not be sure as yet "

## MONNA INNOMINATA.

### A SONNET OF SONNETS.

BEATRICE, immortalised by "altissimo poeta . . . cotanto
amante "; Laura, celebrated by a great though an inferior bard,
—have alike paid the exceptional penalty of exceptional honour,
and have come down to us resplendent with charms, but (at least,
to my apprehension) scant of attractiveness.

These heroines of world-wide fame were preceded by a bevy
of unnamed ladies " donne innominate " sung by a school of less
conspicuous poets ; and in that land and that period which gave
simultaneous birth to Catholics, to Albigenses, and to Trouba-
dours, one can imagine many a lady as sharing her lover's poetic
aptitude, while the barrier between them might be one held
sacred by both, yet not such as to render mutual love incompat-
ible with mutual honour.

Had such a lady spoken for herself, the portrait left us might have appeared more tender, if less dignified, than any drawn even by a devoted friend. Or had the Great Poetess of our own day and nation only been unhappy instead of happy, her circumstances would have invited her to bequeath to us, in lieu of the "Portuguese Sonnets," an inimitable "donna innominata" drawn not from fancy but from feeling, and worthy to occupy a niche beside Beatrice and Laura.

I.

" Lo dì che han detto a' dolci amici addio."—DANTE.
" Amor, con quanto sforzo oggi mi vinci !"—PETRARCA.

COME back to me, who wait and watch for you :—
    Or come not yet, for it is over then,
And long it is before you come again,
So far between my pleasures are and few.
While, when you come not, what I do I do
    Thinking "Now when he comes," my sweetest
        "when :"
For one man is my world of all the men
This wide world holds ; O love, my world is you.
Howbeit, to meet you grows almost a pang
    Because the pang of parting comes so soon ;
    My hope hangs waning, waxing, like a moon
        Between the heavenly days on which we meet :
Ah me, but where are now the songs I sang
    When life was sweet because you called them
        sweet ?

2.

" Era già l'ora che volge il desio."—DANTE.
" Ricorro al tempo ch' io vi vidi prima."—PETRARCA.

I wish I could remember that first day,
 First hour, first moment of your meeting me.
 If bright or dim the season, it might be
Summer or Winter for aught I can say;
So unrecorded did it slip away,
 So blind was I to see and to foresee,
 So dull to mark the budding of my tree
That would not blossom yet for many a May.
If only I could recollect it, such
 A day of days!   I let it come and go
 As traceless as a thaw of bygone snow;
It seemed to mean so little, meant so much;
If only now I could recall that touch,
 First touch of hand in hand—Did one but know!

3.

" O ombre vane, fuor che ne l'aspetto !"—DANTE.
" Immaginata guida la conduce."—PETRARCA.

I dream of you to wake: would that I might
 Dream of you and not wake but slumber on;
 Nor find with dreams the dear companion gone,
As Summer ended Summer birds take flight.

In happy dreams I hold you full in sight,
 I blush again who waking look so wan ;
 Brighter than sunniest day that ever shone,
In happy dreams your smile makes day of night.
Thus only in a dream we are at one,
 Thus only in a dream we give and take
  The faith that maketh rich who take or give ;
 If thus to sleep is sweeter than to wake,
 To die were surely sweeter than to live,
Though there be nothing new beneath the sun.


### 4.

" Poca favilla gran fiamma seconda."—DANTE.
" Ogni altra cosa, ogni pensier va fore,
 E sol ivi con voi rimansi amore."—PETRARCA.

I loved you first : but afterwards your love
 Outsoaring mine, sang such a loftier song
As drowned the friendly cooings of my dove.
 Which owes the other most ? my love was long,
 And yours one moment seemed to wax more strong ;
I loved and guessed at you, you construed me
And loved me for what might or might not be—
 Nay, weights and measures do us both a wrong.
For verily love knows not " mine " or " thine ;"
 With separate " I " and " thou " free love has done,
 For one is both and both are one in love :
Rich love knows nought of " thine that is not mine ;"
 Both have the strength and both the length thereof,
 Both of us, of the love which makes us one.

5.

"Amor che a nullo amato amar perdona."—DANTE.
"Amor m'addusse in sì gioiosa spene."—PETRARCA.

O my heart's heart, and you who are to me
   More than myself myself, God be with you,
   Keep you in strong obedience leal and true
To Him whose noble service setteth free,
Give you all good we see or can foresee,
   Make your joys many and your sorrows few,
   Bless you in what you bear and what you do,
Yea, perfect you as He would have you be.
So much for you; but what for me, dear friend?
   To love you without stint and all I can
To-day, to-morrow, world without an end;
      To love you much and yet to love you more,
      As Jordan at his flood sweeps either shore;
Since woman is the helpmeet made for man.

6.

"Or puoi la quantitate
Comprender de l'amor che a te mi scalda."—DANTE.
"Non vo' che da tal nodo amor mi scioglia."—PETRARCA.

Trust me, I have not earned your dear rebuke,
   I love, as you would have me, God the most;
   Would lose not Him, but you, must one be lost,
Nor with Lot's wife cast back a faithless look
Unready to forego what I forsook;

This say I, having counted up the cost,
This, though I be the feeblest of God's host,
The sorriest sheep Christ shepherds with His crook
Yet while I love my God the most, I deem
That I can never love you overmuch;
I love Him more, so let me love you too;
Yea, as I apprehend it, love is such
I cannot love you if I love not Him,
I cannot love Him if I love not you.

### 7.

"Qui primavera sempre ed ogni frutto."—DANTE.
"Ragionando con meco ed io con lui."—PETRARCA.

"Love me, for I love you"—and answer me,
"Love me, for I love you"—so shall we stand
As happy equals in the flowering land
Of love, that knows not a dividing sea.
Love builds the house on rock and not on sand,
Love laughs what while the winds rave desperately;
And who hath found love's citadel unmanned?
And who hath held in bonds love's liberty?
My heart's a coward though my words are brave—
We meet so seldom, yet we surely part
So often; there's a problem for your art!
Still I find comfort in his Book, who saith,
Though jealousy be cruel as the grave,
And death be strong, yet love is strong as death.

## 8.

"Come dicesse a Dio : D'altro non calme."—DANTE.
"Spero trovar pietà non che perdono."—PETRARCA.

" I, if I perish, perish "—Esther spake :
　And bride of life or death she made her fair
　In all the lustre of her perfumed hair
And smiles that kindle longing but to slake.
She put on pomp of loveliness, to take
　Her husband through his eyes at unaware ;
　She spread abroad her beauty for a snare,
Harmless as doves and subtle as a snake.
She trapped him with one mesh of silken hair,
　She vanquished him by wisdom of her wit,
　　And built her people's house that it should
　　　stand :—
　If I might take my life so in my hand,
　And for my love to Love put up my prayer,
　And for love's sake by Love be granted it !

## 9.

"O dignitosa coscienza e netta !"—DANTE.
"Spirto più acceso di virtuti ardenti."—PETRARCA.

Thinking of you, and all that was, and all
　That might have been and now can never be,
　I feel your honoured excellence, and see
Myself unworthy of the happier call :
For woe is me who walk so apt to fall,

So apt to shrink afraid, so apt to flee,
Apt to lie down and die (ah, woe is me!)
Faithless and hopeless turning to the wall.
And yet not hopeless quite nor faithless quite,
Because not loveless; love may toil all night,
But take at morning; wrestle till the break
Of day, but then wield power with God and
man :—
So take I heart of grace as best I can,
Ready to spend and be spent for your sake.


10.

" Con miglior corso e con migliore stella."—DANTE.
" La vita fugge e non s'arresta un' ora."—PETRARCA.

Time flies, hope flags, life plies a wearied wing;
Death following hard on life gains ground apace;
Faith runs with each and rears an eager face,
Outruns the rest, makes light of everything,
Spurns earth, and still finds breath to pray and sing;
While love ahead of all uplifts his praise,
Still asks for grace and still gives thanks for grace,
Content with all day brings and night will bring.
Life wanes; and when love folds his wings above
Tired hope, and less we feel his conscious pulse,
Let us go fall asleep, dear friend, in peace:
A little while, and age and sorrow cease;
A little while, and life reborn annuls
Loss and decay and death, and all is love.

### I I.

"Vien dietro a me e lascia dir le genti."—DANTE.
"Contando i casi della vita nostra."—PETRARCA.

Many in aftertimes will say of you
" He loved her "—while of me what will they say?
    Not that I loved you more than just in play,
For fashion's sake as idle women do.
Even let them prate; who know not what we knew
    Of love and parting in exceeding pain,
    Of parting hopeless here to meet again,
Hopeless on earth, and heaven is out of view.
But by my heart of love laid bare to you,
    My love that you can make not void nor vain,
Love that foregoes you but to claim anew
        Beyond this passage of the gate of death,
    I charge you at the Judgment make it plain
    My love of you was life and not a breath.

### I 2.

"Amor, che ne la mente mi ragiona."—DANTE.
"Amor vien nel bel viso di costei."—PETRARCA.

If there be any one can take my place
    And make you happy whom I grieve to grieve,
    Think not that I can grudge it, but believe
I do commend you to that nobler grace,
That readier wit than mine, that sweeter face;

Yea, since your riches make me rich, conceive
I too am crowned, while bridal crowns I weave,
And thread the bridal dance with jocund pace.
For if I did not love you, it might be
  That I should grudge you some one dear delight;
    But since the heart is yours that was mine own,
  Your pleasure is my pleasure, right my right,
Your honourable freedom makes me free,
    And you companioned I am not alone.

### 13.

" E drizzeremo glí occhi al Primo Amore."—DANTE.
" Ma trovo peso non da le mie braccia."—PETRARCA.

If I could trust mine own self with your fate,
  Shall I not rather trust it in God's hand?
  Without Whose Will one lily doth not stand,
Nor sparrow fall at his appointed date;
  Who numbereth the innumerable sand,
Who weighs the wind and water with a weight,
To Whom the world is neither small nor great,
  Whose knowledge foreknew every plan we planned.
Searching my heart for all that touches you,
  I find there only love and love's goodwill
  Helpless to help and impotent to do,
    Of understanding dull, of sight most dim;
    And therefore I commend you back to Him
  Whose love your love's capacity can fill.

### 14.

" E la Sua Volontade è nostra pace."—DANTE.
" Sol con questi pensier, con altre chiome."—PETRARCA.

Youth gone, and beauty gone if ever there
 Dwelt beauty in so poor a face as this ;
 Youth gone and beauty, what remains of bliss ?
I will not bind fresh roses in my hair,
To shame a cheek at best but little fair,—
 Leave youth his roses, who can bear a thorn,—
I will not seek for blossoms anywhere,
 Except such common flowers as blow with corn.
Youth gone and beauty gone, what doth remain ?
 The longing of a heart pent up forlorn,
  A silent heart whose silence loves and longs ;
  The silence of a heart which sang its songs
 While youth and beauty made a summer morn,
Silence of love that cannot sing again.

### "LUSCIOUS AND SORROWFUL."

BEAUTIFUL, tender, wasting away for sorrow ;
 Thus to-day ; and how shall it be with thee to-
  morrow ?
 Beautiful, tender—what else ?
 A hope tells.

Beautiful, tender, keeping the jubilee
In the land of home together, past death and sea ;
 No more change or death, no more
  Salt sea-shore.

## ONE SEA-SIDE GRAVE.

UNMINDFUL of the roses,
 Unmindful of the thorn,
A reaper tired reposes
 Among his gathered corn :
 So might I, till the morn !

Cold as the cold Decembers,
 Past as the days that set,
While only one remembers
 And all the rest forget,—
 But one remembers yet.

## DE PROFUNDIS.

OH why is heaven built so far,
 Oh why is earth set so remote ?
I cannot reach the nearest star
 That hangs afloat.

I would not care to reach the moon,
 One round monotonous of change ;
Yet even she repeats her tune
 Beyond my range.

I never watch the scattered fire
 Of stars, or sun's far-trailing train,
But all my heart is one desire,
 And all in vain :

For I am bound with fleshly bands,
   Joy, beauty, lie beyond my scope ;
I strain my heart, I stretch my hands,
   And catch at hope.


## TEMPUS FUGIT.

L OVELY Spring,
     A brief sweet thing,
Is swift on the wing ;
Gracious Summer,
A slow sweet comer,
Hastens past ;
Autumn while sweet
Is all incomplete
With a moaning blast,—
Nothing can last,
Can be cleaved unto,
Can be dwelt upon ;
It is hurried through,
It is come and gone,
Undone it cannot be done,
It is ever to do,
Ever old, ever new,
Ever waxing old
And lapsing to Winter cold.

## GOLDEN GLORIES.

THE buttercup is like a golden cup,
　　The marigold is like a golden frill,
The daisy with a golden eye looks up,
　　And golden spreads the flag beside the rill,
　　And gay and golden nods the daffodil,
The gorsey common swells a golden sea,
　　The cowslip hangs a head of golden tips,
And golden drips the honey which the bee
　　Sucks from sweet hearts of flowers and stores
　　　　and sips.


## JOHNNY.

### FOUNDED ON AN ANECDOTE OF THE FIRST FRENCH REVOLUTION.

JOHNNY had a golden head
　　Like a golden mop in blow,
Right and left his curls would spread
　　In a glory and a glow,
And they framed his honest face
Like stray sunbeams out of place.

Long and thick, they half could hide
　　How threadbare his patched jacket hung;
They used to be his Mother's pride;
　　She praised them with a tender tongue,

And stroked them with a loving finger
That smoothed and stroked and loved to linger

On a doorstep Johnny sat,
   Up and down the street looked he;
Johnny did not own a hat,
   Hot or cold tho' days might be;
Johnny did not own a boot
To cover up his muddy foot.

Johnny's face was pale and thin,
   Pale with hunger and with crying;
For his Mother lay within,
   Talked and tossed and seemed a-dying,
While Johnny racked his brains to think
How to get her help and drink,

Get her physic, get her tea,
   Get her bread and something nice;
Not a penny piece had he,
   And scarce a shilling might suffice;
No wonder that his soul was sad,
When not one penny piece he had.

As he sat there thinking, moping,
   Because his Mother's wants were many,
Wishing much but scarcely hoping
   To earn a shilling or a penny,
A friendly neighbour passed him by
And questioned him: Why did he cry?

Alas ! his trouble soon was told :
 He did not cry for cold or hunger,
Though he was hungry both and cold ;
 He only felt more weak and younger,
Because he wished so to be old
And apt at earning pence or gold.

Kindly that neighbour was, but poor,
 Scant coin had he to give or lend ;
And well he guessed there needed more
 Than pence or shillings to befriend
The helpless woman in her strait,
So much loved, yet so desolate.

One way he saw, and only one :
 He would—he could not—give the advice,
And yet he must : the widow's son
 Had curls of gold would fetch their price ;
Long curls which might be clipped, and sold
For silver, or perhaps for gold.

Our Johnny, when he understood
 Which shop it was that purchased hair,
Ran off as briskly as he could,
 And in a trice stood cropped and bare,
Too short of hair to fill a locket,
But jingling money in his pocket.

Precious money—tea and bread,
 Physic, ease, for Mother dear,
Better than a golden head :

Yet our hero dropped one tear
When he·spied himself close shorn,
Barer much than lamb new born.

His Mother throve upon the money,
　　Ate and revived and kissed her son :
But oh ! when she perceived her Johnny,
　　And understood what he had done
All and only for her sake,
She sobbed as if her heart must break.


## BROTHER BRUIN.

A DANCING Bear grotesque and funny
　　Earned for his master heaps of money,
Gruff yet good-natured, fond of honey,
And cheerful if the day was sunny.
Past hedge and ditch, past pond and wood
He tramped, and on some common stood ;
There cottage children circling gaily,
He in their midmost footed daily.
Pandean pipes and drum and muzzle
Were quite enough his brain to puzzle :
But like a philosophic bear
He let alone extraneous care
And danced contented anywhere.

Still, year on year, and wear and tear,
Age even the gruffest bluffest bear.

A day came when he scarce could prance,
And when his master looked askance
On dancing Bear who would not dance.
To looks succeeded blows : hard blows
Battered his ears and poor old nose.
From bluff and gruff he waxed curmudgeon ;
He danced indeed, but danced in dudgeon,
Capered in fury fast and faster :—
Ah, could he once but hug his master
And perish in one joint disaster !
But deafness, blindness, weakness growing,
Not fury's self could keep him going.
One dark day when the snow was snowing
His cup was brimmed to overflowing :
He tottered, toppled on one side,
Growled once, and shook his head, and died.
The master kicked and struck in vain,
The weary drudge had distanced pain
And never now would wince again.
The master growled : he might have howled
Or coaxed—that slave's last growl was growled.
So gnawed by rancour and chagrin
One thing remained : he sold the skin.

What next the man did is not worth
Your notice or my setting forth,
But hearken what befell at last.
His idle working days gone past,
And not one friend and not one penny
Stored up (if ever he had any

Friends : but his coppers had been many),
All doors stood shut against him, but
The workhouse door which cannot shut.
There he droned on—a grim old sinner
Toothless and grumbling for his dinner,
Unpitied quite, uncared for much
(The ratepayers not favouring such),
Hungry and gaunt, with time to spare:
Perhaps the hungry gaunt old Bear
Danced back, a haunting memory.
Indeed I hope so : for you see
If once the hard old heart relented
The hard old man may have repented.


## "HOLLOW-SOUNDING AND MYSTERIOUS."

THERE'S no replying
   To the Wind's sighing,
Telling, foretelling,
Dying, undying,
Dwindling and swelling,
Complaining, droning,
Whistling and moaning,
Ever beginning,
Ending, repeating,
Hinting and dinning,
Lagging and fleeting—
We've no replying

Living or dying
To the Wind's sighing.

What are you telling,
Variable Wind-tone?
What would be teaching,
O sinking, swelling,
Desolate Wind-moan?
Ever for ever
Teaching and preaching,
Never, ah never
Making us wiser—
The earliest riser
Catches no meaning,
The last who hearkens
Garners no gleaning
Of wisdom's treasure,
While the world darkens:—
Living or dying,
In pain, in pleasure,
We've no replying
To wordless flying
Wind's sighing.

## "A HELPMEET FOR HIM."

WOMAN was made for man's delight ;
  Charm, O woman, be not afraid !
His shadow by day, his moon by night,
  Woman was made.

Her strength with weakness is overlaid ;
  Meek compliances veil her might ;
Him she stays, by whom she is stayed.

World-wide champion of truth and right,
  Hope in gloom and in danger aid,
Tender and faithful, ruddy and white,
  Woman was made.


## MAIDEN MAY.

MAIDEN May sat in her bower,
  In her blush rose bower in flower,
    Sweet of scent ;
Sat and dreamed away an hour,
  Half content, half uncontent.

" Why should rose blossoms be born,
  Tender blossoms, on a thorn
    Though so sweet ?
Never a thorn besets the corn
  Scentless in its strength complete.

" Why are roses all so frail,
 At the mercy of a gale,
   Of a breath ?
 Yet so sweet and perfect pale,
   Still so sweet in life and death."


 Maiden May sat in her bower,
 In her blush rose bower in flower,
   Where a linnet
 Made one bristling branch the tower
   For her nest and young ones in it.


" Gay and clear the linnet trills ;
 Yet the skylark only, thrills
   Heaven and earth
 When he breasts the height, and fills
   Height and depth with song and mirth.


" Nightingales which yield to night
 Solitary strange delight,
   Reign alone :
 But the lark for all his height
   Fills no solitary throne ;


" While he sings, a hundred sing ;
 Wing their flight below his wing
   Yet in flight ;
 Each a lovely joyful thing
   To the measure of its delight.

" Why then should a lark be reckoned
One alone, without a second
    Near his throne ?
He in skyward flight unslackened,
  In his music, not alone."


Maiden May sat in her bower ;
Her own face was like a flower
    Of the prime,
Half in sunshine, half in shower,
  In the year's most tender time.


Her own thoughts in silent song
Musically flowed along,
    Wise, unwise,
Wistful, wondering, weak or strong :
  As brook shallows sink or rise.


Other thoughts another day,
Maiden May, will surge and sway
    Round your heart ;
Wake, and plead, and turn at bay,
  Wisdom part, and folly part.


Time not far remote will borrow
Other joys, another sorrow,
    All for you ;
Not to-day, and yet to-morrow
  Reasoning false and reasoning true.

Wherefore greatest? Wherefore least?
Hearts that starve and hearts that feast?
    You and I?
Stammering Oracles have ceased,
  And the whole earth stands at "why?"

Underneath all things that be
Lies an unsolved mystery;
    Over all
Spreads a veil impenetrably,
  Spreads a dense unlifted pall.

Mystery of mysteries :
*This* creation hears and sees
    High and low—
Vanity of vanities :
  *This* we test and *this* we know.

Maiden May, the days of flowering
Nurse you now in sweet embowering,
    Sunny days;
Bright with rainbows all the showering,
  Bright with blossoms all the ways.

Close the inlet of your bower,
Close it close with thorn and flower,
    Maiden May;
Lengthen out the shortening hour,—
  Morrows are not as to-day.

Stay to-day which wanes too soon,
Stay the sun and stay the moon,
Stay your youth ;
Bask you in the actual noon,
Rest you in the present truth.


Let to-day suffice to-day :
For itself to-morrow may
Fetch its loss,
Aim and stumble, say its say,
Watch and pray and bear its cross.


## TILL TO-MORROW.

LONG have I longed, till I am tired
Of longing and desire ;
Farewell my points in vain desired,
My dying fire ;
Farewell all things that die and fail and tire.


Springtide and youth and useless pleasure
And all my useless scheming,
My hopes of unattainable treasure,
Dreams not worth dreaming,
Glow-worms that gleam but yield no warmth in
gleaming,

Farewell all shows that fade in showing :
   My wish and joy stand over
Until to-morrow ; Heaven is glowing
   Through cloudy cover,
Beyond all clouds loves me my Heavenly Lover.


## DEATH-WATCHES.

THE Spring spreads one green lap of flowers
   Which Autumn buries at the fall,
No chilling showers of Autumn hours
   Can stay them or recall ;
Winds sing a dirge, while earth lays out of sight
Her garment of delight.

The cloven East brings forth the sun,
   The cloven West doth bury him
What time his gorgeous race is run
   And all the world grows dim ;
A funeral moon is lit in heaven's hollow,
And pale the star-lights follow.


## TOUCHING "NEVER."

BECAUSE you never yet have loved me, dear,
   Think you you never can nor ever will ?
  Surely while life remains hope lingers still,
Hope the last blossom of life's dying year.

Because the season and mine age grow sere,
   Shall never Spring bring forth her daffodil,
   Shall never sweeter Summer feast her fill
Of roses with the nightingales they hear?
If you had loved me, I not loving you,
   If you had urged me with the tender plea
Of what our unknown years to come might do
(Eternal years, if Time should count too few),
   I would have owned the point you pressed on me,
Was possible, or probable, or true.

## BRANDONS BOTH.

OH fair Milly Brandon, a young maid, a fair maid!
   All her curls are yellow and her eyes are blue,
And her cheeks were rosy red till a secret care made
   Hollow whiteness of their brightness as a care will
   do.

Still she tends her flowers, but not as in the old
   days,
   Still she sings her songs, but not the songs of
   old:
If now it be high Summer her days seem brief and
   cold days,
   If now it be high Summer her nights are long and
   cold.

If you have a secret keep it, pure maid Milly;
  Life is filled with troubles and the world with scorn;
And pity without love is at best times hard and chilly,
  Chilling sore and stinging sore a heart forlorn.

Walter Brandon, do you guess Milly Brandon's secret?
  Many things you know, but not everything,
With your locks like raven's plumage, and eyes like
      an egret,
  And a laugh that is music, and such a voice to
      sing.

Nelly Knollys, she is fair, but she is not fairer
  Than fairest Milly Brandon was before she turned
      so pale:
Oh, but Nelly's dearer if she be not rarer,
  She need not keep a secret or blush behind a veil.

Beyond the first green hills, beyond the nearest valleys,
  Nelly dwells at home beneath her mother's eyes:
Her home is neat and homely, not a cot and not a
      palace,
  Just the home where love sets up his happiest
      memories.

Milly has no mother; and sad beyond another
  Is she whose blessed mother is vanished out of call:
Truly comfort beyond comfort is stored up in a
      Mother
    Who bears with all, and hopes through all, and loves
      us all.

Where peacocks nod and flaunt up and down the
    terrace,
  Furling and unfurling their scores of sightless eyes,
To and fro among the leaves and buds and flowers
    and berries
  Maiden Milly strolls and pauses, smiles and sighs.

On the hedged-in terrace of her father's palace
  She may stroll and muse alone, may smile or sigh
    alone,
Letting thoughts and eyes go wandering over hills and
    valleys
  To-day her father's, and one day to be all her own.

If her thoughts go coursing down lowlands and up
    highlands,
  It is because the startled game are leaping from
    their lair ;
If her thoughts dart homeward to the reedy river
    islands,
  It is because the waterfowl rise startled here or
    there.

At length a footfall on the steps : she turns, composed
    and steady,
  All the long-descended greatness of her father's
    house
Lifting up her head ; and there stands Walter keen
    and ready
  For hunting or for hawking, a flush upon his brows.

"Good-morrow, fair cousin." "Good-morrow, fairest
    cousin :
The sun has started on his course, and I must start
    to-day.
If you have done me one good turn you've done me
    many a dozen,
And I shall often think of you, think of you away."

"Over hill and hollow what quarry will you follow,
    Or what fish will you angle for beside the river's
    edge ?
There's cloud upon the hill-top and there's mist deep
    down the hollow,
And fog among the rushes and the rustling sedge."

"I shall speed well enough be it hunting or hawking,
    Or casting a bait toward the shyest daintiest fin.
But I kiss your hands, my cousin ; I must not loiter
    talking,
    For nothing comes of nothing, and I'm fain to seek
    and win."

"Here's a thorny rose : will you wear it an hour,
    Till the petals drop apart still fresh and pink and
    sweet ?
Till the petals drop from the drooping perished flower,
    And only the graceless thorns are left of it."

"Nay, I have another rose sprung in another garden,
    Another rose which sweetens all the world for me.

Be you a tenderer mistress and be you a warier
　　warden
　Of your rose, as sweet as mine, and full as fair to
　　see."

" Nay, a bud once plucked there is no reviving,
　Nor is it worth your wearing now, nor worth indeed
　　my own ;
The dead to the dead, and the living to the living.
　It's time I go within, for it's time now you were
　　gone."

" Good-bye, Milly Brandon, I shall not forget you,
　Though it be good-bye between us for ever from
　　to-day ;
I could almost wish to-day that I had never met you,
　And I'm true to you in this one word that I say."

" Good-bye, Walter.　I can guess which thornless rose
　　you covet ;
　Long may it bloom and prolong its sunny morn :
Yet as for my one thorny rose, I do not cease to love it,
　And if it is no more a flower I love it as a thorn."


## A LIFE'S PARALLELS.

NEVER on this side of the grave again,
　　On this side of the river,
On this side of the garner of the grain,
　　Never,—

Ever while time flows on and on and on,
　That narrow noiseless river,
Ever while corn bows heavy-headed, wan,
　　Ever,—

Never despairing, often fainting, rueing,
　But looking back, ah never !
Faint yet pursuing, faint yet still pursuing
　　Ever.


## AT LAST.

MANY have sung of love a root of bane :
　While to my mind a root of balm it is,
　For love at length breeds love ; sufficient bliss
For life and death and rising up again.
Surely when light of Heaven makes all things plain,
　Love will grow plain with all its mysteries ;
　Nor shall we need to fetch from over seas
Wisdom or wealth or pleasure safe from pain.
Love in our borders, love within our heart,
　Love all in all, we then shall bide at rest,
　Ended for ever life's unending quest,
　　Ended for ever effort, change and fear :
Love all in all ;—no more that better part
　　Purchased, but at the cost of all things here.

## GOLDEN SILENCES.

THERE is silence that saith, "Ah me!"
  There is silence that nothing saith;
    One the silence of life forlorn,
    One the silence of death;
  One is, and the other shall be.

One we know and have known for long,
  One we know not, but we shall know,
    All we who have ever been born;
    Even so, be it so,—
  There is silence, despite a song.

Sowing day is a silent day,
  Resting night is a silent night;
    But whoso reaps the ripened corn
    Shall shout in his delight,
  While silences vanish away.


## IN THE WILLOW SHADE.

I SAT beneath a willow tree,
  Where water falls and calls;
While fancies upon fancies solaced me,
  Some true, and some were false.

Who set their heart upon a hope
  That never comes to pass,

Droop in the end like fading heliotrope
   The sun's wan looking-glass.

Who set their will upon a whim
   Clung to through good and ill,
Are wrecked alike whether they sink or swim,
   Or hit or miss their will.

All things are vain that wax and wane.
   For which we waste our breath;
Love only doth not wane and is not vain,
   Love only outlives death.

A singing lark rose toward the sky,
   Circling he sang amain;
He sang, a speck scarce visible sky-high,
   And then he sank again.

A second like a sunlit spark
   Flashed singing up his track;
But never overtook that foremost lark,
   And songless fluttered back.

A hovering melody of birds
   Haunted the air above;
They clearly sang contentment without words,
   And youth and joy and love.

O silvery weeping willow tree
   With all leaves shivering,
Have you no purpose but to shadow me
   Beside this rippled spring?

On this first fleeting day of Spring,
   For Winter is gone by,
And every bird on every quivering wing
   Floats in a sunny sky;

On this first Summer-like soft day,
   While sunshine steeps the air,
And every cloud has gat itself away,
   And birds sing everywhere.

Have you no purpose in the world
   But thus to shadow me
With all your tender drooping twigs unfurled,
   O weeping willow tree?

With all your tremulous leaves outspread
   Betwixt me and the sun,
While here I loiter on a mossy bed
   With half my work undone;

My work undone, that should be done
   At once with all my might;
For after the long day and lingering sun
   Comes the unworking night.

This day is lapsing on its way,
   Is lapsing out of sight;
And after all the chances of the day
   Comes the resourceless night.

The weeping willow shook its head
   And stretched its shadow long;
The west grew crimson, the sun smouldered red,
   The birds forbore a song.

Slow wind sighed through the willow leaves,
   The ripple made a moan,
The world drooped murmuring like a thing that
      grieves;
   And then I felt alone.

I rose to go, and felt the chill,
   And shivered as I went;
Yet shivering wondered, and I wonder still,
   What more that willow meant;

That silvery weeping willow tree
   With all leaves shivering,
Which spent one long day overshadowing me
   Beside a spring in Spring.


## FLUTTERED WINGS.

THE splendour of the kindling day,
   The splendour of the setting sun,
These move my soul to wend its way,
   And have done
With all we grasp and toil amongst and say.

The paling roses of a cloud,
   The fading bow that arches space,
These woo my fancy toward my shroud ;
     Toward the place
Of faces veiled, and heads discrowned and bowed.

The nation of the steadfast stars,
   The wandering star whose blaze is brief,
These make me beat against the bars
     Of my grief ;
My tedious grief, twin to the life it mars.

O fretted heart tossed to and fro,
   So fain to flee, so fain to rest !
All glories that are high or low,
     East or west,
Grow dim to thee who art so fain to go.


## A FISHER-WIFE.

THE soonest mended, nothing said ;
   And help may rise from east or west
But my two hands are lumps of lead,
   My heart sits leaden in my breast.

O north wind swoop not from the north,
   O south wind linger in the south,
Oh come not raving raging forth,
   To bring my heart into my mouth ;

For I've a husband out at sea,
    Afloat on feeble planks of wood;
He does not know what fear may be;
    I would have told him if I could.

I would have locked him in my arms,
    I would have hid him in my heart;
For oh! the waves are fraught with harms,
    And he and I so far apart.


## WHAT'S IN A NAME?

WHY has Spring one syllable less
        Than any its fellow season?
There may be some other reason,
And I'm merely making a guess;
But surely it hoards such wealth
Of happiness, hope and health,
Sunshine and musical sound,
It may spare a foot from its name
Yet all the same
Superabound.

Soft-named Summer,
Most welcome comer,
Brings almost everything
Over which we dream or sing
Or sigh;
But then summer wends its way,

To-morrow,—to-day,—
Good-bye!

Autumn,—the slow name lingers,
While we likewise flag;
It silences many singers;
Its slow days drag,
Yet hasten at speed
To leave us in chilly need
For Winter to strip indeed.

In all-lack Winter,
Dull of sense and of sound,
We huddle and shiver
Beside our splinter
Of crackling pine,
Snow in sky and snow on ground.
Winter and cold
Can't last for ever!
To-day, to-morrow, the sun will shine;
When we are old,
But some still are young,
Singing the song
Which others have sung,
Ringing the bells
Which others have rung,—
Even so!
We ourselves, who else?
We ourselves long
Long ago.

## MARIANA.

NOT for me marring or making,
  Not for me giving or taking;
I love my Love and he loves not me,
I love my Love and my heart is breaking.

Sweet is Spring in its lovely showing,
Sweet the violet veiled in blowing,
  Sweet it is to love and be loved;
Ah, sweet knowledge beyond my knowing!

Who sighs for love sighs but for pleasure,
Who wastes for love hoards up a treasure;
  Sweet to be loved and take no count,
Sweet it is to love without measure.

Sweet my Love whom I loved to try for,
Sweet my Love whom I love and sigh for,
  Will you once love me and sigh for me,
You my Love whom I love and die for?

## MEMENTO MORI.

POOR the pleasure
  Doled out by measure,
Sweet though it be, while brief
As falling of the leaf;
Poor is pleasure
By weight and measure.

Sweet the sorrow
Which ends to-morrow ;
Sharp though it be and sore,
It ends for evermore :
Zest of sorrow,
What ends to-morrow.

## "ONE FOOT ON SEA, AND ONE ON SHORE."

" OH tell me once and tell me twice
    And tell me thrice to make it plain,
When we who part this weary day,
    When we who part shall meet again."

" When windflowers blossom on the sea
    And fishes skim along the plain,
Then we who part this weary day,
    Then you and I shall meet again."

" Yet tell me once before we part,
    Why need we part who part in pain ?
If flowers must blossom on the sea,
    Why, we shall never meet again.

" My cheeks are paler than a rose,
    My tears are salter than the main,
My heart is like a lump of ice
    If we must never meet again."

" Oh weep or laugh, but let me be,
    And live or die, for all's in vain ;
For life's in vain since we must part,
    And parting must not meet again

" Till windflowers blossom on the sea
    And fishes skim along the plain ;
Pale rose of roses let me be,
    Your breaking heart breaks mine again."


## A SONG OF FLIGHT.

WHILE we slumber and sleep
    The sun leaps up from the deep
—Daylight born at the leap !—
Rapid, dominant, free,
Athirst to bathe in the uttermost sea.

While we linger at play
—If the year would stand at May !—
Winds are up and away
Over land, over sea,
To their goal wherever their goal may be.

It is time to arise,
To race for the promised prize,
—The Sun flies, the Wind flies —
We are strong, we are free,
And home lies beyond the stars and the sea.

## BUDS AND BABIES.

A MILLION buds are born that never blow,
   That sweet with promise lift a pretty head
To blush and wither on a barren bed
   And leave no fruit to show.

Sweet, unfulfilled.   Yet have I understood
   One joy, by their fragility made plain :
Nothing was ever beautiful in vain,
   Or all in vain was good.


## A WINTRY SONNET.

A ROBIN said : The Spring will never come,
   And I shall never care to build again.
A Rosebush said : These frosts are wearisome,
   My sap will never stir for sun or rain.
The half Moon said : These nights are fogged and
      slow,
   I neither care to wax nor care to wane.
The Ocean said : I thirst from long ago,
   Because earth's rivers cannot fill the main.—
When Springtime came, red Robin built a nest,
   And trilled a lover's song in sheer delight.
   Gray hoarfrost vanished, and the Rose with might
   Clothed her in leaves and buds of crimson core.
The dim Moon brightened.   Ocean sunned his crest,
   Dimpled his blue, yet thirsted evermore.

## BOY JOHNNY.

" IF you'll busk you as a bride
    And make ready,
It's I will wed you with a ring,
    O fair lady."

" Shall I busk me as a bride,
    I so bonny,
For you to wed me with a ring,
    O boy Johnny?"

" When you've busked you as a bride
    And made ready,
Who else is there to marry you,
    O fair lady?"

" I will find my lover out,
    I so bonny,
And you shall bear my wedding-train,
    O boy Johnny."

## FREAKS OF FASHION.

SUCH a hubbub in the nests,
    Such a bustle and squeak!
Nestlings, guiltless of a feather,
    Learning just to speak,
Ask—" And how about the fashions?"
    From a cavernous beak.

Perched on bushes, perched on hedges,
    Perched on firm hahas,
Perched on anything that holds them,
    Gay papas and grave mammas
Teach the knowledge-thirsty nestlings :
    Hear the gay papas.

Robin says : " A scarlet waistcoat
    Will be all the wear,
Snug, and also cheerful-looking
    For the frostiest air,
Comfortable for the chest too
    When one comes to plume and pair."

" Neat gray hoods will be in vogue,"
    Quoth a Jackdaw : " Glossy gray,
Setting close, yet setting easy,
    Nothing fly-away ;
Suited to our misty mornings,
    *À la négligée.*"

Flushing salmon, flushing sulphur,
    Haughty Cockatoos
Answer—" Hoods may do for mornings,
    But for evenings choose
High head-dresses, curved like crescents
    Such as well-bred persons use."

" Top-knots, yes ; yet more essential
    Still, a train or tail,"
Screamed the Peacock : " Gemmed and lustrous,

Not too stiff, and not too frail;
Those are best which rearrange as
    Fans, and spread or trail."

Spoke the Swan, entrenched behind
    An inimitable neck:
" After all, there's nothing sweeter
    For the lawn or lake
Than simple white, if fine and flaky
    And absolutely free from speck."

" Yellow," hinted a Canary,
    " Warmer, not less *distingué.*"
" Peach colour," put in a Lory,
    " Cannot look *outré.*"
" All the colours are in fashion,
    And are right," the Parrots say.

" Very well.   But do contrast
    Tints harmonious,"
Piped a Blackbird, justly proud
    Of bill aurigerous;
" Half the world may learn a lesson
    As to that from us."

Then a Stork took up the word:
    " Aim at height and *chic:*
Not high heels, they're common; somehow,
    Stilted legs, not thick,
Nor yet thin:" he just glanced downward
    And snapped to his beak.

Here a rustling and a whirring,
　　As of fans outspread,
Hinted that mammas felt anxious
　　Lest the next thing said
Might prove less than quite judicious,
　　Or even underbred.


So a mother Auk resumed
　　The broken thread of speech :
" Let colours sort themselves, my dears,
　　Yellow, or red, or peach ;
The main points, as it seems to me,
　　We mothers have to teach,


" Are form and texture, elegance,
　　An air reserved, sublime ;
The mode of wearing what we wear
　　With due regard to month and clime.
But now, let's all compose ourselves,
　　It's almost breakfast-time."


A hubbub, a squeak, a bustle !
　　Who cares to chatter or sing
With delightful breakfast coming ?
　　Yet they whisper under the wing :
" So we may wear whatever we like,
　　Anything, everything ! "

## AN OCTOBER GARDEN.

IN my Autumn garden I was fain
　　To mourn among my scattered roses ;
　Alas for that last rosebud which uncloses
To Autumn's languid sun and rain
When all the world is on the wane !
　　Which has not felt the sweet constraint of June,
　　Nor heard the nightingale in tune.

Broad-faced asters by my garden walk,
　　You are but coarse compared with roses :
　More choice, more dear that rosebud which uncloses
Faint-scented, pinched, upon its stalk,
That least and last which cold winds balk ;
　　A rose it is though least and last of all,
　　A rose to me though at the fall.


## "SUMMER IS ENDED."

TO think that this meaningless thing was ever a rose
　　　　Scentless, colourless, *this !*
　Will it ever be thus (who knows ?)
　　　　Thus with our bliss,
　　If we wait till the close ?

Though we care not to wait for the end, there comes
　　　　the end
　　　　Sooner, later, at last,
　Which nothing can mar, nothing mend :
　　　　An end locked fast,
　　Bent we cannot re-bend.

## PASSING AND GLASSING.

ALL things that pass
　　Are woman's looking-glass;
They show her how her bloom must fade,
And she herself be laid
With withered roses in the shade;
　With withered roses and the fallen peach,
　Unlovely, out of reach
　　Of summer joy that was.

All things that pass
　　Are woman's tiring-glass;
The faded lavender is sweet,
Sweet the dead violet
Culled and laid by and cared for yet;
　The dried-up violets and dried lavender
　Still sweet, may comfort her,
　　Nor need she cry Alas!

All things that pass
　　Are wisdom's looking-glass;
Being full of hope and fear, and still
Brimful of good or ill,
According to our work and will;
　For there is nothing new beneath the sun;
　Our doings have been done,
　　And that which shall be was.

## "I WILL ARISE."

WEARY and weak,—accept my weariness;
　　Weary and weak and downcast in my soul,
With hope growing less and less,
　　And with the goal
Distant and dim,—accept my sore distress.
I thought to reach the goal so long ago,
　　At outset of the race I dreamed of rest,
Not knowing what now I know
　　Of breathless haste,
　　Of long-drawn straining effort across the waste.

One only thing I knew, Thy love of me;
　　One only thing I know, Thy sacred same
Love of me full and free,
　　A craving flame
Of selfless love of me which burns in Thee.
How can I think of Thee, and yet grow chill;
　　Of Thee, and yet grow cold and nigh to death?
Re-energise my will,
　　Rebuild my faith;
　　I will arise and run, Thou giving me breath.

I will arise, repenting and in pain;
　　I will arise, and smite upon my breast
And turn to Thee again;
　　Thou choosest best,
Lead me along the road Thou makest plain.

Lead me a little way, and carry me
　A little way, and hearken to my sighs,
And store my tears with Thee,
　And deign replies
　To feeble prayers ;—O Lord, I will arise.


## RESURGAM.

FROM depth to height, from height to loftier height,
　The climber sets his foot and sets his face,
　Tracks lingering sunbeams to their halting-place,
And counts the last pulsations of the light.
Strenuous thro' day and unsurprised by night
　He runs a race with Time and wins the race,
　Emptied and stripped of all save only Grace,
Will, Love, a threefold panoply of might.
Darkness descends for light he toiled to seek :
　He stumbles on the darkened mountain-head,
　　Left breathless in the unbreathable thin air,
　Made freeman of the living and the dead :—
He wots not he has topped the topmost peak,
　　But the returning sun will find him there.


## A PRODIGAL SON.

DOES that lamp still burn in my Father's house,
　Which he kindled the night I went away?
I turned once beneath the cedar boughs,
　And marked it gleam with a golden ray ;
　Did he think to light me home some day?

Hungry here with the crunching swine,
  Hungry harvest have I to reap ;
In a dream I count my Father's kine,
  I hear the tinkling bells of his sheep,
  I watch his lambs that browse and leap.

There is plenty of bread at home,
  His servants have bread enough and to spare ;
The purple wine-fat froths with foam,
  Oil and spices make sweet the air,
  While I perish hungry and bare.

Rich and blessed those servants, rather
  Than I who see not my Father's face !
I will arise and go to my Father :—
  " Fallen from sonship, beggared of grace,
  Grant me, Father, a servant's place."


## SŒUR LOUISE DE LA MISÉRICORDE.

### (1674.)

I HAVE desired, and I have been desired ;
  But now the days are over of desire,
Now dust and dying embers mock my fire ;
Where is the hire for which my life was hired ?
  Oh vanity of vanities, desire !

Longing and love, pangs of a perished pleasure,
   Longing and love, a disenkindled fire,
   And memory a bottomless gulf of mire,
And love a fount of tears outrunning measure;
   Oh vanity of vanities, desire!

Now from my heart, love's deathbed, trickles, trickles,
   Drop by drop slowly, drop by drop of fire,
   The dross of life, of love, of spent desire;
Alas, my rose of life gone all to prickles,—
   Oh vanity of vanities, desire!

Oh vanity of vanities, desire;
   Stunting my hope which might have strained up
      higher,
   Turning my garden plot to barren mire;
Oh death-struck love, oh disenkindled fire,
   Oh vanity of vanities, desire!


## TO-DAY'S BURDEN.

" ARISE, depart, for this is not your rest."—
    Oh burden of all burdens, still to arise
  And still depart, nor rest in any wise!
Rolling, still rolling thus to east from west
Earth journeys on her immemorial quest,
   Whom a moon chases in no different guise:
   Thus stars pursue their courses, and thus flies
The sun, and thus all creatures manifest.

Unrest the common heritage, the ban
  Flung broadcast on all humankind, on all
    Who live ; for living, all are bound to die :
That which is old, we know that it is man :
    These have no rest who sit and dream and sigh,
  Nor have those rest who wrestle and who fall.


## AN "IMMURATA" SISTER.

LIFE flows down to death ; we cannot bind
    That current that it should not flee :
Life flows down to death, as rivers find
    The inevitable sea.

Men work and think, but women feel ;
    And so (for I'm a woman, I)
    And so I should be glad to die
And cease from impotence of zeal,
And cease from hope, and cease from dread,
    And cease from yearnings without gain,
    And cease from all this world of pain,
And be at peace among the dead.

Hearts that die, by death renew their youth,
    Lightened of this life that doubts and dies ;
Silent and contented, while the Truth
    Unveiled makes them wise.

Why should I seek and never find
  That something which I have not had?
  Fair and unutterably sad
The world hath sought time out of mind;
The world hath sought and I have sought,—
  Ah, empty world and empty I!
For we have spent our strength for nought,
  And soon it will be time to die.

Sparks fly upward toward their fount of fire,
  Kindling, flashing, hovering :—
Kindle, flash, my soul; mount higher and higher,
  Thou whole burnt-offering!


## "THERE IS A BUDDING MORROW IN MIDNIGHT."

WINTRY boughs against a wintry sky;
  Yet the sky is partly blue
    And the clouds are partly bright :—
Who can tell but sap is mounting high
    Out of sight,
Ready to burst through?

Winter is the mother-nurse of Spring,
  Lovely for her daughter's sake,
    Not unlovely for her own:
For a future buds in everything;
    Grown, or blown,
Or about to break.

## "IF THOU SAYEST, BEHOLD, WE KNEW IT NOT."—Proverbs xxiv. 11, 12.

### 1.

I HAVE done I know not what,—what have I done?
  My brother's blood, my brother's soul, doth cry:
And I find no defence, find no reply,
No courage more to run this race I run
Not knowing what I have done, have left undone;
  Ah me, these awful unknown hours that fly
Fruitless it may be, fleeting fruitless by
Rank with death-savour underneath the sun.
For what avails it that I did not know
  The deed I did? what profits me the plea
That had I known I had not wronged him so?
  Lord Jesus Christ, my God, him pity Thou;
  Lord, if it may be, pity also me:
  In judgment pity, and in death, and now.

### 2.

Thou Who hast borne all burdens, bear our load,
  Bear Thou our load whatever load it be;
  Our guilt, our shame, our helpless misery,
Bear Thou Who only canst, O God my God.
  Seek us and find us, for we cannot Thee

Or seek or find or hold or cleave unto :
We cannot do or undo ; Lord, undo
    Our self-undoing, for Thine is the key
Of all we are not though we might have been.
    Dear Lord, if ever mercy moved Thy mind,
        If so be love of us can move Thee yet,
If still the nail-prints in Thy Hands are seen,
        Remember us,—yea, how shouldst Thou forget ?
    Remember us for good, and seek, and find.


3.

Each soul I might have succoured, may have slain,
    All souls shall face me at the last Appeal,
    That great last moment poised for woe or weal,
That final moment for man's bliss or bane.
Vanity of vanities, yea all is vain
    Which then will not avail or help or heal :
    Disfeatured faces, worn-out knees that kneel,
Will more avail than strength or beauty then.
Lord, by Thy Passion,—when Thy Face was marred
    In sight of earth and hell tumultuous,
        And Thy heart failed in Thee like melting wax,
And Thy Blood dropped more precious than the
                nard,—
        Lord, for Thy sake, not our's, supply our lacks,
    For Thine own sake, not our's, Christ, pity us.

## THE THREAD OF LIFE.

### I.

THE irresponsive silence of the land,
 The irresponsive sounding of the sea,
 Speak both one message of one sense to me :—
Aloof, aloof, we stand aloof, so stand
Thou too aloof bound with the flawless band
 Of inner solitude ; we bind not thee ;
 But who from thy self-chain shall set thee free?
What heart shall touch thy heart? what hand thy
  hand?—
And I am sometimes proud and sometimes meek,
 And sometimes I remember days of old
When fellowship seemed not so far to seek
 And all the world and I seemed much less cold,
 And at the rainbow's foot lay surely gold,
And hope felt strong and life itself not weak.

### 2.

Thus am I mine own prison. Everything
 Around me free and sunny and at ease :
 Or if in shadow, in a shade of trees
Which the sun kisses, where the gay birds sing
And where all winds make various murmuring ;

Where bees are found, with honey for the bees ;
Where sounds are music, and where silences
Are music of an unlike fashioning.
Then gaze I at the merrymaking crew,
And smile a moment and a moment sigh
Thinking : Why can I not rejoice with you ?
But soon I put the foolish fancy by :
I am not what I have nor what I do ;
But what I was I am, I am even I.


3.


Therefore myself is that one only thing
I hold to use or waste, to keep or give ;
My sole possession every day I live,
And still mine own despite Time's winnowing.
Ever mine own, while moons and seasons bring
From crudeness ripeness mellow and sanative ;
Ever mine own, till Death shall ply his sieve ;
And still mine own, when saints break grave and
sing.
And this myself as king unto my King
I give, to Him Who gave Himself for me ;
Who gives Himself to me, and bids me sing
A sweet new song of His redeemed set free ;
He bids me sing : O death, where is thy sting ?
And sing : O grave, where is thy victory ?

## AN OLD-WORLD THICKET.

. . . " Una selva oscura."—DANTE.

A WAKE or sleeping (for I know not which)
　I was or was not mazed within a wood
Where every mother-bird brought up her brood
　Safe in some leafy niche
Of oak or ash, of cypress or of beech,

Of silvery aspen trembling delicately,
　Of plane or warmer-tinted sycomore,
　Of elm that dies in secret from the core,
　　Of ivy weak and free,
Of pines, of all green lofty things that be.

Such birds they seemed as challenged each desire ;
　Like spots of azure heaven upon the wing,
　Like downy emeralds that alight and sing,
　　Like actual coals on fire,
Like anything they seemed, and everything.

Such mirth they made, such warblings and such chat
　With tongue of music in a well-tuned beak,
　They seemed to speak more wisdom than we speak,
　　To make our music flat
And all our subtlest reasonings wild or weak.

Their meat was nought but flowers like butterflies,
　　With berries coral-coloured or like gold ;
　　Their drink was only dew, which blossoms hold
　　　Deep where the honey lies ;
Their wings and tails were lit by sparkling eyes.


The shade wherein they revelled was a shade
　　That danced and twinkled to the unseen sun ;
　　Branches and leaves cast shadows one by one,
　　　And all their shadows swayed
In breaths of air that rustled and that played.


A sound of waters neither rose nor sank,
　　And spread a sense of freshness through the air ;
　　It seemed not here or there, but everywhere,
　　　As if the whole earth drank,
Root fathom deep and strawberry on its bank.


But I who saw such things as I have said,
　　Was overdone with utter weariness ;
　　And walked in care, as one whom fears oppress,
　　　Because above his head
Death hangs, or damage, or the dearth of bread.


Each sore defeat of my defeated life
　　Faced and outfaced me in that bitter hour ;
　　And turned to yearning palsy all my power,
　　　And all my peace to strife,
Self stabbing self with keen lack-pity knife.

Sweetness of beauty moved me to despair,
   Stung me to anger by its mere content,
   Made me all lonely on that way I went,
     Piled care upon my care,
Brimmed full my cup, and stripped me empty and bare:

For all that was but showed what all was not,
   But gave clear proof of what might never be ;
   Making more destitute my poverty,
     And yet more blank my lot,
And me much sadder by its jubilee.

Therefore I sat me down : for wherefore walk ?
   And closed mine eyes : for wherefore see or hear ?
   Alas, I had no shutter to mine ear,
     And could not shun the talk
Of all rejoicing creatures far or near.

Without my will I hearkened and I heard
   (Asleep or waking, for I know not which),
   Till note by note the music changed its pitch;
     Bird ceased to answer bird,
And every wind sighed softly if it stirred.

The drip of widening waters seemed to weep,
   All fountains sobbed and gurgled as they sprang,
Somewhere a cataract cried out in its leap
     Sheer down a headlong steep ;
   High over all cloud-thunders gave a clang.

Such universal sound of lamentation
   I heard and felt, fain not to feel or hear ;
   Nought else there seemed but anguish far and near ;
     Nought else but all creation
   Moaning and groaning wrung by pain or fear,

Shuddering in the misery of its doom :
   My heart then rose a rebel against light,
   Scouring all earth and heaven and depth and height,
     Ingathering wrath and gloom,
   Ingathering wrath to wrath and night to night.

Ah me, the bitterness of such revolt,
   All impotent, all hateful, and all hate,
That kicks and breaks itself against the bolt
     Of an imprisoning fate,
   And vainly shakes, and cannot shake the gate.

Agony to agony, deep called to deep,
   Out of the deep I called of my desire ;
   My strength was weakness and my heart was fire ;
     Mine eyes that would not weep
Or sleep, scaled height and depth, and could not sleep;

The eyes, I mean, of my rebellious soul,
   For still my bodily eyes were closed and dark :
   A random thing I seemed without a mark,
     Racing without a goal,
   Adrift upon life's sea without an ark.

More leaden than the actual self of lead
   Outer and inner darkness weighed on me.
  The tide of anger ebbed.   Then fierce and free
     Surged full above my head
   The moaning tide of helpless misery.


Why should I breathe, whose breath was but a sigh?
  Why should I live, who drew such painful breath?
Oh weary work, the unanswerable why!—
    Yet I, why should I die,
  Who had no hope in life, no hope in death?


Grasses and mosses and the fallen leaf
   Make peaceful bed for an indefinite term;
  But underneath the grass there gnaws a worm—
    Haply, there gnaws a grief—
Both, haply always; not, as now, so brief.


The pleasure I remember, it is past;
   The pain I feel, is passing passing by;
  Thus all the world is passing, and thus I:
    All things that cannot last
  Have grown familiar, and are born to die.


And being familiar, have so long been borne
   That habit trains us not to break but bend:
Mourning grows natural to us who mourn
    In foresight of an end,
  But that which ends not who shall brave or mend?

Surely the ripe fruits tremble on their bough,
  They cling and linger trembling till they drop:
I, trembling, cling to dying life; for how
    Face the perpetual Now?
    Birthless and deathless, void of start or stop,

Void of repentance, void of hope and fear,
  Of possibility, alternative,
  Of all that ever made us bear to live
    From night to morning here,
  Of promise even which has no gift to give.

The wood, and every creature of the wood,
  Seemed mourning with me in an undertone;
  Soft scattered chirpings and a windy moan,
    Trees rustling where they stood
And shivered, showed compassion for my mood.

Rage to despair; and now despair had turned
  Back to self-pity and mere weariness,
With yearnings like a smouldering fire that burned,
    And might grow more or less,
  And might die out or wax to white excess.

Without, within me, music seemed to be;
  Something not music, yet most musical,
Silence and sound in heavenly harmony;
    At length a pattering fall
  Of feet, a bell, and bleatings, broke through all.

Then I looked up. The wood lay in a glow
   From golden sunset and from ruddy sky;
   The sun had stooped to earth though once so high;
    Had stooped to earth, in slow
Warm dying loveliness brought near and low.

Each water drop made answer to the light,
   Lit up a spark and showed the sun his face;
   Soft purple shadows paved the grassy space
    And crept from height to height,
   From height to loftier height crept up apace.

While opposite the sun a gazing moon
   Put on his glory for her coronet,
Kindling her luminous coldness to its noon,
    As his great splendour set;
   One only star made up her train as yet.

Each twig was tipped with gold, each leaf was edged
   And veined with gold from the gold-flooded west;
Each mother-bird, and mate-bird, and unfledged
    Nestling, and curious nest,
   Displayed a gilded moss or beak or breast.

And filing peacefully between the trees,
   Having the moon behind them, and the sun
Full in their meek mild faces, walked at ease
    A homeward flock, at peace
   With one another and with every one.

A patriarchal ram with tinkling bell
   Led all his kin ; sometimes one browsing sheep
   Hung back a moment, or one lamb would leap
     And frolic in a dell ;
Yet still they kept together, journeying well,

And bleating, one or other, many or few,
   Journeying together toward the sunlit west ;
   Mild face by face, and woolly breast by breast,
     Patient, sun-brightened too,
   Still journeying toward the sunset and their rest.

## EXULTATE DEO.

MANY a flower hath perfume for its dower,
     And many a bird a song,
And harmless lambs milkwhite beside their dams
     Frolic along ;
Perfume and song and whiteness offering praise
     In humble, peaceful ways.

Man's high degree hath will and memory,
     Affection and desire,
By loftier ways he mounts of prayer and praise ;
     Fire unto fire,
Deep unto deep responsive, height to height,
     Until he walk in white.

## " ALL THY WORKS PRAISE THEE, O LORD."

### A PROCESSIONAL OF CREATION.

#### ALL.

I ALL-CREATION sing my song of praise
To God Who made me and vouchsafes my days,
And sends me forth by multitudinous ways.

#### SERAPH.

I, like my Brethren, burn eternally
With love of Him Who is Love, and loveth me ;
The Holy, Holy, Holy Unity.

#### CHERUB.

I, with my Brethren, gaze eternally
On Him Who is Wisdom, and Who knoweth me ;
The Holy, Holy, Holy Trinity.

#### ALL ANGELS.

We rule, we serve, we work, we store His treasure,
Whose vessels are we brimmed with strength and
pleasure ;
Our joys fulfil, yea, overfill our measure.

### HEAVENS.

We float before the Presence Infinite,
We cluster round the Throne in our delight,
Revolving and rejoicing in God's sight.

### FIRMAMENT.

I, blue and beautiful, and framed of air,
At sunrise and at sunset grow most fair;
His glory by my glories I declare.

### POWERS.

We Powers are powers because He makes us strong;
Wherefore we roll all rolling orbs along,
We move all moving things, and sing our song.

### SUN.

I blaze to Him in mine engarlanding
Of rays, I flame His whole burnt-offering
While as a bridegroom I rejoice and sing.

### MOON.

I follow, and am fair, and do His Will;
Through all my changes I am faithful still,
Full-orbed or strait His mandate to fulfil.

### STARS.

We Star-hosts numerous, innumerous,
Throng space with energy untumultuous,
And work His Will Whose eye beholdeth us.

### Galaxies and Nebulæ.

No thing is far or near; and therefore we
Float neither far nor near; but where we be
Weave dances round the Throne perpetually.


### Comets and Meteors.

Our lights dart here and there, whirl to and fro,
We flash and vanish, we die down and glow;
All doing His Will Who bids us do it so.


### Showers.

We give ourselves; and be we great or small,
Thus are we made like Him Who giveth all,
Like Him Whose gracious pleasure bids us fall.


### Dews.

We give ourselves in silent secret ways,
Spending and spent in silence full of grace;
And thus are made like God, and show His praise.


### Winds.

We sift the air and winnow all the earth;
And God Who poised our weights and weighs our
    worth
Accepts the worship of our solemn mirth.

### FIRE.

My power and strength are His Who fashioned me,
Ordained me image of His Jealousy,
Forged me His weapon fierce exceedingly.

### HEAT.

I glow unto His glory, and do good :
I glow, and bring to life both bud and brood ;
I glow, and ripen harvest-crops for food.

### WINTER AND SUMMER.

Our wealth and joys and beauties celebrate
His wealth of beauty Who sustains our state,
Before Whose changelessness we alternate.

### SPRING AND AUTUMN.

I hope,—
                 And I remember,—
                                        We give place
Either to other with contented grace,
Acceptable and lovely all our days.

### FROST

I make the unstable stable, binding fast
The world of waters prone to ripple past :
Thus praise I God, Whose mercies I forecast.

### COLD.

I rouse and goad the slothful apt to nod,
I stir and urge the laggards with my rod:
My praise is not of men, yet I praise God.

### SNOW.

My whiteness shadoweth Him Who is most fair,
All spotless: yea, my whiteness which I wear
Exalts His Purity beyond compare.

### VAPOURS.

We darken sun and moon, and blot the day.
The good Will of our Maker to obey:
Till to the glory of God we pass away.

### NIGHT.

Moon and all stars I don for diadem
To make me fair: I cast myself and them
Before His feet, Who knows us gem from gem.

### DAY.

I shout before Him in my plenitude
Of light and warmth, of hope and wealth and food;
Ascribing all good to the Only Good.

### Light and Darkness.

I am God's dwelling-place,—
                            And also I
Make His pavilion,—
                            Lo, we bide and fly
Exulting in the Will of God Most High.

### Lightning and Thunder.

We indivisible flash forth His Fame,
We thunder forth the glory of His Name,
In harmony of resonance and flame.

### Clouds.

Sweet is our store, exhaled from sea or river:
We wear a rainbow, praising God the Giver
Because His mercy is for ever and ever.

### Earth.

I rest in Him rejoicing: resting so
And so rejoicing, in that I am low;
Yet known of Him, and following on to know.

### Mountains.

Our heights which laud Him, sink abased before
Him higher than the highest evermore:
God higher than the highest we adore.

### Hills.

We green-tops praise Him, and we fruitful heads,
Whereon the sunshine and the dew He sheds :
We green-tops praise Him, rising from our beds.

### Green Things.

We all green things, we blossoms bright or dim,
Trees, bushes, brushwood, corn and grasses slim,
We lift our many-favoured lauds to Him.

### Rose,—Lily,—Violet.

I praise Him on my thorn which I adorn,—
And I, amid my world of thistle and thorn,—
And I, within my veil where I am born.

### Apple,—Citron,—Pomegranate.

We Apple-blossom, Citron, Pomegranate,
We clothed of God without our toil and fret,
We offer fatness where His Throne is set.

### Vine,—Cedar,—Palm.

I proffer Him my sweetness, who am sweet,—
I bow my strength in fragrance at His feet,—
I wave myself before His Judgment Seat.

### MEDICINAL HERBS.

I bring refreshment,—
                    I bring ease and calm,—
I lavish strength and healing,—
                    I am balm,—
We work His pitiful Will and chant our psalm.

### A SPRING.

Clear my pure fountain, clear and pure my rill,
My fountain and mine outflow deep and still,
I set His semblance forth and do His Will.

### SEA.

To-day I praise God with a sparkling face,
My thousand thousand waves all uttering praise :
To-morrow I commit me to His Grace.

### FLOODS.

We spring and swell meandering to and fro,
From height to depth, from depth to depth we flow,
We fertilise the world, and praise Him so.

### WHALES AND SEA MAMMALS.

We Whales and Monsters gambol in His sight
Rejoicing every day and every night,
Safe in the tender keeping of His Might.

### FISHES.

Our fashions and our colours and our speeds
Set forth His praise Who framed us and Who feeds,
Who knows our number and regards our needs.

### BIRDS.

Winged Angels of this visible world, we fly
To sing God's praises in the lofty sky ;
We scale the height to praise our Lord most High.

### EAGLE AND DOVE.

I the sun-gazing Eagle,—
             I the Dove
With plumes of softness and a note of love,—
We praise by divers gifts One God above.

### BEASTS AND CATTLE.

We forest Beasts,—
          We Beasts of hill or cave,—
We border-loving Creatures of the wave,—
We praise our King with voices deep and grave.

### SMALL ANIMALS.

God forms us weak and small, but pours out all
We need, and notes us while we stand or fall :
Wherefore we praise Him, weak and safe and small.

### LAMB.

I praise my loving Lord, Who maketh me
His type by harmless sweet simplicity :
Yet He the Lamb of lambs incomparably.

### LION.

I praise the Lion of the Royal Race,
Strongest in fight and swiftest in the chase :
With all my might I leap and lavish praise.

### ALL MEN.

All creatures sing around us, and we sing :
We bring our own selves as our offering,
Our very selves we render to our King.

### ISRAEL.

Flock of our Shepherd's pasture and His fold,
Purchased and well-beloved from days of old,
We tell His praise which still remains untold.

### PRIESTS.

We free-will Shepherds tend His sheep and feed ;
We follow Him while caring for their need ;
We follow praising Him, and them we lead.

### SERVANTS OF GOD.

We love God, for He loves us ; we are free
In serving Him, who serve Him willingly :
As kings we reign, and praise His Majesty.

### HOLY AND HUMBLE PERSONS.

All humble souls He calls and sanctifies ;
All holy souls He calls to make them wise ;
Accepting all, His free-will sacrifice.

### BABES.

He maketh me,—
       And me,—
              And me,—
                   To be
His blessed little ones around His knee,
Who praise Him by mere love confidingly.

### WOMEN.

God makes our service love, and makes our wage
Love : so we wend on patient pilgrimage,
Extolling Him by love from age to age

### MEN.

God gives us power to rule : He gives us power
To rule ourselves, and prune the exuberant flower
Of youth, and worship Him hour after hour.

### SPIRITS AND SOULS—

Lo, in the hidden world we chant our chant
To Him Who fills us that we nothing want,
To Him Whose bounty leaves our craving scant.


### OF BABES—

With milky mouths we praise God, from the breast
Called home betimes to rest the perfect rest,
By love and joy fulfilling His behest.


### OF WOMEN—

We praise His Will which made us what He would,
His Will which fashioned us and called us good,
His Will our plenary beatitude.


### OF MEN.

We praise His Will Who bore with us so long,
Who out of weakness wrought us swift and strong,
Champions of right and putters-down of wrong.


### ALL.

Let everything that hath or hath not breath,
Let days and endless days, let life and death,
Praise God, praise God, praise God, His creature
    saith.

## LATER LIFE: A DOUBLE SONNET OF SONNETS.

### 1.

BEFORE the mountains were brought forth, before
 Earth and the world were made, then God was
  God :
And God will still be God, when flames shall roar
 Round earth and heaven dissolving at His nod :
 And this God is our God, even while His rod
Of righteous wrath falls on us smiting sore :
And this God is our God for evermore
 Through life, through death, while clod returns to
  clod.
For though He slay us we will trust in Him ;
 We will flock home to Him by divers ways :
 Yea, though He slay us we will vaunt His praise,
Serving and loving with the Cherubim,
Watching and loving with the Seraphim,
 Our very selves His praise through endless days.


### 2.

Rend hearts and rend not garments for our sins ;
 Gird sackcloth not on body but on soul ;
 Grovel in dust with faces toward the goal
Nor won, nor neared : he only laughs who wins.

Not neared the goal, the race too late begins ;
   All left undone, we have yet to do the whole ;
   The sun is hurrying west and toward the pole
Where darkness waits for earth with all her kins.
Let us to-day while it is called to-day
   Set out, if utmost speed may yet avail—
   The shadows lengthen and the light grows pale :
      For who through darkness and the shadow of
        death,
Darkness that may be felt, shall find a way,
      Blind-eyed, deaf-eared, and choked with failing
        breath ?

### 3.

Thou Who didst make and knowest whereof we are
      made,
   Oh bear in mind our dust and nothingness,
   Our wordless tearless dumbness of distress :
Bear Thou in mind the burden Thou hast laid
Upon us, and our feebleness unstayed
   Except Thou stay us : for the long long race
   Which stretches far and far before our face
Thou knowest,—remember Thou whereof we are
      made.
If making makes us Thine then Thine we are,
   And if redemption we are twice Thine own :

If once Thou didst come down from heaven afar
   To seek us and to find us, how not save?
Comfort us, save us, leave us not alone,
   Thou Who didst die our death and fill our grave.

### 4.

So tired am I, so weary of to-day,
   So unrefreshed from foregone weariness,
   So overburdened by foreseen distress,
So lagging and so stumbling on my way,
I scarce can rouse myself to watch or pray,
   To hope, or aim, or toil for more or less,—
   Ah, always less and less, even while I press
Forward and toil and aim as best I may.
Half-starved of soul and heartsick utterly,
   Yet lift I up my heart and soul and eyes
   (Which fail in looking upward) toward the prize:
Me, Lord, Thou seest though I see not Thee;
   Me now, as once the Thief in Paradise,
Even me, O Lord my Lord, remember me.

### 5.

Lord, Thou Thyself art Love and only Thou;
   Yet I who am not love would fain love Thee;
   But Thou alone being Love canst furnish me

With that same love my heart is craving now.
Allow my plea! for if Thou disallow,
  No second fountain can I find but Thee;
  No second hope or help is left to me,
No second anything, but only Thou.
O Love accept, according my request;
  O Love exhaust, fulfilling my desire:
  Uphold me with the strength that cannot tire,
Nerve me to labour till Thou bid me rest,
  Kindle my fire from Thine unkindled fire,
And charm the willing heart from out my breast.


### 6.

We lack, yet cannot fix upon the lack:
  Not this, nor that; yet somewhat, certainly.
  We see the things we do not yearn to see
Around us: and what see we glancing back?
Lost hopes that leave our hearts upon the rack,
  Hopes that were never ours yet seemed to be,
  For which we steered on life's salt stormy sea
Braving the sunstroke and the frozen pack.
If thus to look behind is all in vain,
  And all in vain to look to left or right,
Why face we not our future once again,
Launching with hardier hearts across the main,
  Straining dim eyes to catch the invisible sight,
And strong to bear ourselves in patient pain?

7.

To love and to remember; that is good :
  To love and to forget; that is not well :
  To lapse from love to hatred ; that is hell
And death and torment, rightly understood.
Soul dazed by love and sorrow, cheer thy mood ;
  More blest art thou than mortal tongue can tell :
  Ring not thy funeral but thy marriage bell,
And salt with hope thy life's insipid food.
Love is the goal, love is the way we wend,
  Love is our parallel unending line
    Whose only perfect Parallel is Christ,
Beginning not begun, End without end :
  For He Who hath the Heart of God sufficed,
  Can satisfy all hearts,—yea, thine and mine.

8.

We feel and see with different hearts and eyes :—
  Ah Christ, if all our hearts could meet in Thee
  How well it were for them and well for me,
Our hearts Thy dear accepted sacrifice.
Thou, only Life of hearts and Light of eyes,
  Our life, our light, if once we turn to Thee,
  So be it, O Lord, to them and so to me ;
Be all alike Thine own dear sacrifice.

Thou Who by death hast ransomed us from death,
　Thyself God's sole well-pleasing Sacrifice,
　　Thine only sacred Self I plead with Thee :
　Make Thou it well for them and well for me
That Thou hast given us souls and wills and breath,
　And hearts to love Thee, and to see Thine eyes.


9.

Star Sirius and the Pole Star dwell afar
　Beyond the drawings each of other's strength :
　　One blazes through the brief bright summer's length
Lavishing life-heat from a flaming car ;
　While one unchangeable upon a throne
　Broods o'er the frozen heart of earth alone,
Content to reign the bright particular star
　Of some who wander or of some who groan.
They own no drawings each of other's strength,
　Nor vibrate in a visible sympathy,
　　Nor veer along their courses each toward each :
　Yet are their orbits pitched in harmony
Of one dear heaven, across whose depth and length
　　Mayhap they talk together without speech.

10.

Tread softly ! all the earth is holy ground.
 It may be, could we look with seeing eyes,
 This spot we stand on is a Paradise
Where dead have come to life and lost been found,
Where Faith has triumphed, Martyrdom been crowned,
 Where fools have foiled the wisdom of the wise ;
 From this same spot the dust of saints may rise,
And the King's prisoners come to light unbound.
O earth, earth, earth, hear thou thy Maker's Word :
 " Thy dead thou shalt give up, nor hide thy slain "—
Some who went weeping forth shall come again
 Rejoicing from the east or from the west,
As doves fly to their windows, love's own bird
 Contented and desirous to the nest.[1]


11.

Lifelong our stumbles, lifelong our regret,
 Lifelong our efforts failing and renewed,
 While lifelong is our witness, " God is good ·'·
Who bore with us till now, bears with us yet,

---

[1] " Quali colombe dal disio chiamate
 Con l'ali aperte e ferme al dolce nido
 Volan per l'aer dal voler portate."
    DANTE.

Who still remembers and will not forget,
　Who gives us light and warmth and daily food ;
　And gracious promises half understood,
And glories half unveiled, whereon to set
Our heart of hearts and eyes of our desire ;
　Uplifting us to longing and to love,
Luring us upward from this world of mire,
　Urging us to press on and mount above
　Ourselves and all we have had experience of,
Mounting to Him in love's perpetual fire.

12

A dream there is wherein we are fain to scream,
　While struggling with ourselves we cannot speak :
　And much of all our waking life, as weak
And misconceived, eludes us like the dream.
For half life's seemings are not what they seem,
　And vain the laughs we laugh, the shrieks we shriek;
　Yea, all is vain that mars the settled meek
Contented quiet of our daily theme.
When I was young I deemed that sweets are sweet:
　But now I deem some searching bitters are
　Sweeter than sweets, and more refreshing far,
　And to be relished more, and more desired,
And more to be pursued on eager feet,
　　On feet untired, and still on feet though tired.

## 13.

Shame is a shadow cast by sin : yet shame
　　Itself may be a glory and a grace,
　　Refashioning the sin-disfashioned face ;
A nobler bruit than hollow-sounded fame,
A new-lit lustre on a tarnished name,
　　One virtue pent within an evil place,
　　Strength for the fight, and swiftness for the race,
A stinging salve, a life-requickening flame.
A salve so searching we may scarcely live,
　　A flame so fierce it seems that we must die,
　　　An actual cautery thrust into the heart :
　　　Nevertheless, men die not of such smart ;
And shame gives back what nothing else can give,
　　Man to himself,—then sets him up on high.

## 14.

When Adam and when Eve left Paradise
　　Did they love on and cling together still,
　　Forgiving one another all that ill
The twain had wrought on such a different wise ?
She propped upon his strength, and he in guise
　　Of lover though of lord, girt to fulfil

Their term of life and die when God should will ;
Lie down and sleep, and having slept arise.
Boast not against us, O our enemy !
   To-day we fall, but we shall rise again ;
We grope to-day, to-morrow we shall see :
      What is to-day that we should fear to-day ?
      A morrow cometh which shall sweep away
   Thee and thy realm of change and death and pain.

## 15.

Let woman fear to teach and bear to learn,
   Remembering the first woman's first mistake.
   Eve had for pupil the inquiring snake,
Whose doubts she answered on a great concern ;
But he the tables so contrived to turn,
   It next was his to give and her's to take ;
   Till man deemed poison sweet for her sweet sake,
And fired a train by which the world must burn.
Did Adam love his Eve from first to last ?
   I think so ; as we love who works us ill,
   And wounds us to the quick, yet loves us still.
Love pardons the unpardonable past :
Love in a dominant embrace holds fast
   His frailer self, and saves without her will.

### 16.

Our teachers teach that one and one make two :
   Later, Love rules that one and one make one :
   Abstruse the problems! neither need we shun,
But skilfully to each should yield its due.
The narrower total seems to suit the few,
   The wider total suits the common run ;
   Each obvious in its sphere like moon or sun ;
Both provable by me, and both by you.
Befogged and witless, in a wordy maze
   A groping stroll perhaps may do us good ;
   If cloyed we are with much we have understood,
If tired of half our dusty world and ways,
   If sick of fasting, and if sick of food ;—
And how about these long still-lengthening days?

### 17.

Something this foggy day, a something which
   Is neither of this fog nor of to-day,
   Has set me dreaming of the winds that play
Past certain cliffs, along one certain beach,
   And turn the topmost edge of waves to spray :
   Ah pleasant pebbly strand so far away,
So out of reach while quite within my reach,
   As out of reach as India or Cathay!
I am sick of where I am and where I am not.

I am sick of foresight and of memory,
I am sick of all I have and all I see,
　I am sick of self, and there is nothing new;
Oh weary impatient patience of my lot!—
　　Thus with myself: how fares it, Friends, with you?


## 18.

So late in Autumn half the world's asleep,
　And half the wakeful world looks pinched and pale;
　For dampness now, not freshness, rides the gale;
And cold and colourless comes ashore the deep
With tides that bluster or with tides that creep;
　Now veiled uncouthness wears an uncouth veil
　Of fog, not sultry haze; and blight and bale
Have done their worst, and leaves rot on the heap.
So late in Autumn one forgets the Spring,
　Forgets the Summer with its opulence,
The callow birds that long have found a wing,
　The swallows that more lately gat them hence:
Will anything like Spring, will anything
　Like Summer, rouse one day the slumbering sense?


## 19.

Here now is Winter.　Winter, after all,
　Is not so drear as was my boding dream

While Autumn gleamed its latest watery gleam
On sapless leafage too inert to fall.
Still leaves and berries clothe my garden wall
 Where ivy thrives on scantiest sunny beam ;
 Still here a bud and there a blossom seem
Hopeful, and robin still is musical.
Leaves, flowers and fruit and one delightful song
 Remain ; these days are short, but now the nights
 Intense and long, hang out their utmost lights ;
Such starry nights are long, yet not too long ;
Frost nips the weak, while strengthening still the strong
 Against that day when Spring sets all to rights.

### 20.

A hundred thousand birds salute the day :—
 One solitary bird salutes the night :
Its mellow grieving wiles our grief away,
 And tunes our weary watches to delight ;
It seems to sing the thoughts we cannot say,
 To know and sing them, and to set them right ;
Until we feel once more that May is May,
 And hope some buds may bloom without a blight.
This solitary bird outweighs, outvies,
 The hundred thousand merry-making birds
Whose innocent warblings yet might make us wise
Would we but follow when they bid us rise,
 Would we but set their notes of praise to words
And launch our hearts up with them to the skies.

### 21.

A host of things I take on trust : I take
  The nightingales on trust, for few and far
  Between those actual summer moments are
When I have heard what melody they make.
So chanced it once at Como on the Lake :
  But all things, then, waxed musical ; each star
  Sang on its course, each breeze sang on its car,
All harmonies sang to senses wide awake.
All things in tune, myself not out of tune,
  Those nightingales were nightingales indeed :
  Yet truly an owl had satisfied my need,
And wrought a rapture underneath that moon,
  Or simple sparrow chirping from a reed ;
For June that night glowed like a doubled June.

### 22.

The mountains in their overwhelming might
  Moved me to sadness when I saw them first,
And afterwards they moved me to delight ;
  Struck harmonies from silent chords which burst
  Out into song, a song by memory nursed ;
For ever unrenewed by touch or sight
Sleeps the keen magic of each day or night,
  In pleasure and in wonder then immersed.
All Switzerland behind us on the ascent,

All Italy before us we plunged down
  St. Gothard, garden of forget-me-not :
  Yet why should such a flower choose such a spot?
Could we forget that way which once we went
  Though not one flower had bloomed to weave its
    crown?

### 23.

Beyond the seas we know, stretch seas unknown
  Blue and bright-coloured for our dim and green,
  Beyond the lands we see, stretch lands unseen
With many-tinted tangle overgrown ;
And icebound seas there are like seas of stone,
  Serenely stormless as death lies serene ;
  And lifeless tracts of sand, which intervene
Betwixt the lands where living flowers are blown.
This dead and living world befits our case
  Who live and die : we live in wearied hope,
We die in hope not dead ; we run a race
To-day, and find no present halting-place ;
  All things we see lie far within our scope,
And still we peer beyond with craving face.

### 24.

The wise do send their hearts before them to
  Dear blessed Heaven, despite the veil between ;

The foolish nurse their hearts within the screen
Of this familiar world, where all we do
Or have is old, for there is nothing new :
   Yet elder far that world we have not seen ;
   God's Presence antedates what else hath been :
Many the foolish seem, the wise seem few.
Oh foolishest fond folly of a heart
   Divided, neither here nor there at rest !
      That hankers after Heaven, but clings to earth ;
      That neither here nor there knows thorough mirth,
Half-choosing, wholly missing, the good part :—
   Oh fool among the foolish, in thy quest.


25.

When we consider what this life we lead
   Is not, and is : how full of toil and pain,
   How blank of rest and of substantial gain,
Beset by hunger earth can never feed,
And propping half our hearts upon a reed ;
   We cease to mourn lost treasures, mourned in vain,
   Lost treasures we are fain and yet not fain
To fetch back for a solace of our need.
For who that feel this burden and this strain,
   This wide vacuity of hope and heart,
Would bring their cherished well-beloved again :
   To bleed with them and wince beneath the smart,
To have with stinted bliss such lavish bane,
   To hold in lieu of all so poor a part ?

26.

This Life is full of numbness and of balk,
　Of haltingness and baffled short-coming,
　Of promise unfulfilled, of everything
That is puffed vanity and empty talk :
Its very bud hangs cankered on the stalk,
　Its very song-bird trails a broken wing,
　Its very Spring is not indeed like Spring,
But sighs like Autumn round an aimless walk.
This Life we live is dead for all its breath ;
　Death's self it is, set off on pilgrimage,
　Travelling with tottering steps the first short stage :
　　The second stage is one mere desert dust
　　Where Death sits veiled amid creation's rust :—
Unveil thy face, O Death who art not Death.

27.

I have dreamed of Death :—what will it be to die
　Not in a dream, but in the literal truth
　With all Death's adjuncts ghastly and uncouth,
The pang that is the last and the last sigh ?
Too dulled, it may be, for a last good-bye,
　Too comfortless for any one to soothe,
　A helpless charmless spectacle of ruth
Through long last hours, so long while yet they fly.

So long to those who hopeless in their fear
    Watch the slow breath and look for what they
        dread :
While I supine with ears that cease to hear,
    With eyes that glaze, with heart pulse running
        down
    (Alas ! no saint rejoicing on her bed),
    May miss the goal at last, may miss a crown.


## 28.

In life our absent friend is far away :
    But death may bring our friend exceeding near,
    Show him familiar faces long so dear
And lead him back in reach of words we say.
He only cannot utter yea or nay
    In any voice accustomed to our ear ;
    He only cannot make his face appear
And turn the sun back on our shadowed day.
The dead may be around us, dear and dead ;
    The unforgotten dearest dead may be
        Watching us with unslumbering eyes and heart
Brimful of words which cannot yet be said,
    Brimful of knowledge they may not impart,
    Brimful of love for you and love for me.

## "FOR THINE OWN SAKE, O MY GOD."

WEARIED of sinning, wearied of repentance,
    Wearied of self, I turn, my God, to Thee ;
To Thee, my Judge, on Whose all-righteous sentence
    Hangs mine eternity :
I turn to Thee, I plead Thyself with Thee,—
    Be pitiful to me.

Wearied I loathe myself, I loathe my sinning,
    My stains, my festering sores, my misery :
Thou the Beginning, Thou ere my beginning
    Didst see and didst foresee
Me miserable, me sinful, ruined me,—
    I plead Thyself with Thee.

I plead Thyself with Thee Who art my Maker,
    Regard Thy handiwork that cries to Thee ;
I plead Thyself with Thee Who wast partaker
    Of mine infirmity,
Love made Thee what Thou art, the love of me,—
    I plead Thyself with Thee.

## UNTIL THE DAY BREAK.

WHEN will the day bring its pleasure ?
    When will the night bring its rest ?
Reaper and gleaner and thresher
    Peer toward the east and the west :—
    The Sower He knoweth, and He knoweth best.

Meteors flash forth and expire,
　　Northern lights kindle and pale ;
These are the days of desire,
　　Of eyes looking upward that fail ;
　　Vanishing days as a finishing tale.


Bows down the crop in its glory
　　Tenfold, fiftyfold, hundredfold ;
The millet is ripened and hoary,
　　The wheat ears are ripened to gold :—
　　Why keep us waiting in dimness and cold ?


The Lord of the harvest, He knoweth
　　Who knoweth the first and the last :
The Sower Who patiently soweth,
　　He scanneth the present and past :
　　He saith, "What thou hast, what remaineth, hold
　　　　fast."


Yet, Lord, o'er Thy toil-wearied weepers
　　The storm-clouds hang muttering and frown :
On threshers and gleaners and reapers,
　　O Lord of the harvest, look down ;
　　Oh for the harvest, the shout, and the crown !


"Not so," saith the Lord of the reapers,
　　The Lord of the first and the last :
"O My toilers, My weary, My weepers,
　　What ye have, what remaineth, hold fast.
　　Hide in My heart till the vengeance be past."

## A HOPE CAROL.

A NIGHT was near, a day was near,
   Between a day and night
I heard sweet voices calling clear,
   Calling me :
I heard a whirr of wing on wing,
   But could not see the sight ;
I long to see my birds that sing,
   I long to see.

Below the stars, beyond the moon,
   Between the night and day
I heard a rising falling tune
   Calling me :
I long to see the pipes and strings
   Whereon such minstrels play ;
I long to see each face that sings,
   I long to see.

To-day or may be not to-day,
   To-night or not to-night,
All voices that command or pray
   Calling me,
Shall kindle in my soul such fire
   And in my eyes such light
That I shall see that heart's desire
   I long to see.

## "OF HIM THAT WAS READY TO PERISH."

LORD, I am waiting, weeping, watching for Thee :
    My youth and hope lie by me buried and dead,
My wandering love hath not where to lay its head
    Except Thou say " Come to Me."

My noon is ended, abolished from life and light,
    My noon is ended, ended and done away,
    My sun went down in the hours that still were day,
    And my lingering day is night.

How long, O Lord, how long in my desperate pain
    Shall I weep and watch, shall I weep and long for
        Thee ?
    Is Thy grace ended, Thy love cut off from me ?
    How long shall I long in vain ?

O God Who before the beginning hast seen the end,
    Who hast made me flesh and blood, not frost and
        not fire,
    Who hast filled me full of needs and love and
        desire
    And a heart that craves a friend,

Who hast said " Come to Me and I will give thee rest,"
    Who hast said " Take on thee My yoke and learn
        of Me,"
    Who calledst a little child to come to Thee,
    And pillowedst John on Thy breast ;

Who spak'st to women that followed Thee sorrowing,
　Bidding them weep for themselves and weep for
　　　their own ;
　Who didst welcome the outlaw adoring Thee all
　　　alone,
　And plight Thy word as a King,—

By Thy love of these and of all that ever shall be,
　By Thy love of these and of all the born and unborn,
　Turn Thy gracious eyes on me and think no scorn
　　Of me, not even of me.

Beside Thy Cross I hang on my cross in shame,
　My wounds, weakness, extremity cry to Thee :
　Bid me also to Paradise, also me
　　For the glory of Thy Name.


## CHRISTMAS CAROLS.

### I.

WHOSO hears a chiming for Christmas at the
　nighest,
　Hears a sound like Angels chanting in their glee,
Hears a sound like palm boughs waving in the highest,
　Hears a sound like ripple of a crystal sea.

Sweeter than a prayer-bell for a saint in dying,
　Sweeter than a death-bell for a saint at rest,
Music struck in Heaven with earth's faint replying
　" Life is good, and death is good, for Christ is Best."

2.

A holy, heavenly chime
Rings fulness in of time,
And on His Mother's breast
Our Lord God ever-Blest
Is laid a Babe at rest.

Stoop, Spirits unused to stoop,
Swoop, Angels, flying swoop,
Adoring as you gaze,
Uplifting hymns of praise :—
" Grace to the Full of Grace !"

The cave is cold and strait
To hold the angelic state :
More strait it is, more cold,
To foster and infold
Its Maker one hour old.

Thrilled through with awestruck love,
Meek Angels poised above,
To see their God, look down :
" What, is there never a Crown
For Him in swaddled gown ?

" How comes He soft and weak
With such a tender cheek,
With such a soft small hand ?—
The very Hand which spann'd
Heaven when its girth was plann'd.

" How comes He with a voice
Which is but baby-noise ?—
That Voice which spake with might
—' Let there be light '—and light
Sprang out before our sight.

" What need hath He of flesh
Made flawless now afresh ?
What need of human heart ?—
Heart that must bleed and smart
Choosing the better part.

" But see : His gracious smile
Dismisses us a while
To serve Him in His kin.
Haste we, make haste, begin
To fetch His brethren in."

Like stars they flash and shoot,
The Shepherds they salute :
" Glory to God " they sing :
" Good news of peace we bring,
For Christ is born a King."

### 3.

Lo ! newborn Jesus
  Soft and weak and small,
Wrapped in baby's bands

By His Mother's hands,
  Lord God of all.

Lord God of Mary,
  Whom His Lips caress
While He rocks to rest
On her milky breast
  In helplessness.

Lord God of shepherds
  Flocking through the cold.
Flocking through the dark
To the only Ark,
  The only Fold.

Lord God of all things
  Be they near or far,
Be they high or low;
Lord of storm and snow,
  Angel and star.

Lord God of all men,—
  My Lord and my God!
Thou who lovest me,
Keep me close to Thee
  By staff and rod.

Lo! newborn Jesus
  Loving great and small,
Love's free Sacrifice,
Opening Arms and Eyes
  To one and all.

## A CANDLEMAS DIALOGUE.

"LOVE brought Me down: and cannot love
make thee
Carol for joy to Me?
Hear cheerful robin carol from his tree,
Who owes not half to Me
I won for thee."

"Yea, Lord, I hear his carol's wordless voice;
And well may he rejoice
Who hath not heard of death's discordant noise.
So might I too rejoice
With such a voice."

"True, thou hast compassed death: but hast not thou
The tree of life's own bough?
Am I not Life and Resurrection now?
My Cross balm-bearing bough
For such as thou."

"Ah me, Thy Cross!——but that seems far away;
Thy Cradle-song to-day
I too would raise and worship Thee and pray:
Not empty, Lord, to-day
Send me away."

"If thou wilt not go empty, spend thy store;
And I will give thee more,

Yea, make thee ten times richer than before.
Give more and give yet more
Out of thy store."

"Because Thou givest me Thyself, I will
Thy blessed word fulfil,
Give with both hands, and hoard by giving still:
Thy pleasure to fulfil,
And work Thy Will."

## "BEHOLD THE MAN!"

SHALL Christ hang on the Cross, and we not look?
  Heaven, earth and hell stood gazing at the first,
  While Christ for long-cursed man was counted cursed;
Christ, God and Man, Whom God the Father strook
And shamed and sifted and one while forsook:—
  Cry shame upon our bodies we have nursed
  In sweets, our souls in pride, our spirits immersed
In wilfulness, our steps run all acrook.
Cry shame upon us! for He bore our shame
  In agony, and we look on at ease
With neither hearts on flame nor cheeks on flame:
  What hast thou, what have I, to do with peace?
Not to send peace but send a sword He came,
  And fire and fasts and tearful night-watches.

## THE DESCENT FROM THE CROSS.

IS this the Face that thrills with awe
  Seraphs who veil their face above?
Is this the Face without a flaw,
  The Face that is the Face of Love?
Yea, this defaced, a lifeless clod,
  Hath all creation's love sufficed,
Hath satisfied the love of God,
  This Face the Face of Jesus Christ.

## MARY MAGDALENE AND THE OTHER MARY.

### A SONG FOR ALL MARIES.

OUR Master lies asleep and is at rest:
  His Heart has ceased to bleed, His Eye to weep:
The sun ashamed has dropt down in the west:
  Our Master lies asleep.

Now we are they who weep, and trembling keep
Vigil, with wrung heart in a sighing breast,
  While slow time creeps, and slow the shadows creep.

Renew Thy youth, as eagle from the nest;
  O Master, who hast sown, arise to reap:—
No cock-crow yet, no flush on eastern crest:
  Our Master lies asleep.

## "IT IS FINISHED."

DEAR Lord, let me recount to Thee
    Some of the great things Thou hast
       done
    For me, even me
    Thy little one.

It was not I that cared for Thee,—
But Thou didst set Thy heart upon
    Me, even me
    Thy little one.

And therefore was it sweet to Thee
To leave Thy Majesty and Throne,
    And grow like me
    A Little One,

A swaddled Baby on the knee
Of a dear Mother of Thine own,
    Quite weak like me
    Thy little one.

Thou didst assume my misery,
And reap the harvest I had sown,
    Comforting me
    Thy little one.

Jerusalem and Galilee,—
Thy love embraced not those alone,

But also me
Thy little one.

Thy unblemished Body on the Tree
Was bared and broken to atone
    For me, for me
    Thy little one.

Thou lovedst me upon the Tree,—
Still me, hid by the ponderous stone,—
    Me always,—me
    Thy little one.

And love of me arose with Thee
When death and hell lay overthrown :
    Thou lovedst me
    Thy little one.

And love of me went up with Thee
To sit upon Thy Father's Throne :
    Thou lovest me
    Thy little one.

Lord, as Thou me, so would I Thee
Love in pure love's communion,
    For Thou lov'st me
    Thy little one :

Which love of me bring back with Thee
To Judgment when the Trump is blown,
    Still loving me
    Thy little one.

## AN EASTER CAROL.

SPRING bursts to-day,
    For Christ is risen and all the earth's
      at play.

Flash forth, thou Sun,
The rain is over and gone, its work is done.

Winter is past,
Sweet Spring is come at last, is come at last.

Bud, Fig and Vine,
Bud, Olive, fat with fruit and oil and wine.

Break forth this morn
In roses, thou but yesterday a Thorn.

Uplift thy head,
O pure white Lily through the Winter dead.

Beside your dams
Leap and rejoice, you merry-making Lambs.

All Herds and Flocks
Rejoice, all Beasts of thickets and of rocks.

Sing, Creatures, sing,
Angels and Men and Birds and everything.

All notes of Doves
Fill all our world : this is the time of loves.

## "BEHOLD A SHAKING."

### I.

MAN rising to the doom that shall not err,—
    Which hath most dread : the arouse of all or
      each ;
  All kindreds of all nations of all speech,
Or one by one of *him* and *him* and *her ?*
While dust reanimate begins to stir
  Here, there, beyond, beyond, reach beyond reach ;
  While every wave refashions on the beach
Alive or dead-in-life some seafarer.
Now meeting doth not join or parting part ;
  True meeting and true parting wait till then,
    When whoso meet are joined for evermore,
Face answering face and heart at rest in heart :—
  God bring us all rejoicing to the shore
  Of happy Heaven, His sheep home to the pen.

### 2.

Blessed that flock safe penned in Paradise ;
  Blessed this flock which tramps in weary ways ;
  All form one flock, God's flock ; all yield Him
    praise
By joy or pain, still tending toward the prize.
Joy speaks in praises there, and sings and flies

Where no night is, exulting all its days ;
Here, pain finds solace, for, behold, it prays ;
In both love lives the life that never dies.
Here life is the beginning of our death,
  And death the starting-point whence life ensues ;
    Surely our life is death, our death is life :
      Nor need we lay to heart our peace or strife,
But calm in faith and patience breathe the breath
God gave, to take again when He shall choose.


## ALL SAINTS.

THEY are flocking from the East
    And the West,
They are flocking from the North
And the South,
Every moment setting forth
From realm of snake or lion.
Swamp or sand,
Ice or burning ;
Greatest and least,
Palm in hand
And praise in mouth,
They are flocking up the path
To their rest,
Up the path that hath
No returning.

Up the steeps of Zion
They are mounting,
Coming, coming,
Throngs beyond man's counting;
With a sound
Like innumerable bees
Swarming, humming
Where flowering trees
Many tinted,
Many scented,
All alike abound
With honey,—
With a swell
Like a blast upswaying unrestrainable
From a shadowed dell
To the hill-tops sunny,—
With a thunder
Like the ocean when in strength
Breadth and length
It sets to shore ;
More and more
Waves on waves redoubled pour
Leaping flashing to the shore
(Unlike the under
Drain of ebb that loseth ground
For all its roar).

They are thronging
From the East and West,
From the North and South,

Saints are thronging, loving, longing,
To their land
Of rest,
Palm in hand
And praise in mouth.


## "TAKE CARE OF HIM."

" THOU whom I love, for whom I died,
        Lovest thou Me, My bride?"—
Low on my knees I love Thee, Lord,
    Believed in and adored.

" That I love thee the proof is plain :
        How dost thou love again?"—
In prayer, in toil, in earthly loss,
    In a long-carried cross.

" Yea, thou dost love : yet one adept
        Brings more for Me to accept."—
I mould my will to match with Thine,
    My wishes I resign.

" Thou givest much : then give the whole
        For solace of My soul."—
More would I give, if I could get :
    But, Lord, what lack I yet?

" In Me thou lovest Me : I call
        Thee to love Me in all."—

Brim full my heart, dear Lord, that so
  My love may overflow.

" Love Me in sinners and in saints,
    In each who needs or faints."—
Lord, I will love Thee as I can
    In every brother man.

" All sore, all crippled, all who ache,
    Tend all for My dear sake."—
All for Thy sake, Lord : I will see
    In every sufferer Thee.

" So I at last, upon My Throne
    Of glory, Judge alone,
So I at last will say to thee :
    Thou diddest it to Me."


## PATIENCE OF HOPE.

THE flowers that bloom in sun and shade
    And glitter in the dew,
  The flowers must fade.
The birds that build their nest and sing
    When lovely Spring is new,
    Must soon take wing.

The sun that rises in his strength
    To wake and warm the world,
    Must set at length.

The sea that overflows the shore
　　With billows frothed and curled,
　　　Must ebb once more.

All come and go, all wax and wane,
　　O Lord, save only Thou
　　　Who dost remain
The Same to all eternity.
　　All things which fail us now
　　　We trust to Thee.


## A MARTYR.

### THE VIGIL OF THE FEAST.

INNER not outer, without gnash of teeth
　　Or weeping, save quiet sobs of some who pray
And feel the Everlasting Arms beneath,—
Blackness of darkness this, but not for aye;
　　Darkness that even in gathering fleeteth fast,
　　Blackness of blackest darkness close to day.
Lord Jesus, through Thy darkened pillar cast,
　　Thy gracious eyes all-seeing cast on me
　　Until this tyranny be overpast.
Me, Lord, remember who remember Thee,
　　And cleave to Thee, and see Thee without sight,
　　And choose Thee still in dire extremity,
And in this darkness worship Thee my Light,
　　And Thee my Life adore in shadow of death,
　　Thee loved by day, and still beloved by night.

It is the Voice of my Beloved that saith :
" I am the Way, the Truth, the Life, I go
    Whither that soul knows well that followeth "—
O Lord, I follow, little as I know ;
    At this eleventh hour I rise and take
    My life into my hand, and follow so,
With tears and heart-misgivings and heart-ache ;
    Thy feeblest follower, yet Thy follower
    Indomitable for Thine only sake.
To-night I gird my will afresh, and stir
    My strength, and brace my heart to do and dare,
    Marvelling : Will to-morrow wake the whirr
Of the great rending wheel, or from his lair
    Startle the jubilant lion in his rage,
    Or clench the headsman's hand within my hair,
Or kindle fire to speed my pilgrimage,
    Chariot of fire and horses of sheer fire
    Whirling me home to heaven by one fierce stage ?—
Thy Will I will, I Thy desire desire ;
    Let not the waters close above my head,
    Uphold me that I sink not in this mire :
For flesh and blood are frail and sore afraid ;
    And young I am, unsatisfied and young,
    With memories, hopes, with cravings all unfed,
My song half sung, its sweetest notes unsung,
    All plans cut short, all possibilities,
    Because my cord of life is soon unstrung.
Was I a careless woman set at ease
    That this so bitter cup is brimmed for me ?
    Had mine own vintage settled on the lees ?

A word, a puff of smoke, would set me free;
  A word, a puff of smoke, over and gone : . . .
  Howbeit, whom have I, Lord, in heaven but Thee?
Yea, only Thee my choice is fixed upon
  In heaven or earth, eternity or time :—
  Lord, hold me fast, Lord, leave me not alone,
Thy silly heartless dove that sees the lime
  Yet almost flutters to the tempting bough :
  Cover me, hide me, pluck me from this crime.
A word, a puff of smoke, would save me now : . . .
  But who, my God, would save me in the day
  Of Thy fierce anger? only Saviour Thou.
Preoccupy my heart, and turn away
  And cover up mine eyes from frantic fear,
  And stop mine ears lest I be driven astray :
For one stands ever dinning in mine ear
  How my gray Father withers in the blight
  Of love for me, who cruel am and dear;
And how my Mother through this lingering night
  Until the day, sits tearless in her woe,
  Loathing for love of me the happy light
Which brings to pass a concourse and a show
  To glut the hungry faces merciless,
  The thousand faces swaying to and fro,
Feasting on me unveiled in helplessness
  Alone,—yet not alone : Lord, stand by me
  As once by lonely Paul in his distress.
As blossoms to the sun I turn to Thee ;
  Thy dove turns to her window, think no scorn;
  As one dove to an ark on shoreless sea,

To Thee I turn mine eyes, my heart forlorn;
    Put forth Thy scarred right Hand, kind Lord, take
      hold
Of me Thine all-forsaken dove who mourn :
For Thou hast loved me since the days of old,
    And I love Thee Whom loving I will love
    Through life's short fever-fits of heat and cold ;
Thy Name will I extol and sing thereof,
    Will flee for refuge to Thy Blessed Name.
    Lord, look upon me from Thy bliss above :
Look down on me, who shrink from all the shame
    And pangs and desolation of my death,
    Wrenched piecemeal or devoured or set on flame,
While all the world around me holds its breath
    With eyes glued on me for a gazing-stock,
    Pitiless eyes, while no man pitieth.
The floods are risen, I stagger in their shock,
    My heart reels and is faint, I fail, I faint :
    My God, set Thou me up upon the rock,
Thou Who didst long ago Thyself acquaint
    With death, our death ; Thou Who didst long ago
    Pour forth Thy soul for sinner and for saint.
Bear me in mind, whom no one else will know ;
    Thou Whom Thy friends forsook, take Thou my
      part,
    Of all forsaken in mine overthrow ;
Carry me in Thy bosom, in Thy heart,
    Carry me out of darkness into light,
    To-morrow make me see Thee as Thou art.
Lover and friend Thou hidest from my sight :—

Alas, alas, mine earthly love, alas,
  For whom I thought to don the garments white
And white wreath of a bride, this rugged pass
  Hath utterly divorced me from thy care ;
  Yea, I am to thee as a shattered glass
Worthless, with no more beauty lodging there,
  Abhorred, lest I involve thee in my doom :
  For sweet are sunshine and this upper air,
And life and youth are sweet, and give us room
  For all most sweetest sweetnesses we taste :
  Dear, what hast thou in common with a tomb ?
I bow my head in silence, I make haste
  Alone, I make haste out into the dark,
  My life and youth and hope all run to waste.
Is this my body cold and stiff and stark,
  Ashes made ashes, earth becoming earth,
  Is this a prize for man to make his mark ?
Am I that very I who laughed in mirth
  A while ago, a little little while,
  Yet all the while a-dying since my birth ?
Now am I tired, too tired to strive or smile ;
  I sit alone, my mouth is in the dust :
  Look Thou upon me, Lord, for I am vile.
In Thee is all my hope, is all my trust,
  On Thee I centre all my self that dies,
  And self that dies not with its mortal crust,
But sleeps and wakes, and in the end will rise
  With hymns and hallelujahs on its lips,
  Thee loving with the love that satisfies.
As once in Thine unutterable eclipse

The sun and moon grew dark for sympathy,
   And earth cowered quaking underneath the drips
Of Thy slow Blood priceless exceedingly,
   So now a little spare me, and show forth
   Some pity, O my God, some pity of me.
If trouble comes not from the south or north,
   But meted to us by Thy tender hand,
   Let me not in Thine eyes be nothing worth:
Behold me where in agony I stand,
   Behold me no man caring for my soul,
   And take me to Thee in the far-off land,
Shorten the race and lift me to the goal.


## WHY?

LORD, if I love Thee and Thou lovest me,
   Why need I any more these toilsome days;
   Why should I not run singing up Thy ways
Straight into heaven, to rest myself with Thee?
What need remains of death-pang yet to be,
   If all my soul is quickened in Thy praise;
   If all my heart loves Thee, what need the amaze,
Struggle and dimness of an agony?—
Bride whom I love, if thou too lovest Me,
   Thou needs must choose My Likeness for thy dower:
      So wilt thou toil in patience, and abide
   Hungering and thirsting for that blessed hour
When I My Likeness shall behold in thee,
   And thou therein shalt waken satisfied.

## "LOVE IS STRONG AS DEATH."

I HAVE not sought Thee, I have not found Thee,
    I have not thirsted for Thee:
And now cold billows of death surround me,
Buffeting billows of death astound me,—
    Wilt Thou look upon, wilt Thou see
    Thy perishing me?"

"Yea, I have sought thee, yea, I have found thee,
    Yea, I have thirsted for thee,
Yea, long ago with love's bands I bound thee:
Now the Everlasting Arms surround thee,—
    Through death's darkness I look and see
    And clasp thee to Me."

# DISTRIBUTORS
*for the Wordsworth Poetry Library*

## AUSTRALIA, BRUNEI, MALAYSIA & SINGAPORE

Reed Editions
22 Salmon Street
Port Melbourne
Vic 3207
Australia

Tel: (03) 646 6716
Fax: (03) 646 6925

## GREAT BRITAIN & IRELAND

Wordsworth Editions Ltd
Cumberland House
Crib Street
Ware
Hertfordshire SG12 9ET

## HOLLAND & BELGIUM

Uitgeverij en Boekhandel
Van Gennup BV, Spuistraat 283
1012 VR Amsterdam, Holland

## INDIA

Om Book Service
1690 First Floor
Nai Sarak, Delhi - 110006

Tel: 3279823/3265303
Fax: 3278091

## ITALY

Magis Books
Piazza della Vittoria 1/C
42100 Reggio Emilia

Tel: 0522-452303
Fax: 0522-452845

## NEW ZEALAND

Whitcoulls Limited
Private Bag 92098, Auckland

## SOUTHERN AFRICA

Struik Book Distributors (Pty) Ltd
Graph Avenue
Montague Gardens
7441
P O Box 193
Maitland
7405
South Africa

Tel: (021) 551-5900
Fax: (021) 551-1124

## USA, CANADA & MEXICO

Universal Sales & Marketing
230 Fifth Avenue
Suite 1212
New York, NY 10001 USA

Tel: 212-481-3500
Fax: 212-481-3534